The

as

The Marx Brothers as Social Critics

*Satire and Comic
Nihilism in Their Films*

Martin A. Gardner

McFarland & Company, Inc., Publishers

Jefferson, North Carolina, and London

The photographs used in this book are from Photofest

LIBRARY OF CONGRESS CATALOGUING-IN-PUBLICATION DATA

Gardner, Martin A.
    The Marx Brothers as social critics : satire and comic nihilism
in their films / Martin A. Gardner.
        p.   cm.
    Includes bibliographical references and index.

    ISBN 978-0-7864-3942-3
    softcover : 50# alkaline paper ∞

    1. Marx Brothers.   2. Comedy films — United States — History
and criticism.   I. Title.
PN2297.M3G37   2009
791.4302'8092273 — dc22   2009023169

British Library cataloguing data are available

On the cover: The Marx Brothers in the 1930s — (clockwise from
upper left) Zeppo, Groucho, Harpo and Chico (Photofest)

Manufactured in the United States of America

*McFarland & Company, Inc., Publishers
    Box 611, Jefferson, North Carolina 28640
        www.mcfarlandpub.com*

Contents

Preface   1

  1. An Indifferent World   5

  2. Triumphs, Tryouts, and Turkeys: The Film Career   15

  3. The Writers   27

  4. You Can Get Stucco   40

  5. Is It Swordfish?   54

  6. The Seven-Cent Nickel   63

  7. A Job in the Mint   72

  8. A Standing Army   80

  9. Dear Old Ivy   89

10. A Coed with Two Pair of Pants   97

11. The Whole Wig   102

12. It's Tough on My Suspenders   113

13. Three Hardboiled Eggs   119

14. Ice Water in 318   127

15. The Main Hungerdunger   136

16. Grand Slam   145

17. A Very Strange Interlude   152

18. A Brace of Woodpeckers   164

19. Upside Down   171

20. Whim Wham   174

Appendix: Credits of the Films Discussed   185

Chapter Notes   189

Bibliography   199

Index   209

Preface

"Whatever it is, I'm against it." This pithy expression of nihilism is the theme of a song in the Marx Brothers film *Horse Feathers.* The lyrics are a comic device for Groucho's character, who sings them at his inauguration as the new president of Huxley College and is critical of Huxley's inept administration and faculty. But it's more than that. It is just one satirical element in the film about more important matters than cloistered university life. The comic nihilism captures the essence of all the Marx Brothers films.

This book is about that essence. Critics usually analyze the Marx Brothers films from a viewpoint of broad comedy, loosely defined as satire. They offer some insight into the characters played by the Brothers and their significance. Most people view the films as farcical, and it's true: The Marx Brothers films are replete with slapstick and obvious gags, puns, pratfalls, and mimicry.

If we look beneath the outer patina of roughhouse comedy, we see the essence. The films are a serious and biting condemnation of American culture.

Placed within the socio-cultural background of the period, this book shows how their films comment on historical events, political practices, economic conditions, manners and customs, literary subjects, and popular entertainment. We see the films aim at Prohibition, the Florida land boom, political speeches on radio exemplified by Franklin D. Roosevelt's "Fireside Chats," and international diplomacy with its concomitant problem of war. As well, there's a focus on higher education, college sports, speechmaking, big business practices, salesmen's techniques, department store merchandising, letter writing, business and professional clubs, social introductions, ocean travel, legal contracts, dancing, romantic attitudes, card playing, marriage and divorce, crime detection, hotel customs, theatre and entertainment, with references to Dreiser's *An American Tragedy*, O'Neill's *Strange Interlude*, John Cecil Holm and George Abbott's *Three Men on a Horse*, Western movies, detective films, Greta Garbo, Humphrey Bogart, and Lauren Bacall.

Growing up, I loved the slapstick and pratfalls of the Marx Brothers. Who doesn't? Of course, I didn't understand all the jokes or puns until one evening my older brother and I went to see a re-release of *A Day at the Races* (it was the first time for me). On our way to the theatre he told me a little about the Hollywood Production Code of the 1930s and how it was censorious to films that had lewd content. He also told me that the Brothers had some of that in their early films, even though it was fairly mild. I didn't believe it. No, not the madcap Marx Brothers! Watch Groucho's eyebrows, he said, and listen to the puns. I did. None of this diminished my enjoyment of the superficial comedy, but I started to realize that there was something else going on: a serious purpose beneath the laughter. This made the film more enjoyable for me. And so I tried to see any of the Brothers' films whenever they played in theatres or on television (this was before VCRs or DVDs).

Flash forward 15 years. It was time for me to select a subject for my doctoral dissertation, and I had to decide on one that had academic significance as well as enough primary material for a serious study. I thought about what I had been seeing in the Marx Brothers for all those years. I proposed to the university that I would do an analytical study of the social satire in their films. My proposal was accepted and I wrote a doctoral dissertation about the Marx Brothers films. This book is an outgrowth of that study. What came from that academic exploration is the evidence to support the greater importance of the films.

Of course, the films are the primary material for the research for this book. To identify the satirical social criticism in the films, I explored general and social histories of the 1920s and '30s for a diversified picture of those times. For example, I investigated the economic situation in the United States during and just prior to the period in which the Brothers made the films. I became familiar with domestic and international politics. I looked at general trends in social and cultural history during that period, and their bearing on human conduct. I read about the general changes in social and cultural climate as well as the historical, economic, and political causes for those changes. This enabled me to see how the social criticism in the films reflected the attitudes of the time. I looked for evidence of social criticism as a conscious effort by the writers of the films, too.

Collections of original and secondary materials about the Marx Brothers and their films are available and plentiful. The Groucho Marx Papers owned by the Library of Congress include both Groucho's personal correspondence and some of the film scripts. There are several biographies and autobiographies about the Marx Brothers and their writers, as well as biographical material in periodicals and newspapers that reported the activities of the Brothers. I did most of my research at the New York Public Library and the

Library of Congress. For the academic study I went to movie theatres or was able to have private screenings where I would take notes in the dark and try to record the soundtracks of the films. Wherever I could see the films on television I would. My living room has better lighting, but the process of note-taking and recording was the same. For this book, I've been able to use DVDs to see the films again and search databases or the general Internet. Both these contemporary electronic resources can be a helpful supplement to basic library research.

Most of the time I refer to Margaret Dumont by her real name and the Brothers by the names everyone knows. Who remembers Martha Phelps? But people know Margaret Dumont. Occasionally I use the names of the characters that the Brothers play, especially Groucho's roles. Sometimes I analyze a scene twice in different chapters, each with a different insight, because there is more than one interpretation for the same scene, and they are disparate enough so that if both interpretations are included in the same chapter they are too digressive.

I did not intend my academic study or this book to be a biography of the Brothers. However, I have included one chapter that traces their film history, as well as a little segment about a formative event that occurred during their years in vaudeville. I've included some of the background of their primary writers to help understand how the writing evolved. I did not do a comparative analysis of scripts, either shooting scripts or any pre-production versions. I worked exclusively with the films that are available. There have been many versions of the films available at any time. There are things that are cut from the films in the current versions on television, DVD, or online. For example, in one version shown on television an editor has excised the entire canoe scene in *A Day at the Races* even though it is noteworthy for its parody of *An American Tragedy*.

Many books have covered the biographical and autobiographical materials quite thoroughly, and I simply consulted and/or cited several of them. The first biography, Kyle Crichton's *The Marx Brothers* (1950), was mostly about their vaudeville years and some of the early film career. Crichton's book, well-written and entertaining, seems to rely on anecdotal evidence rather than disciplined historical research. Groucho wrote several anecdotal autobiographies, and Harpo wrote one (*Harpo Speaks*). Groucho's son, Arthur, wrote *Life with Groucho*, filled with personal memories and observations. Allen Eyles' *The Marx Brothers: Their World of Comedy* is a film-by-film critical and complete analysis. Wes Gehring's *The Marx Brothers: A Bio-biography* is an excellent analytic study, as is Simon Louvish's *Monkey Business: The Lives and Legends of The Marx Brothers*. Stefan Kanfer's thorough biography, *Groucho: The Life and Times of Julius Henry Marx* is written in a captivating style.

Thomas Doherty's *Pre-Code Hollywood* offers intelligent insights about filmmaking between 1930 and 1934. He includes a major section about *Duck Soup* that is impeccably detailed and informative.

A variety of authors have published dozens of books about the Brothers covering a range of topics and themes, from uncomplicated photo books to serious critical film studies. As an example of the scope of specialized interest in the Marx Brothers, two academic studies offer thoughtful exploration: David James LeMaster's Ph.D. dissertation "Charlie Chaplin and Harpo Marx as Masks of the Commedia dell'Arte: Theory and Practice" and Christine Wigell's Master's thesis "A Comparison of the Nonverbal and Verbal Lazzi Performed by the Zanni of the Commedia dell'Arte and the Visual and Verbal Gags of the Marx Brothers." Another specialized study is Michael Yann's book *Music of the Marx Brothers*.

Finally, I found that revisiting the Marx Brothers critically has been an enlightening experience. As I re-read what I had written in my dissertation and then proceeded to work on this book, I discovered new and interesting things about the films, based on research that was not required for my academic work because, as interesting as they are, they deviated from the main theme of the dissertation. I became conscious of something else, too.

In 1935, Irving Thalberg sat in the audience at the Golden Gate Theatre in San Francisco on closing night of the tryout pre-filming road show performances of *A Night at the Opera*. The Brothers were anxious because Thalberg, the producer of the film, was there to give his verdict. Groucho watched Thalberg carefully for a reaction, but Thalberg remained expressionless throughout the show, even as the rest of the audience was figuratively rolling in the aisles with laughter. After the performance, Thalberg came backstage and congratulated them hardily. Groucho asked him why he hadn't laughed. Thalberg explained that he had been sitting secretly in the audience for four days. He implied that because he had heard the jokes repeatedly for the past four days, he wasn't able to laugh at them.

Never mind Thalberg's four days. I realized that even after years of watching the Marx Brothers and knowing what they're going to do before they do it, they still make me laugh.

1. An Indifferent World

Several hundred people appeared at the Gallery of Modern Art in New York in the early evening of April 18, 1967, to attend the gala opening of a three-week retrospective devoted to the Marx Brothers' film comedies. Among the invited guests were representatives of various news media, members of the Marxes' family, long-time friends, collaborators, and fans. The collected guests saw *Animal Crackers*, the second Marx Brothers film. In itself, this was a spectacular gambit, guaranteed to draw an eager audience. No one had shown the film publicly for more than thirty years because of copyright restrictions. Even more exciting, after the film, Groucho Marx spoke to the audience. Stefan Kanfer in his biography of Groucho reported that this was the moment when the audience "turned a comedian into an icon."[1] Surprisingly, the assembled spectators didn't seem to respond to Groucho's remarks. He couldn't engage them. Kanfer suggests that the audience was more interested in the Groucho on film than the Groucho speaking in front of them, in person. "For more than half a century, Groucho Marx had been able to turn any audience to his advantage, offering a leer, wiggling an eyebrow, waggling a cigar, creating merriment with the ease of a man jingling change in his pockets. Not now."[2]

The reception, held in a different room at the museum, was more intimate. There was no stage, no barrier — the implicit, translucent "fourth wall" of the theatre — between speaker and audience. The crowd pushed forward and gathered close to Groucho, perhaps out of curiosity or perhaps to hear better. The guests were crowded together. Groucho, as usual, was the center of attention. If you had arrived late and had to stand at the outer perimeter of the crowd and hadn't been to the film or had never seen him in person before, but only in films or on television, he was difficult to identify because, unlike his haphazard attire in films and the casual clothing he usually wore as a guest on television programs, he was dressed in a conservative suit, button-down shirt, and paisley tie. He looked like a Wall Street banker or lawyer. On screen, Groucho appears to be tall but in person he was surprisingly short and slightly bent over — not in the comic stoop he assumed while scampering around the stage or movie set as Captain Spaulding et al., but more the result of his age. He was 76.

Speaking to the audience about his brothers and their films, Groucho reminisced for a few minutes. Just six days earlier, in an interview with Vincent Canby, the chief film critic of *The New York Times*, Groucho said that he was "allergic to nostalgia," and then "promptly cued Zeppo into a lengthy vaudeville tale."[3] Here at the fête, without the benefit of a microphone, his voice was softened and muted. After nearly seven decades of performing as a bombastic anti-establishment slayer of social, cultural, and establishment dragons, he was difficult to hear. Although he exhibited a wry smile during this speech, the gentle timbre of his voice was far removed from the days in his prime as the *de facto* leader of the loud, brassy, supremely confident Marx Brothers of *The Cocoanuts, Animal Crackers, Duck Soup*, and *A Night at the Opera*. He spoke slowly, appearing to be hesitant, almost uncomfortably confused. Kanfer described him as appearing disoriented.[4] Ironically, the Marx Brothers had been performers and popular entertainers on both stage and in films, and were comfortable with being the focus of attention.

In their early performances on stage, and later, in a more structured manner in their films, the Marx Brothers literally and figuratively destroyed conventional language and the scenery around them. Their stage shows were masterpieces of improvised chaos. The characters they played, created by themselves and constantly honed to perfection in small-town and small-city vaudeville theatres (prevalent throughout America at that time), reflected an undercurrent of mockery that was raffish, louche, lascivious, and deprecating. By the time they graduated to playing a major vaudeville circuit in New York, Chicago, San Francisco and other major entertainment centers, they had formed their characters fully, suitable to express a more urbane impertinence. And sophisticated it was to be. Some of America's best writers of comedy and satire retooled their naturally impertinent rants and took them to new heights. The Brothers welcomed the contribution of these writers.

And thus, the rebellious and newly refined nature of their derision delighted critics and made them a symbol of dynamic, irreverent comedy. Audiences flocked to their stage extravaganzas knowing that they would see and hear riotous performances complete with ad lib comments, extemporized language, and blatant physical action.[5]

Underlying their heretofore simple irreverence and absurd mockery, there was an urbane texture that was both wildly humorous and critical of American society. For the most part, this added element of social criticism came from the vision of their writers and reflected a perplexity about the world surrounding the Marx Brothers; a "realization of confusion and chaos in life."[6]

Considerable erudition has followed the course of satire and satirical social criticism through the history of literature, primarily because such criticism is a method of achieving the correction of man's foibles and follies.[7] When we discover a contemporary offering of satire, interest in it and its creators or performers burgeons anew. The Marx Brothers, who created interest as popular entertainers both on the Broadway stage and in films, had the added texture of social satire present in their material. The social satire injected by their writers and subsequently supporting the Brothers' characters grew out of a realization and confusion about the chaos in the world around them, as Edgar Johnson suggests.

Groucho Marx acknowledged his personal confusion in a letter to Leonard Lyons, the *New York Post* columnist, in 1960. Lyons had written to him citing a letter he had received from Thornton Wilder: "Re Groucho and *Finnegans Wake*—I have long thought that he was in the book. Weren't the Marx Brothers once in a skit about Napoleon? I seem to remember them wearing tricornes, etc. Anyway, on pages 8 and 9 there is a visit to the Wellington Museum at Waterloo and I read ... 'This is the three lipoleum Coyne Grouching down in the living detch.'" Lyons continued, saying that Wilder "once tried to explain to me the key to *Finnegans Wake*—involving his constant use of puns. The three lipoleum Coyne must be a reference to the Napoleon-type hats. And Grouching makes you a verb."[8] Groucho answered:

> There is no reason why I shouldn't appear in *Finnegans Wake*. I'm certainly as bewildered about life as Joyce was. Well, let Joyce be unconfined.
> Tracing this item down from the *Wake* could be a life project and I question whether I'm up to it. Is it possible that Joyce at one time was in the U.S.A. and saw *I'll Say She Is!*? Or did some New York policeman on his way back to Ireland to see his dear old Mother Machree encounter Joyce in some peat bog and patiently explain to him in detail that at the Casino Theatre at 39th and Broadway there were three young Jewish fellows running around the stage shouting to an indifferent world that they were all Napoleon?[9]

Bewildered about life as Groucho seemed to be, audiences have not ignored the Marx Brothers' well-scripted shouts. Unlike many popular entertainers whose pertinence is evanescent, the Marx Brothers have remained relevant. We can identify the imprint of their work and the characters they created in various other works that have appeared throughout the years, continuing to the present. In fact, playwrights, authors, and artists have specifically credited them with affecting their creative thinking.

In 1937 Salvador Dalí went to Hollywood and while there he met Harpo. Dalí concluded that he was the most surreal of all the Brothers.[10] He thought that Harpo was the funniest man in Hollywood.[11] Dalí presented an idea to Harpo for a new Marx Brothers film that he titled *Giraffes on Horseback Salad*.

The giraffes were to wear gas masks. One scene shows Chico wearing a deep-diving suit while playing the piano. Chico's scene was a case of art imitating art. Years earlier, Dalí had played piano at a performance wearing a diving suit. Inadvertently someone had locked the helmet, and his assistants were trying frantically to pry him free before he suffocated.[12] The audience thought it was all part of the act, and applauded wildly.

Dalí wanted Cole Porter to write the score for his Marx Brothers film. Although Harpo liked the idea, the Brothers never made the film.[13] Still, the Brothers so inspired Dalí with the surrealistic aspect of their work that he painted Harpo's portrait in 1939.[14]

John Willett in his book about Bertolt Brecht thought that Brecht had reflected the Marx Brothers in *A Night at the Opera* when he wrote the wedding scene for *The Caucasian Chalk Circle*.[15] In 1960, Eugene Ionesco told the audience at the American premiere of *The Shepherd's Chameleon* that the three biggest influences on his work had been Groucho, Chico, and Harpo Marx.[16]

François Truffaut in his classic 1960 film, *Shoot the Piano Player*, names a character Chico, an obvious plain-spoken reference to Chico Marx, the brother of the protagonist of the film, named Saroyan (apparently a reference to the author William Saroyan). The film's title itself could be considered an ironic reference to Chico's humorous "shooting the piano keys" with his right forefinger, his own irreverent comment on the intricacies of serious piano technique.

Philip Roth said that he would have liked to have seen a film made of Franz Kafka's *The Castle* with Groucho Marx as K. and Chico and Harpo as the two "assistants."[17]

Transcending time, the references to the Marx Brothers continue to appear in various forms, showing no abatement. In the television series *M*A*S*H*, the character Hawkeye, played by Alan Alda, frequently lapses into an imitation of Groucho. Woody Allen created an entire film referring to the Brothers and entitled *A New Kind of Love*, from one of the songs performed by Zeppo in the film *Monkey Business*. This song, made popular by Maurice Chevalier a decade earlier, was a reference to French music hall performances of the 1920s. Chevalier was one of the leading performers of that genre in Paris. In one of the scenes in Allen's movie, all of the characters at a Parisian masked ball, men and women, are dressed as Groucho and his brothers; one of the characters in the film actually calls the scene "The Groucho Party." Children and adults buy thousands of plastic party masks of Groucho's distinctive mustache, eyebrows, and glasses every year. In the 1970s, Robert Volpe, the first and only detective in the New York City Police Department's art-theft squad, would track down fiendishly clever art criminals dressed in a unique uniform. Appropriate to his role, he favored a sweeping mustache, shoulder-length hair and flamboyant clothing to fit the part. He wore Armani suits to art auctions and a Groucho Marx disguise for no known reason.[18] In 1985 The Groucho Club opened in London, England. It is the antithesis of traditional gentlemen's clubs. The club's owners named it as a tribute to Groucho's letter in the 1940s giving up his membership in a private club in Hollywood. Groucho had written to its president: "Please accept my resignation. I don't care to belong to any club that will have me as a member."[19]

The Marx Brothers films exhibit several aspects of varied literary and artistic movements. But their most pronounced intellectual facet is the overriding social criticism. Although the brothers were successful in vaudeville and musical comedy on Broadway prior to their work in Hollywood, they made their most outstanding and widespread contribution in a portfolio of thirteen films they made between 1929 and 1949 when three or four of the Brothers appeared in prominent roles.[20] These are the Marx Brothers films, defined.

Not all of the films in which they appeared are Marx Brothers films. They made films as a group or individually from 1929 to 1968. The major Hollywood studios produced original scripts (with the exception of *Room Service*) from 1929 to 1949 that emanated social criticism. These are the Marx Brothers films that are the subject of this book.

Of course, satirical social criticism presented to a mass audience did not originate with the Marx Brothers. It has had a long history; social criticism was an important aspect of Greek theatre. Aristophanes in the fifth century B.C. used satire as a powerful weapon to attack social and political follies.[21] Traditionally defined, its true nature is personal and social criticism.[22] Satire is a critical statement of amused disgust about a person or group of people, a social class or a national structure as opposed to another form of literature which may be purely mimetic.[23]

Every society needs some form of satire to ridicule man's foolish acts or ideas, to help remove them.[24] It can be criticism or comment, both friendly and unfriendly. James K. Feibleman takes the position that satirical criticism aims at the formal structure of the object of criticism in order to produce reform. "Formal structure is alone responsible for the paucity of actual value; and it is this lack with which comedy expresses dissatisfaction." But Feibleman warns us about a grave danger that lurks in this fact. "It is a mistake to suppose that ridicule leveled at the limitations of any actual system is being directed at the idea of system itself.... To deride our government's shortcomings is not to deride the necessity for some sort of government but it is rather a demand for better government."[25]

Comedy is most effective when it aims at old customs that are no longer useful, and which stand in the way of progress[26]; it tries to illustrate that nothing actual is completely logical. Although comedy is a method of criticism, its goal is to attain perfection.[27] But it recognizes the reality of the limitations of experience and actuality. "Comedy ... may ... be achieved (1) by means of direct ridicule of the categories of actuality (such as found in current customs and institutions), or it may be achieved (2) by confusing the categories of actuality as an indication of their ultimate unimportance, and as a warning against taking them too seriously. Comedians from Aristophanes to Chaplin, from Daumier to the Marx Brothers, have been occupied with the illustration of these approaches."[28]

Molière, in his preface to *Tartuffe*, discusses the purpose of satire, and justifies it as a means to bring about social reform. For Molière, satire was a more effective way of correcting the ills of society, than was a serious, moral statement of correction: "If the function of comedy is to correct man's vices, I do not see why any should be exempt. Such a condition in our society would be much more dangerous than the thing itself; and we have seen that the theater is admirably suited to provide correction. The most forceful lines of a serious moral statement are usually less powerful than those of satire; and nothing will reform most men better than the depiction of their faults."[29]

Satire can ask for perfection or reform, without making direct suggestions about what should be done to put this reform into effect. Satire can be merely a sharp comment on an aspect of contemporary society to illustrate its absurdity in the hope that merely by focusing attention on the social problem a reform will be enacted eventually.[30] Change, or at least re–examination of that facet which is being satirized, is implied. Sigmund Freud, in his analysis of wit, contends that we are asking for reform of society indirectly, for he says, "By belittling and humbling our enemy; by scorning and ridiculing him, we indirectly obtain the pleasure of his defeat...."[31] He also thought that wit and satire was a way to prevent violence — that we are prevented from actively expressing our hostility about some aspect of society, therefore, as in sexual expression, wit and satire is a technique of substituting invectives for violence.[32] Freud's suggestion about the use of invective to assuage our suppressed hostility refers to the original technique of satire. Effective satire is not invective only, but it is rather a calculated distortion of the object being ridiculed to bring about a pointed attack.[33]

The subjects of satire are always man in society, sex, and politics. Simple comedy differs from satire in attacking these subjects. "[C]omedy laughs joyously over the norms of contemporary society, [whereas] satire laughs sardonically at those norms...."[34]

Comedy has greater freedom than straight drama to achieve the goals of reform, modification, and improvement within a society. Traditionally, it was the Court Jester who sometimes influenced a change of law by virtue of his freedom to satirically insult the king or society.[35] To this day, a typical form of satire is often a "monologue spoken virtually without interruption by one man, either by the author or his mouthpiece."[36] It is an apt description of contemporary stand-up comics.

Notwithstanding the intellectual side of Marx Brothers films, they really were created to be basic entertainment for a mass audience whether or not that audience appreciated or cared about the intrinsic criticism in the dialogue, subtle or obvious. Parents often brought their children to Marx Brothers films simply because they were suitable for viewing by children; they were easy to understand, not burdened by violence or serious "adult" issues, and a perfect escape from the harsh reality of the economically depressed 1930s for audience members of all ages. Whatever sexual references that were made in their films released in the years before or after the enforcement of the guidelines established by the Hollywood Production Code were mild and ambiguous enough so that they were not noticeable to children. (Groucho to Esther Muir: "If I were any closer [to you], I'd be behind you.") Youngsters, even if they understood them, usually ignored them anyway. They were more interested in the slapstick.

Generally, children preferred comedies (and they still do). The broader comedies — unvarnished, obvious, pure slapstick — were the films of choice; a steady diet of popular culture that filled an insatiable appetite, just as television programs and video games do today. Children loved watching the Marx Brothers films. Often they were included in the "Saturday afternoons at the movies" social menu.

Ah, the Saturday afternoon social menu! From the 1930s to the '50s, and to some degree the '60s, it was *de rigueur* for urban children to go to the movies on Saturday afternoons, usually without their parents; it was an opportunity to escape from the usual rules of acceptable social conduct imposed by adults. For parents, this Saturday afternoon interlude served as a symbolic popular-culture baby sitter. When children went to the movies "all alone," usually their siblings or a group of friends accompanied them.

Aside from what was unfolding on the screen, what was happening in the audience was just as entertaining to the analytical observer. Trying to follow the plot of the films was disconcerting to anyone in the audience who wanted to listen to the dialogue. The children wanted action, pure and simple; anything else bored them. During the scenes that focused on exposition of plot, there was always an underlying, constant hubbub running through the audience — chatter, giggling, outright laughter, popcorn throwing, spitball shooting — making it difficult, if not impossible, to hear the soundtrack until the next action scene. It was true with comedies as well: Unsophisticated preadolescent audiences only wanted to see broad, unvarnished slapstick. They ignored any dialogue calculated to amuse, ridicule, or condemn; they thought it was tedious.

A Marx Brothers film had the same effect on children. They screamed with joy at the slapstick portions, and were indifferent to the clever and barbed dialogue, if they understood it at all. The subtlety of the anger embedded in the social criticism spewing forth on the screen was completely lost on them, as it may have been to some adults.

Most people didn't think that the films were anything more than crazy comedies, and that the Marx Brothers were the craziest of all the comedians making movies. This was the theme that movie studio advertising perpetrated to promote the Marx Brothers. But for those who heard the substance of some of the dialogue, and empathized with the acidic vitriol that tried to neutralize the prevalent social, political, and business establishment, the films were a glittering jewel in a field of dross. They were a refreshing way to denigrate a smug, uninformed, haughty, and often pompous American society, more often than not, surrounded by a seemingly impenetrable battlement of social, cultural, and mercantile arrogance. The films were a metaphor: the four Marx Brothers lobbing verbal grenades over the impregnable walls of Caroline Astor's designated Four Hundred.

This is the essential underpinning of their humor. The physical humor was simple slapstick, but the verbal humor, expressing outrage about the world surrounding us, was more trenchant and provocative. Perhaps this is why writers and critics adored and idolized the Marx Brothers when they appeared in shows on Broadway; they loved the physical energy on the stage, but they looked beyond the broad and quotidian humor of the vaudevillian jokes to what the dialogue was really saying. Much of the humor and satire in their vaudeville days and their stage shows (and subsequently in the films) emanated from contemporary social and cultural references. This has always been the operative construction of comedy. The references to the world around us are the basis of the humor in comedy.

These references abound. As we look at the Marx Brothers' films today, some of the references to the culture of that time may be difficult to understand fully, because of the temporary nature of most topical references. It's as if you were to tell a joke five years from now with a punchline based on something in today's newspaper. Your audience, for the most part, won't "get it." Contemporary audiences simply may not identify or understand the "dated" topical references in the films and their relevance to everyday life, then or now.

A perfect example of how quickly a reference may become obsolete occurred during a performance of the Broadway stage version of *Animal*

Crackers. George S. Kaufman reputedly said that Groucho uttered the ad lib that produced "the greatest single explosive laugh in Broadway history."[37] Harpo was in the middle of a leisurely, and probably boring, harp solo when Groucho, with pained ennui, said to the audience, "I wonder what ever happened to Rhinelander?" The topical reference juxtaposed with Harpo's "serious" turn on the harp ignited an explosion of laughter from the attentive and subdued audience. Most contemporary audiences will not understand the joke and its reference. Appreciating the comment makes it wittier and more pointed.[38]

Short-lived references have always been the *bête noire* of comedy. When we know what the comments are referring to, and therefore when we understand the contemporaneous allusions in the humor of the Marx Brothers films, they become more interesting and the humor more pertinent. If we don't know what the references are, it takes some explanation in order to understand them. The purpose of my examination in this book is not just to dissect the jokes, but also to understand the topical references and their shadings of meaning and to put them into context. And thus, not only to explore, where possible, the layers of meaning beneath the outer patina of slapstick in the Marx Brothers films, but also to try to elevate the appreciation of the films to a more sophisticated level, and understand their significance.

Nevertheless, there is a difference between mere topical reference and satire. The attitude and scope of the comedic attack makes the difference. A topical reference implies disappointment with that aspect within a larger society, whereas sardonic laughter calls for reform. Joyous laughter over a topical reference does not imply any larger meaning than the immediate. This is Albert Cook's explanation, in a nutshell.[39]

Originally, during their years in vaudeville, the sophisticated, impromptu topical references came from the Brothers themselves, notably Groucho who was an inveterate reader.[40] Groucho's extra-curricular reading was his *modus operandi* throughout his life. He resented not having had the opportunity to finish his formal education (he went on the vaudeville circuit when he was twelve years old, followed by his brothers shortly thereafter) and so he compensated by reading as much as possible.

Groucho's random education wasn't the primary source of the pointed topical humor of their performances, especially when they "graduated" to Broadway (although he was a master of the ad lib parry and thrust). It actually came from the men who wrote Broadway shows and movies for them, all accepted as among the best in the field of rebellious and irreverent comedy: notably George S. Kaufman (*New York Times* drama critic, playwright, and winner of the Pulitzer Prize, along with Moss Hart, for their play *You Can't Take It with You*), S. J. Perelman (a consistent contributor to *The New Yorker* magazine, his humorous essays and reminiscences were consistently flavored with a massive and rancorous vocabulary), Harry Ruby and Bert Kalmar (clever creators of comic songs in the Brothers' movies, as well as the writers of *Duck Soup*), Al Boasberg (celebrated for writing the famous "stateroom scene" in *A Night at the Opera*, the Marx Brothers' most commercially successful film), Morris (Morrie) Ryskind (a playwright, gag writer, and screenwriter who collaborated with Kaufman on several projects), and even Buster Keaton, who worked on sight gags for the Brothers. Metaphorically, when life threw lemons at these men, instead of passively offering resistance by "making lemonade," they pitched the lemons back, along with anything else they could — a bouillabaisse of cutting insults, quicksilver ripostes, verbal jabs, puns, and wordplay that would make even the diehard advocate of the *bon mot* cringe. As always, these writers aimed their punches at a figurative solar plexus.

■ ■ ■

Just as with the other performing arts, not all films are art. Some are produced for the purpose of entertainment, just as some of the other arts are not meant to be statements of the artist's philosophy. If we watch films with the viewpoint that they are only entertainment, many of the possible richer meanings can be lost. Movies are both an art form and a form of entertainment, and frequently a single film can be both simultaneously.[41] The condemnation of American society is the more significant meaning of the Marx Brothers films, although when asked, the brothers denied it. They claimed that they were "just four brothers," entertainers, trying to make a living.[42] Nonetheless, beneath the superficial patina of slapstick and broad comedy, we discover glimpses of a more serious purpose presented by the Brothers and their writers — specifically, that the films scrutinized and attacked a variety of aspects of American life at that time: WASP arrogance, higher education, war, politics, grand opera, retailing, advertising, "western" movies, shifty real estate offerings, horse races, boxing, gambling, Prohibition, et al. References to events of the day were a comedic frosting, heightening the understanding of the dialogue. As well, their assault on their societal, social, and political surroundings helps the films pass the test of time. Their irreverence continues to be cogent. Coated with this icing of penetrating, irreverent, and often lowbrow comedy, the films themselves are timeless.

2. Triumphs, Tryouts, and Turkeys: The Film Career

When the Marx Brothers began making films, they brought to the screen the same iconic characters that they had developed with success throughout their years on the stage (first in vaudeville and then in musical comedies on Broadway). These characterizations were distinct, yet traditional, in the history of theatre. Groucho was the cynical wit of the group, a sharp-tongued "fast talker who is forever trying to take someone in," and who was continually pricking the bubble of social pomposity with his verbal jabs.[1] The Marx Brothers were all about words (their films were "talkies," after all). Especially with Groucho and Chico, dialogue was the primary method of expression. One critic contends that Groucho "killed" his targets verbally.[2] Harpo was a silent buffoon, having started in their vaudeville days playing a country moron in a school act where he was "the bumpkin with the idiotic stare and the lolling mouth."[3]

By the time the Marx Brothers had refined and developed their characters many years later, Harpo had flowered as a mime. He was a carefree cherub, a Pan-like *naïf* who seemed to float through the films as master of his own world. If comedy writers created his sight gags, it wasn't obvious. He took great joy in energetically (and musically) leading children (and some adults, especially in the barn scene from *A Day at the Races*) with him toward an imaginary world of fun-filled days. It was always sunny in Harpo's child-like world. Children in movie theatre audiences on those long Saturday afternoons were willing and ready to follow Harpo from the moment he plucked a warm and lyrical arpeggio on his harp, or appeared as a Punch and Judy puppet in *Monkey Business*. He never appeared to be serious, even in scenes where he was supposedly fighting. He would strike a boxer's stance, raising both fists, and swing his left arm like a pendulum or a baseball pitcher winding up to throw a fastball. Then he would "punch" his opponent by kicking him in the rear with his right foot as if he was making fun of the entire fight. Some twenty years later, Milton Berle, America's first television superstar and comedian, mimicked Harpo's disarming gesture. Berle would hold up his left hand in a humble gesture, palm outward, to a studio audience in the middle of their wild applause, silently begging ironically that they stop their accolade. At the same time, with his right hand below the camera's focus, he would motion to the audience to applaud more vigorously, like a traffic cop at a busy intersection commanding a speedier free-flow of vehicles in one direction while holding up his other hand to intersecting traffic, wordlessly commanding them to halt. These contradictory gestures (rear kicking by Harpo and the hand-waving comic deception revealed as the camera panned down on Berle) always delighted audiences.

Richard Schickel contends that Harpo "was the last great silent comedian, supplying the Marx Brothers films with pantomime comparable to that of silent days."[4] In his silence, Harpo displayed an unblemished innocence as if it were the essence of a perfectly ripened piece of fruit, like a chef's reduction, always ready for him to use as a powerful grace note of flavoring. His character was straightforward, and understood by everyone. He was the geometric opposite of Groucho's devious hostility, even vaulting international language and social barriers as any great mimetic character does. Revered by both the hoi polloi and the privileged, by the 1950s he was a colleague and friend of the French mime, Marcel Marceau.[5]

Chico always appeared as an immigrant — an ignorant, casual, yet crafty partner to Groucho's schemes, and a willing colleague of Harpo's. Chico used a pseudo–Italian accent in the American vaudeville tradition of the comic character who represents a recent émigré. Between 1890 and 1920, immigration from Europe was at its peak, so "when Irish, German, Italian, Jewish and other immigrants passed through the gates of Ellis Island, each nationality had its stock prototype on the stage, usually portrayed at the level of the lowest common denominator."[6]

Zeppo usually was costumed fashionably, as opposed to the assortment of seemingly haphazard costumes worn by his brothers. He played conventional romantic roles on stage and in their films, although his portrayals appeared wooden and dispassionate. Zeppo's character was the Establishment, in manner and dress, always playing straight man to his brothers.

In their early vaudeville days they were just a singing act, similar to many other acts with bookings scheduled on any one of a multitude of vaudeville circuits touring throughout the United States. Gradually they started to add comedy because their audiences didn't want to hear four guys just singing.[7] Their comedy skits were not distinctive; they copied those of other performers. Sometimes their famous uncle, Al Shean, wrote their material. Shean, whose success came from years of performing with Edward Gallagher in their legendary ("Absolutely, Mr. Gallagher?" "Positively, Mr. Shean") vaudeville routine, would incorporate outrageous, sometimes witless puns in his scripts for the Brothers.

The Brothers depended on these scripts by Shean, and whatever they could construct from their recollection of other acts, observed over the years. But they came into their own in Texas. And so it goes: Apparently a single incident nurtured their unique style of comedy. Kyle Crichton identifies this incident as the moment when the Marx Brothers were "born."[8]

Arguably, their "birth" occurred during a performance in Nacogdoches, Texas, in 1907[9] or 1912[10] or September 25, 1916,[11] when they first broke away from their heretofore established format with its primary emphasis on music and moth-eaten comedy. In the middle of a matinee, someone ran into the auditorium and interrupted their performance by shouting the news to the audience that there was a runaway mule on the street in front of the theatre. Suddenly everyone left to watch this attention-grabbing event. The Brothers went outside to see this spectacle, too. But they were furious that a runaway mule upstaged their performance. Finally, as the local citizens trickled back to their seats, Groucho, venting his resentment and frustration at the interruption to their performance, began to ridicule the town and its population for its boorishness and provincial stupor. It was the first concerted effort at an ad lib performance by the Brothers.[12] And it provided the spark to what amounted to the eventual conflagration called The Marx Brothers, as we know them today.

In the middle of a pause in a sentimental song that they had always considered "one of their more important dramatic moments," Groucho inserted a few lines ("Nacogdoches is full of roaches"). It wasn't quicksilver wit on a par with Oscar Wilde, but it did defuse the anger that the Brothers felt and restored their youthful vigor, mentally and physically. They began to ham up the rest of the song ironically until it was in ruins. At the next pause Groucho inserted "The jack-ass is the finest flower of Tex-ass."[13] Instead of being insulted, the audience loved it. The Marx Brothers were the hit of the day, perhaps the entire theatrical season in Nacogdoches. So memorable was this historical theatrical event that a marker commemorating it still stands in downtown Nacogdoches at the site of the former opera house and theatre. And, so memorable and important was this groundbreaking matinee to the Brothers that it hardly seems coincidental that they probably contributed the idea of naming their mythical kingdom Freedonia in *Duck Soup*, after the Republic of Fredonia of 1826 in Nacogdoches. The Fredonia uprising was one of the several attempts at freeing Texas from Mexico and subsequent to forming an independent republic.[14] The leaders of the uprising named the territory around Nacogdoches Fredonia, derived from the word freedom. It became a common name for Nacogdoches, just as Columbia was a common name for the United States in the eighteenth century. Local area residents sometimes use the name Fredonia even today as a sobriquet for Nacodogches.[15]

The Marx Brothers made thirteen films. Paramount made the first two, *The Cocoanuts* and *Animal Crackers*, as adaptations of the triumphant Broadway musicals having the same names. Several writers wrote ten of the remaining eleven as original screenplays. *Room Service* (1938) was an exception. It was an adaptation of a same-name Broadway play that opened in 1937, written by John Murray and Alan Boretz.

Paramount also produced their third, fourth, and fifth films, *Monkey Business, Horse Feathers,* and *Duck Soup*. After the release of *Horse Feathers*, the Brothers decided to produce their next film themselves. It was to be an adaptation of George S. Kaufman and Morrie Ryskind's *Of Thee I Sing*.[16] The Brothers dropped their plans for this production because they could not raise sufficient financing. Instead, they made *Duck Soup* (1933) for Paramount. After the release of *Duck Soup*, two major changes occurred in their career. First, Zeppo left the act to work in business. He no longer wanted to be their straight man.[17] Second, their association with Paramount ended, and the Marx Brothers moved to Metro-Goldwyn-Mayer.

A change in management at Paramount during the completion of *Duck Soup* prompted the Brothers to move to MGM. Chico, who was managing the Brothers at the time, was wary of these executive changes. He feared that the studio would not renew their contract.[18] More telling than different personnel at Paramount, the freezing wind of criticism about *Duck Soup* was blowing in from audiences and exhibitors. Thomas Doherty reports that exhibitors were angry about the box office terms demanded by Paramount, criticizing the film as not appealing to a mass audience because it was "just a lot of gags" with no harp solo from Harpo or piano interlude from Chico. One exhibitor was so angry that he referred to the Marx Brothers as the Wisecrack Brothers, while another remonstrated that each new Marx Brothers movie "gets worse."[19] The film's cynicism shocked audiences at a time when newly elected President Franklin D. Roosevelt was trying to solve the problems of the Great Depression and the rise of Hitler and the Nazis in Germany.[20]

Suspicious that Paramount might not renew, Chico managed to get Irving Thalberg, MGM's head of production, interested in the Brothers. During the first meeting with them, Thalberg was highly critical of their Paramount films. Thalberg's remarks incensed Groucho. Thalberg analyzed their five Paramount films, suggesting improvements that he would like to make.[21] He stressed the need for a coherent plot to temper their antics and add some dramatic flesh to their wildly comic interludes. This was Thalberg's

The Marx Brothers. Taking a break at Paramount in Hollywood: (from left) Harpo,
Chico, Groucho, Zeppo (early 1930s).

usual approach to filmmaking: He believed emphatically in the value and importance of a good story in movies, and thus "took an active role in story and script conferences."[22]

Thalberg expanded on his theme. He said that the trouble was that although the films were funny, they had no story. According to Arthur Marx, Groucho's son, Thalberg had a firmly conceived concept of film comedy. He believed that he could sacrifice comedy for plot, and that it was better to have a story that audiences would be interested in, rather than an endless chain of comedy scenes held together by a flimsy story. As well, Thalberg thought that comedy should help a sympathetic character as well as further the plot, rather than appearing out of context with the story line.[23] Thalberg thought that the Brothers were only funny when their characters were helping someone else.[24]

Thalberg's concept was antithetical to the way the Marx Brothers had been working for the previous twenty years; however, they acquiesced, at the urging of Samuel Goldwyn, and signed with Metro-Goldwyn-Mayer to make two pictures for Thalberg.[25] Groucho, whose attitude toward movie producers was usually acerbic, was impressed with Thalberg. He changed his mind completely. "I finally met a Hollywood producer who knows what he's talking about," he said.[26]

Their first film for MGM was *A Night at the Opera*, and for it Thalberg contributed a pre-production idea that Arthur Marx, Groucho's son, considered "a revolutionary way of making screen comedies."[27] After the writers had completed the script, at a story conference with all the Brothers, Thalberg asked Groucho what he thought the chances were of having a successful film. Groucho was skeptical because in making a movie there was no way to predict with any certainty if, or how, an audience would respond to any of the comedy scenes or jokes. He recalled their experience with legitimate theatre when the Marx Brothers had a chance to preview a show on the road for several weeks before opening in New York. With such an extensive tryout, writers could revamp weak scenes to make them more successful.

Thalberg tried preview screenings of his films to help decide whether or not to rewrite, reshoot, or reedit.[28] After Groucho's comments, Thalberg suggested a variation of his usual method of testing: He wanted to try some of the *A Night at the Opera* scenes as a "vaudeville" show, as a preview in front of a live audience, interspersed with flashing some of the narrative on the screen so that the audience would be able to follow the plot. If they tried this method of testing their films, they could rewrite weak comedy scenes. After playing on the road for several weeks, they would return to Hollywood and shoot the movie with the rewrites in place.[29] This gave them a better chance to diminish Groucho's justifiable skepticism and to produce a hit movie.

Thalberg's idea was a smart and simple form of market testing. It was a variation of the out-of-town previews described by Groucho and prevalent in drama and comedy productions for live theatre to help producers, writers, and directors determine which scenes were working, and which weren't. But the boys were unenthusiastic about the quality of writing usually found in Hollywood. Thalberg challenged them to make a suggestion and Groucho responded by saying that Kaufman and Ryskind were their choice, but they couldn't persuade them because Kaufman disliked being away from New York. So adamant was Kaufman that he said that he wouldn't "go any place where he can't be in Times Square in twenty minutes."[30] Supremely confident, Thalberg said that he could persuade Kaufman with a single telephone call. He did. Thalberg guaranteed Kaufman $100,000 just for working on *A Night at the Opera*. It was a huge fee in those Depression years and was enough to entice him to come to Hollywood and work on the movie with Ryskind.[31]

Thalberg's concept of taking the selected scenes on the road was vaudeville reborn. In vaudeville and the legitimate theatre, writers could refine their scripts based on audience reaction. Vaudeville comics, after playing countless weeks and years on the vaudeville circuit, knew exactly what worked, having refined their acts accordingly. For the Brothers it was like being home again. These road shows of selected comedy scenes had them regressing 15 years or more, returning to their roots as an itinerant music and comedy act on the vaudeville circuit, but this time without the need to stay in fleabag hotels or cheap rooming houses for traveling actors.

Thalberg used this market testing experiment for *A Day at the Races* as well, allowing the Brothers to try several comedy ideas before the production team settled on the best ones for filming. One report states how they had tried eleven different versions of scenes in eleven consecutive shows. In fact, the writers revised scenes so rapidly, there was hardly time for the boys to learn the new material before appearing with it in front of an audience. Prompters had to coach the Brothers from the wings while they were on stage.[32] How delicious it would have been to be present at these performances, script in hand, just to see how much ad lib material the boys were creating to bridge the gaps between what they knew and what they couldn't remember! Apparently this road testing was so successful that Thalberg thought of trying it with other MGM films, not just Marx Brothers comedies.[33]

A brilliant refinement in the actual shooting and editing of the films emerged from these pre-production, on-the-road tryouts. It was a way to edit the films to accommodate audience laughter. Thalberg hired young writers George Seaton and Robert Pirosh to work on both *A Night at the Opera* and *A Day at the Races*. As part of their duties, they traveled with the cast for the road show tryouts of both films and rewrote (Seaton called it a little "patchwork") some of the troublesome scenes. Pirosh and Seaton would sit in the audience at every performance and time the length of the laughs. Then they would calculate the average of all the time the audience would laugh at each joke. When they returned to Hollywood after six or eight weeks on the road, they informed Sam Wood, the director, how long each laugh would be; Wood could "cut to a reaction shot" of Harpo and Chico just standing there during some of the joke lines "until a laugh died down." Because they knew approximately how long the laughs would take, they would time the reaction shots accordingly. Thus, audiences in movie theaters wouldn't miss the next line of dialogue, essential to the verbal acuity of the Marxian films. If you look at *A Night at the Opera* or *A Day at the Races*, you can see how they keep cutting to shots of Chico or Harpo doing nothing. This was all predetermined, and worked well with a full movie theatre audience.[34]

Upon reflection, Thalberg's pre-testing was not a perfect solution. Doherty suggests that the timing of the audio track of a film was difficult because of the variations in audiences, even in the same theatre. On the stage, "wisecrack" comedians, especially the Marx Brothers or Mae West, could refine their deliveries instantly; they could pause in response to "bursts of hilarity" before delivering the next line, or move on quickly if a joke fell flat. No amount of previewing scenes in front of live audiences could ensure complete success once a movie was on film.

Another obstacle was the cultural and regional differences in America. The disparity between big cities and smaller towns and rural areas was greater in the 1930s than it is today, because of the limitations and lack of immediacy of mass communications at that time. Radio was not as omnipresent then, television was practically unknown, and not every town had a movie theatre. American language was still the result of pockets of regional and cultural variations. Today, as a consequence of faster media and the broader scope of mass communication, the regional differences in American English, both in pronunciation and references, are less of a stumbling block to understanding. Now, language, even coming from the big cities, is more comprehensible to the entire population, no matter how far-flung it may be. That's why a vast television audience can understand sophisticated references made by a late-night talk show comic. In the 1930s it was difficult, almost impossible, for someone who grew up in a rural area to understand the language and references in those wisecracks that came from the polyglot population and ethnic ghettos of big cities, and often were part of screen dialogue.[35] This was especially true for the Marx Brothers, aka "The Wisecrack Brothers."

Although we might consider Thalberg's concept of writing comedy naive, it was logical. Thalberg guided his writers to remember his preliminary analysis of what was wrong with the earlier films produced by Paramount. As he planned it, the *Night at the Opera* comedy scenes are more cohesive with the story. As well, the Brothers help a sympathetic character (Ricardo Baroni, played by Allan Jones) to achieve his dream of singing grand opera in New York. The story, as slight as it may be, works even if you take the Marx Brothers out of the film.[36]

They tried Thalberg's innovation and it helped make *A Night at the Opera* one of the most successful that the Marx Brothers ever had.[37] In its first release it apparently made a profit of more than $3,000,000 at a time when admission to movies ranged from 25 to 40 cents.[38]

Unfortunately, Thalberg died during the shooting of *A Day at the Races*. Groucho took his death as both a personal and professional loss. He thought that Thalberg had been the only producer in Hollywood who understood how to make a good Marx Brothers movie.[39]

After completing *A Day at the Races*, there appeared to be a lack of interest in negotiating a new contract between the studio and the Brothers, just as there had been at Paramount four years earlier at the end of shooting *Duck Soup*. In October 1937, four months after MGM released *Races*, the Marx Brothers announced that they had signed a contract with RKO Radio for three films. First was to be *Room Service*.[40] This film was a departure in style for the Brothers, because it was a straight comedy rather than the type of musical comedy usually written for them. The film did not include many of the usual devices used by Harpo, Chico and Groucho. Harpo did not honk the automobile bulb horn he usually carried, nor did he play the harp. Chico did not play the piano. Groucho, who had a dance sequence (usually the tango) in every one of their previous films, did not dance.[41] They tried to follow the script as written for the stage. But some of their signature devices remained: Groucho still wore his silver-rimmed glasses, Chico still played the role of an Italian, and Harpo was still a mime.

Chico did not like the film. He characterized it as the first time they had appeared in a play that they hadn't created themselves, and he thought that they were no good at it. He was emphatic in saying that he and his brothers had to originate the characters and the situations. "Then they're us," he stated. "If we get a gag that suits our characters we can work it out and make it ours. But we can't do gags or play characters that aren't ours. We tried it and we'll never do it again."[42]

The Brothers did not make three films for RKO as they had announced. Upon finishing *Room Service* they returned to MGM for their next three films, *At the Circus*, *Go West*, and *The Big Store*. Arthur Marx thought that their ardor for making films had cooled by this time, partly because of Thalberg's death. Apparently, MGM felt a little cool toward the Marx Brothers, too.[43]

An erosion of enthusiasm for making films began to show in correspondence between Groucho and his associates and friends. During a two-year period between June 1939 and June 1941 he wrote several letters to Arthur Sheekman, a screenwriter and personal friend. In one letter, he was cautiously optimistic about the outcome of *At the Circus*.[44] When he saw the finished film, he was no longer cautious; he was openly antagonistic. Groucho mildly described his feelings by writing that he "didn't much care for" *At the Circus*. In the next sentence he was more vehement. "I realize I'm not much of a judge but I'm kind of sick of the whole thing and, on leaving the theatre, vowed that I'd never see it again." As disappointed as he was about *Circus*, he was still proud of *A Night at the Opera* and "to a lesser degree" *A Day at the Races*. He described his feelings about the rest of their films by saying that they "sicken me, and I'll stay clear of them in the future."[45]

When they made *Go West*, the Brothers once again performed the comedy scenes in theatres prior to actually filming. But by this time, Groucho's bitterness toward making movies was more apparent. Even before they began making the film, he was negatively inclined toward it. He wrote several letters to Sheekman during various stages during the making of *Go West* displaying an increasing sarcasm, but with a comedic bite in several of them, both toward this film and (in general) about making movies. Even before they began filming *Go West*, Groucho was skeptical.

> The boys at the studio have lined up another turkey for us and there's a strong likelihood that we'll be shooting in about three or four weeks. I'm not looking forward to it but I guess it's just as well to get it over with.[46]

Groucho was particularly impatient with the personal interplay among the studio production staff during the making of the film. He thought that the politics, intrigue, and chicanery involved in producing the film were appalling. Production meetings were the most torturous for him and he wrote to Sheekman that if he had to try to take these meetings seriously he'd probably kill himself. As surcease to this depressing thought, he noted that as soon as he was able to get away from the meetings and the studio, "it all recedes into a shadowy insignificance and I play the guitar and think of other things."[47]

Groucho thought that the road tryout of *Go West* had accomplished its purpose "even though we were ready for a sanitarium" at the end of "those haunted weeks."[48] Aside from his rancor, he concluded that they were able to get many more laughs at the close of the trip than they had been getting at the beginning.[49]

However, studio executives postponed filming several times, the result of office politics. Groucho feared that he and his brothers had forgotten all the dialogue they had carefully rehearsed on the road.[50] After reading the revised script, Groucho wrote to Sheekman with vitriolic irony that he didn't blame the producers for postponing production. "If they were smart," he wrote, "they'd pay us off and get three other fellows to take all that money and open up a big, gaudy cat house. Perhaps a drive-in with girls between the layers of bread. For dressing they could use mayonnaise."[51]

Near the end of filming *Go West*, Groucho began to think seriously of abandoning his film career. "I'm shaping my ambitions in other directions and discussing a radio show that I might do," he wrote to Sheekman.[52] The Marx Brothers formally announced their retirement from films at the conclusion of shooting *The Big Store*.[53] Groucho and Harpo had decided a month earlier that they were going to disband. Groucho reported this to Sheekman, still with a negative evaluation of their current efforts. "We are starting our picture next week and it stinks!" he wrote. "[T]his will ring down my Marx Brothers career. I'm firm about disbanding, as is Harpo, and from now on I'm strictly on my own."[54]

Although the brothers decided that *The Big Store* was to be their last film, Groucho was still censorious. He was critical of the production, commenting on some revisions in the dialogue by a new writer, hired specifically to rewrite a comedy scene, resulting in Groucho's condemnation that "these jokes will be six times as unfunny when they reach the screen." Groucho further disagreed with the producer, who had thought that the audience, during a preview of the film, reacted negatively because the plot was confusing. Groucho demurred. He thought that the audience hadn't laughed because they didn't understand the jokes.[55] Stoic about the film after all, Groucho was happy to retire. He wanted to "escape from this kind of picture and the character I'm playing" for he described his feelings as "wholly repulsive" about the character he was playing.[56] Groucho's public explanation was different. He called the retirement a move motivated by audience reaction rather than personal animosities by the Marx Brothers. He described their retirement to a newspaper reporter by saying that the audience was tired of the Marx Brothers, and their retirement was anticipating public demand "by a very short margin. Our stuff is stale. So are we," he said.[57]

This was not the first time the brothers had discussed retirement; they did not make their previous discussions public. Groucho and Harpo had "pretended" to retire once before, solely for Chico's benefit.

Chico gambled obsessively during his entire life, often irresponsibly. George S. Kaufman once described Chico as "an odd combination of business acumen and financial idiocy, a man who will bet you that three Rolls-Royces will pass the next corner within three minutes. Or they won't."[58] When the brothers completed *Room Service*, Groucho and Harpo hesitated to sign their new contract with MGM in order to frighten Chico, who was anxious to sign. He needed the money to pay gambling debts he had incurred. At the height of Chico's anxiety, his brothers agreed to sign; however, they forced Chico to turn fifty percent of his weekly salary over to them to save and invest with their stockbroker.[59] According to Arthur Whitelaw, even this ploy did not prove to be successful, because Chico eventually gambled away his trust fund, and died practically broke.[60]

As early as 1942, Chico wanted to come out of retirement; he predicted that shortly he and his brothers would return to making films.[61] But it wasn't until 1946 that the next Marx Brothers film appeared.

Returning to work in 1945, they made *A Night in Casablanca* for United Artists. Time had not mellowed Groucho. He commented to Sam Zolotow, a writer for the *New York Times*, on the uselessness of protesting about the movie business; however, he speculated about the reasons that "so much bilge appears in your neighborhood theatre."[62] He also complained to Zolotow about *A Night in Casablanca*, writing a long (for Groucho) letter and including an ironic, and probably apocryphal, anecdote remembered from his days in vaudeville. He described his labors in making the film as a parallel to one of the rats in a long, forgotten, two-a-day act called Swain's Rat and Cat Act. Groucho described Swain's vaudeville act in detail, remembering that it consisted of six rats dressed as jockeys, who were perched on six cats, dressed as horses. They galloped furiously around a miniature race track.

He also conceded that he earned more money in the movies than Swain paid his actors; Swain paid them in cheese. He deduced that although it didn't sound like much salary, it was all net: The rats didn't have an agent, they booked themselves independently. Ergo, there was no agent's commission to pay. Groucho speculated that he wasn't as well off as the rats were. Of course, his salary was in money, but most of it he used to pay for fuel, shelter, and income taxes. With the remainder, Groucho said that he was able to buy cheese, but he had no manager to deliver it to him, and he had to take a bus to the grocery store and shop for his. Groucho concluded by saying that if *A Night in Casablanca* turns out disastrously, and there was no reason why it shouldn't, he was going to look up Swain and ask him to revive his act with Groucho playing one of the jockeys.[63]

After *A Night in Casablanca*, the Brothers made *Love Happy*, based on a story by Harpo and released in 1949. It was a far cry from the films they made in their prime, with practically no satire to add spice to its dialogue. It was the last film in which the Brothers were preeminent. It was the last Marx Brothers movie.

3. The Writers

He was the most illustrious playwright in America. The author of more than 40 Broadway plays, usually collaborating with other playwrights, he was a successful and famous director — the most eminent on Broadway — both of his own work and the work of others. He was a "play doctor," with the ability to home in on how to "surgically repair" the weak spots during tryouts in plays by other authors. (He would continuously look for weak spots in his own work, too.) In addition to these prominent accomplishments there were other achievements: He was a journeyman writer in the theatre, writing "blackout sketches" for musical revues, as well as the author of humorous verse and prose for newspapers and magazines. When Hollywood beckoned, he became a script doctor, author, and director, even though he disliked being away from Broadway for too long. George S. Kaufman was all of that, and more. Starting his lifetime career as a newspaper reporter from Pittsburgh, Kaufman was eventually the drama editor for *The New York Times* for 13 years, at the same time turning out a continual stream of extracurricular writing for theatre and magazines. In his job as drama editor, he had plenty of time for other writing.[1]

Kaufman's style of writing was laconic and pointed. The discipline needed to be a newspaper reporter contributed to that. He wrote dialogue that was sharp and believable, and funny. Being a reporter probably taught him to be skeptical of anything, and irreverent toward everything. Personally he was mordant, and his writing for theatre reflected his personality. It was satiric and caustic, heavily flavored with wisecracks and deflating comments. Howard Teichmann, a collaborator and friend for the last ten years of Kaufman's life, noted that "anything that was mighty was fair game for him.... Taxes, the Congress, the Presidency, the Supreme Court, Big Business, Hollywood."[2] Deflating pomposity was his war, words were his weapons.

He hated sentimentality and even though he wrote comedies that often contained love scenes, he consciously avoided writing these romantic episodes, actually going so far as to tell his collaborators, whenever a love scene had to be inserted, "I'll walk around the block while you do the love scene."[3] Kaufman despised sentimentality in any shape or form.[4] When Irving Berlin presented a new song, entitled "Always," to Kaufman for inclusion in the stage version of *The Cocoanuts*, Kaufman said that the lyrics were too sentimental. He claimed that he knew nothing about music; words were his strength. He analyzed the first line of the refrain, "I'll be loving you — Always," to support his case. He thought that "always" was a long time for romance, citing a multitude of newspaper stories about "middle-aged husbands who had bricked their wives up in the cellar wall and left for Toledo with the maid." He suggested, cynically, that Berlin should change the lyric to something more in touch with reality, such as "I'll be loving you — Thursday."[5]

This dismissal of sentimentality was in tandem with the change in social attitude that was a result of World War I (called naively "the war to end all wars"). Malcom Goldstein suggests that the war, more violent than any others, erupting without rational thought, brought about disillusion about life that had been the norm before 1914, and was reflected in attitudes toward society, labor, and sex, and unmistakably evident in the arts.[6]

Kaufman's work with the Marx Brothers came about gradually, first after his introduction to and friendship with Harpo, and then, after meeting Groucho. Kaufman and Groucho had a mutual respect for each other's professional abilities; Groucho thought that Kaufman was the wittiest man he had ever known. As well, Groucho thought that Kaufman's literary style led him to develop his own style further.[7]

Nonetheless, Kaufman was not keen about working with the entire Marx Brothers clan. Their reputation for unpredictability had not only preceded them, it was unacceptable for Kaufman. He simply did not like the idea of anyone changing or cutting his lines, even the glib and lightning-fast purveyor of ad libs that Groucho Marx was. He accepted the assignment of writing *The Cocoanuts* for the Broadway stage with assurances from Sam Harris that Harris would keep the Marx Brothers' stage behavior at a manageable level. Although Kaufman had started working on the script alone, and took credit for it, he invited Morrie Ryskind to collaborate with him. Ryskind was delighted.

At this point in their career (before the stage play was written and produced and became a hit), the Marx Brothers were anxious about working with Kaufman and Harris. Both of these Broadway veterans were more famous than they were. Moving to *bona fide* Broadway musical comedies was a huge step forward for the Brothers; heretofore, the professional quality of the writing and production of their performances was dubious, at best. The Brothers thought that it was important, even critical, to be allied with Kaufman and Harris. The course of their professional future depended on it. And so, they departed from their usual disregard of a script or direction during the tryouts and early months of the run of *The Cocoanuts* on Broadway. It was clear to them. Kaufman and Ryskind had established rules that they were expected to follow. Kaufman's rules were not just for the Marx Brothers, he expected professional conduct from everyone throughout his career. When the Marx Brothers were late for a rehearsal during the tryout in Boston, Kaufman hit the roof, threatening to leave the production immediately. Finally, Ryskind persuaded him to stay.[8]

When Kaufman and Ryskind started working on *The Cocoanuts* it was like the casting had come from heaven. The Marx Brothers were perfect candidates to espouse Kaufman and Ryskind's vivisection of the chicanery of the Florida land boom and the sleazy business practices associated with it because the Brothers shared their distaste for silly or pompous social and cultural habits, as well as business, government, and political deceit.

Kaufman established self-imposed writing guidelines for Ryskind and himself. Simon Louvish notes that before writing the Broadway version of *The Cocoanuts*, Kaufman understood that he shouldn't alter the characters developed and refined by the Brothers, but rather shape their "naturally anarchic inclinations" with a more focused, sharper satire.[9] He wanted to enhance their satiric impulses with a more worldly focus and to give greater importance to the humor than the Brothers could themselves. Although he wanted to shape the satire, he didn't want to change the characters that the Brothers had already established; he just wanted to "get into their heads" and create a more socially critical Marx Brothers stance, refining what the Brothers had been doing for years, and take them to a new level of sophistication amid their muscular and destructive physicality. It wasn't enough to comment on the roaches in Nacogdoches, or to simply run amuck, chase pretty blondes, and make outrageous puns. He broadened the humor with a subtext that was critical of greater components in modern life. And it wasn't enough for Harpo to simply destroy a grand piano on stage. It was a more pointed comment for Harpo to pull the framework and strings out of the wreckage, fashion them into a harp, and play a semi-classical etude. Wisely, Kaufman applied his writing guidelines to create Marx Brothers films, too. Harpo claimed that he only knew one or two songs, and certainly nothing that came close to classical music. In fact, as his career progressed, with the added direction of more sophisticated writers heeding Kaufman's guidelines, Harpo's solos became more intense, more ironic, as they climbed up the musical ladder toward classical music.

Morris ("Morrie") Ryskind collaborated with some of the best known comedy writers in America, as well as writing entirely on his own. His professional identity came from his work on Broadway, but in fact he also wrote lyrics, plays, and film scripts throughout his career. Visibly questioning authority was evident even in his college days. Columbia University expelled him. In writing for the college magazine, *Jester*, in 1917, he referred to Nicholas Murray Butler, the president of the university, as "Czar Nick" because he refused to allow Count Nikolai Tolstoy, Leo Tolstoy's nephew, to speak there. His expulsion didn't faze him at all. His anarchistic streak served him well when he wrote for the Marx Brothers both on Broadway and in films.

His work with Kaufman on the stage play of *The Cocoanuts* came about when they accidentally met on the street in New York. Kaufman decided that he wanted a collaborator, even though he had started writing the book for the show already. On the sidewalk that day, he asked Ryskind to work with him. Ryskind was ecstatic about the idea. They had known each other for some ten years before that, when both were contributing humor to Franklin P. Adams's newspaper column, "The Conning Tower." In the early years of the twentieth century, young writers who wanted to gain more experience and exposure could submit their unsolicited work to newspapers — poetry, prose, humor — in the hope that it would appear in those papers and that the striving authors would eventually be recognized, and ultimately compensated for their efforts. Of all the New York papers that had columns devoted to light verse, prose, and humor, Adams's column was the most famous and popular with readers. Starting in 1909, Adams printed contributions by Kaufman regularly. He also printed work by Edna Ferber, Ring Lardner, Sinclair Lewis, Dorothy Parker, Alexander Woollcott, and Marc Connelly. All of them ultimately published elsewhere and became famous writers in their time.[10]

Although Ryskind worked with Kaufman on the stage production of *The Cocoanuts*, Kaufman took sole credit as the author. The credits show that Ryskind provided "additional text."[11] Kaufman did not deny Ryskind's contribution; he acknowledged it openly.[12] Ryskind did get screen credit for adapting the play to film. He had full collaborative credit as author with Kaufman on the stage play of *Animal Crackers*.

The Depression brought about changes in the nation's economic life, but it also created new themes in theatre and films illustrating the drastic shift in the political and economic environment. Ryskind, in a reflection of his undergraduate days at Columbia, was the most politically minded of all of Kaufman's collaborators. His distrust of government turned him from a liberal, as he had been at Columbia, to a political conservative by the time Franklin D. Roosevelt ran for a third term in 1940.[13] Kaufman and Ryskind wrote *Of Thee I Sing*, a biting satirical musical comedy about American politics and the presidency. It was natural that Kaufman, having the need to deflate the bombast of the Establishment, especially in politics, and Ryskind, the old liberal, would feel at home writing this. *Of Thee I Sing* was so successful that its winning of the Pulitzer Prize was notable because it was not predictable as the winner, and more unusual because it was the winner in the drama category.

In all of their collaborative efforts, Kaufman and Ryskind delighted in turning the accepted order of things upside down, both in ideas and with the words that described them. But it was another Quixote who entered the realm of the Marx Brothers — a fresh and innovative satiric voice in the American idiom — who made a further contribution to the Brothers' best work. S. J. Perelman not only tilted at the windmills of high society, big business, theatre, movies, celebrities, and politics, but he upended language, with a Herculean vocabulary that was a fluid and lyric delight. Perelman, in his days as an undergraduate at Brown University, had problems similar to Ryskind at Columbia. In his senior year he was editor of the *Brown Jug*, the university's humor magazine. Soon after taking this post, he began to rail against the provincialism at the university and the inconsequential intellectual interests of the student body, at the same time trying to broaden the magazine's appeal to off-campus readers, who made up two-thirds of the distribution of the magazine, by making the humor worldlier. In the January 1925 issue he wrote a serious and venomous diatribe that encompassed "almost everything he found shallow and adolescent at Brown."[14] Perelman left Brown that year because of academic deficiencies. He couldn't pass trigonometry, even though he took the course several times. He was three credits short of getting his degree.

Perelman frequently drew cartoons for the *Brown Jug* and even designed sets for student theatrical productions. His writing was serious, but occasionally his riotous comic imagination came through, a foreshadowing of things to come in his professional life. Once, writing a student editorial about parricide, a flight of wild humor emerged when he cited the story of a student at Harvard who had murdered his parents and disposed of their bodies with an eye toward making money. The Harvard student, "reported" Perelman, had fed his parents on raisins and rusty well water until they were chemically about 95 percent iron. He sold their bodies to a dealer in scrap iron. The dealer sold them to a foundry that melted them and made them into tenpenny nails and doorknobs.[15]

When Perelman left Brown, he moved to New York. The comic magazine *Judge* offered him a job drawing cartoons. At the same time, he began to focus more on writing, and had two novels published. The first, *Dawn Ginsbergh's Revenge*, published in 1929, was filled with typical, irreverent Perelmanesque humor (one chapter that takes place in New York's Chinatown is entitled "Vandal Explosion Rocks Chow Mains").[16] In October 1931, Perelman and his wife, Laura, went to see a performance of *Animal Crackers* on Broadway.[17] Groucho had written a blurb for the *Dawn Ginsbergh* book that the publisher edited to be: "From the moment I picked up your book until

I laid it down, I was convulsed with laughter. Someday I intend reading it."[18] It was typical Groucho Marx humor, and in keeping with the flavor that Perelman favored: the turning of language around into a delicious insult. At the theatre that night, Perelman sent Groucho a note thanking him for the blurb, and Groucho invited Perelman and his wife to come to his dressing room after the performance. Perhaps to control the meeting by adding a shocking and *gauche* element to the setting, Groucho entered the dressing room wearing nothing but his under shorts. He confessed that he had an ulterior motive for this impromptu meeting. He wondered if Perelman might want to write a radio show for the Brothers. Perelman was flattered, but confessed that he had never written a radio script and wouldn't know how to begin. "Neither has Will Johnstone," Groucho announced.[19] In Groucho's mind, it was a *fait accompli*: Perelman would collaborate with Johnstone. Groucho went on to explain that Johnstone, like Perelman, was a comic artist and a staff member of the *Evening World*, a New York newspaper. Johnstone was also the author of *I'll Say She Is*, the Broadway show that helped the Marx Brothers make the chasm-spanning leap from vaudeville to musical comedy. Groucho insisted that Perelman's anxiety about writing a radio script was no obstacle. Perelman thought that Groucho's logic was perverse. Groucho couldn't imagine two writers who were more ill-equipped to create this radio script than Perelman and Johnstone, but he reasoned that because of their ingenuousness they might come up with something fresh.

Perelman and Johnstone started to work together, and began by getting to know each other. Johnstone, in his late fifties, was a cheerful newspaperman; a jovial raconteur with a "fund of newspaper stories."[20] After a couple of enjoyable working sessions, the only idea they had was something vaguely to do with stowaways on shipboard. However, they thought it was too silly to develop. Shortly thereafter, they had a meeting scheduled with the Brothers, but thought that because of the inadequacy of their stowaway idea, they should withdraw from the project in defeat. In a meeting with the Marx Brothers a few days later, they told them the stowaway idea thinking that the Brothers would reject it. To their surprise, Groucho, after a quick conference with his brothers, announced that Perelman and Johnstone had stumbled onto "something big," not just a fly-by-night radio serial. The Marx Brothers had decided that it would be their next movie.[21]

Perelman and Johnstone went to Hollywood to start the script. Aware of their shortcomings as screenwriters, and to make their work more acceptable, they included as many technical terms as they could, i.e., Jackman and Dunning shots, even a Vorkapich. Six weeks from the day that they started work, they read the screenplay to the brothers. The reading was to be on a Friday evening at the Roosevelt Hotel.[22] Fearful about the evening, Perelman and Johnstone flipped a coin to see who would read the script to the brothers. Perelman lost; he had to read it. With trepidation, Perelman read the script to an audience of the brothers, their wives, relatives, and, by Perelman's count, another 19 people — friends, gag writers, their "supervisor" at the studio Herman Mankiewicz, studio executives, "several cold-eyed vultures obviously dispatched by the studio" — and various dogs, domestic pets of the Brothers. A total of twenty-seven people and five dogs were the entire audience. With great anticipation from the assembly, Perelman began reading the 126-page screenplay. Although there was some mild laughter at some of the jokes at the beginning of the reading, this soon dissipated to a deathly silence, partly exemplified by the fact that many of the audience had fallen asleep. When Perelman finished with a final "fade out," there was silence. Dead silence. Chico turned to Groucho to ask his opinion. Groucho said, "It stinks." Immediately, Groucho stood up and left, followed by the rest of the audience. Perelman and Johnstone thought that their participation in the project was doomed; the Brothers had rejected their work conclusively, leaving no doubt about their thoughts. The next day, they learned that the Marxes thought that they could salvage the script. It took five months of rewriting before they were ready to film *Monkey Business*.[23]

Even before they came to Hollywood, Johnstone had predicted that their first meeting with the Brothers, lunch at the Astor Hotel in New York, would be "disorganized." But Herman Mankiewicz (who was to write *Citizen Kane* with Orson Welles in 1940) was more direct. He said that no matter what script they produced, the Marx Brothers were "mercurial, devious, and ungrateful. I hate to depress you," he added, "but you'll rue the day you ever took the assignment. This is an ordeal by fire. Make sure you wear asbestos pants."[24] Years later, Jack Benny was furious with Groucho for the same reason. Benny had invited him to appear on his show as a guest; Groucho had praised Benny's radio show, and thought it was very funny. But he couldn't understand how it was consistent week after week. Benny explained that the consistency came from the fact that the writers, working on weekly situations, knew the characters better. Benny asked Groucho to be a guest on his show. Groucho agreed. He sent his writers to Groucho with the script, and Benny said that Groucho "thought it was lousy." Benny explained that these were the same writers who had written all his shows, those who Groucho had praised. Benny described Groucho as always being nervous: "Even before he read a script he would think it wasn't any good."[25]

It is reasonable to conclude that during the years at Paramount, the writers of the Marx Brothers films created their most satiric and most anarchic films. Kaufman was one of the most acerbic and anti-establishment voices in America. Ryskind and S. J. Perelman had burst forth as political and social gadflies in their college days. All of them retained their youthful indignation for their entire careers. These three men, along with a handful of others, practically set the tone for satiric humor for the first half of the twentieth century.

Hollywood studios made it a practice to hire other writers to help with scripts, writing what they termed "additional material." Sometimes there were two (or more) sets of these freelance writers working on the same scenes, not knowing of each other's existence.[26] It was secretive and grueling (with unrealistic deadlines set by producers and directors) and, naturally, extremely competitive. When the brothers started working with Irving Thalberg on *A Night at the Opera*, they made it clear that they wanted Kaufman to write the movie. When Kaufman finally agreed, as usual he collaborated, and his partner was Ryskind. Of course, in the established *modus operandi* of writing a movie script, there were three other writers involved: James McGuinness, who conceived the original story, Buster Keaton, the great silent film star and gag writer, and Al Boasberg, one of the most prolific and respected comedy writers in Hollywood in the 1930s.

Boasberg was the ultimate script doctor. He had been writing for vaudeville, nightclub acts, radio, and eventually movies. Jack Benny paid him $1,000 a week just to have him review his scripts. Benny paid him whether or not he actually wrote anything.[27] Boasberg also wrote gags and routines for Keaton's silent films, some of them the most respected of the Keaton oeuvre. Bob Hope, Sophie Tucker, Eddie Cantor, George Burns and Gracie Allen, among many others, turned to Boasberg for help with their vaudeville and radio shows.

Although he did not have a screen credit for *A Night at the Opera*, Boasberg in his usual role as a script doctor wrote "additional dialogue." According to some accounts, he wrote the famous stateroom scene by himself, but there is no documented evidence to prove it, just anecdotal. Arthur Marx reports that when he was writing, Boasberg hated to be rushed. He would slow his efforts purposely if a producer called for more speed. After a couple of weeks of writing the stateroom scene, after much "hounding" by Thalberg, Boasberg telephoned him to say that he had finished, but that if Thalberg wanted the scene, he'd have to go to Boasberg's office to get it because he was going home for the day. The Brothers were just as anxious to see the scene, so they walked with Thalberg to Boasberg's office. They couldn't find it, even after going through desk drawers and filing cabinets. Groucho looked up and saw that Boasberg had torn the script into tiny pieces, "each just large enough for one line of dialogue," and tacked them to the ceiling. Groucho reported that it took them five hours to put it together.[28]

In all, there were at least 29 writers credited with creating the films during those 20 years. Some worked on multiple films; others made minor or fleeting contributions, often not credited. Boasberg worked on only two of the films. Hired by the studio just to be a script doctor, he deserves attention because of his stature and longevity in show business. His renown came from his ability to focus on weak spots in a script, just as Kaufman did. His strength came from the fact that he could find a weak spot in a script and sometimes with just a word or two he could heal the ailing scenario. But, unlike Kaufman, Boasberg was not a household name. He probably preferred to bask in the reflected luminous spotlight of the famous comedians for whom he provided material. Although Jack Benny reputedly paid him that $1,000 a week (all this during the Depression, when 25 percent of the American workforce was unemployed), he knew Boasberg's limitations, and said that he wouldn't pay him ten cents to write an original script.[29]

After the first seven films, the scripts (with the exception of *Room Service*, a straightforward filmed version of a Broadway stage play) began to appear formulaic and, according to Groucho, "tired." Groucho's viewpoint was more than a casual observation aimed at garnering a laugh or two. It was a damning criticism; he expressed his thinking clearly in his letters to Arthur Sheekman.

Sheekman had been a newspaper reporter in Chicago. He had interviewed Groucho backstage after a stage performance of *Animal Crackers* in Chicago, but Groucho actually wrote the column for Sheekman, and Sheekman used it.[30] They became friends and Groucho was influential in getting Sheekman work as a writer, working with Perelman and Johnstone on *Monkey Business* and *Duck Soup*.

Kyle Crichton thinks that the Brothers' method of comedy was a reflection of the irrelevant illogic displayed in the humor of S. J. Perelman and Robert Benchley, but not directly influenced by it. Generally, his conclusion is correct, but not for all the Brothers. Except for Groucho, the clan would not have been reading *Judge* or *Life* (the comic magazine, not the weekly journalistic photography-news magazine published from 1936 to 1972) during the time just after World War I, while they were traveling from town to town doing two shows a day in vaudeville. They certainly would not have been reading Kaufman or Ryskind, Perelman or Benchley. Crichton suggests that there was something in the air that brought about their irreverence.[31] They were not alone. On both sides of the Atlantic Ocean, attitudes were changing. Both the Dada artists and the surrealists in Europe were equally a wild and heady circus creating irreverent art and ideas, with Salvador Dalí as one of their chief ringmasters. In America in the Twenties and the beginning of the Thirties (before the grim reality of the Depression overshadowed everything), a similar flaunting of the pre-war social norms was prevalent; overriding everything was the quest for fun and diversion, although without serious titles as Dada or Surrealism that their European counterparts affixed to their occupational frivolity. When Harpo joined some of his fun-seeking, pun-seeking cohorts from the Algonquin Round Table for a summer on the Côte d'Azur in the south of France, their antics became the talk of the Riviera among the American and British literary and theatre colony. Crichton described it as the Age of Wonderful Nonsense.[32] Among the literary crowd at the Algonquin Round Table, irreverent to a fault, their attitude toward pre–World War I social notions showed in their work and in their personal lives.[33]

One of the techniques used by the writers to define Groucho's characters was the reversal of the method of the most popular style of humor of the day — that of making large matters trivial. Faced with dangerous and maybe even life-threatening situations, Harry Langdon or Eddie Cantor, even Chaplin, would be likely to wave them off as inconsequential. Groucho's characters would do the opposite, building from something inconsequential to full-blown, angry outrage. Sheekman analyzed Groucho's characters thoroughly, saying that if a man met Groucho and politely asked, "How are you?" Groucho would reply by asking "You want to know how I am? A man can't even feel bad without a lot of nosy people wanting to make something of it. How am I? As if you cared. A hypocrite. Next thing you'll be asking me to lend you a match. I lend you a match and then you want me to lend you my wife, and eventually ... lend you a fortune. I can see it in your eye. Just a passing acquaintance, and you say, lend me a fortune."[34]

We see this angry outrage in *Duck Soup* when Groucho's Rufus Firefly provokes a war between Freedonia and Sylvania by verbally turning a tiny slight into a monumental climax leading to a real conflict between the two countries.

Making mountains out of molehills was one of Groucho's predictable methods of creating humorous outrage throughout the Brothers' films, just as the musical interludes by Chico and Harpo were predictable nonverbal breathers always placed after the comedy scenes in their films as they had been in their vaudeville and Broadway performances. But these were just techniques. A more meaningful observation of the role of their writers was how and why the writing changed from the first films for Paramount, then under Thalberg at MGM, and finally, to the ensuing years after the films at MGM.

The evolution started simply enough. There was nothing different about the writing in the first Marx Brothers films produced by Paramount; they were adaptations of their Broadway successes *The Cocoanuts* and *Animal Crackers*. Perelman and Johnstone tapped the same anarchic vein as the previous two films when they wrote *Horse Feathers*, with the plot subservient to the Brothers' antics, some of which were their vaudeville routines, recycled. One can almost sense the tone of these first films changing, when they cut from the high antics of Marxian energy to a subdued exposition of their flimsy plots. It was as if each film were two movies: a wildly comic section followed by a snippet of mundane plot. This format was the same as many musical revues and Broadway musical comedies at that time. They juxtaposed the high energy of the singers and dancers in the musical scenes to the more becalmed exposition of their skimpy plots. No one bought tickets for these traditional Broadway musicals because of their serious and incisive ideas about which an audience could reflect and discuss afterward.

After the failure of *Duck Soup* to capture an audience and Paramount's disenchantment with the Brothers, Thalberg's insistence on a stronger, more coherent story took the films in a new direction. It didn't matter that Kaufman and some of his rebellious coterie continued writing the films, Thalberg had a clearly defined vision for the writers. His concept was artistically sound. As the chief architect of *Opera* and *Races*, he tempered his productions to encourage box office sales, as all the studios did. More than ever, the plunge of ticket sales during the Depression had a sobering effect throughout Hollywood. By 1935 an even more severe change affected the industry: Hollywood producers, Thalberg among them, were particularly careful to adhere to the guidelines of the Production Code. The Code was instrumental in changing filmmaking for decades.

Groucho's distaste for what their films had become came only from his viewpoint. From a different perspective, the fall from the über-satirical Paramount years to the more story-conscious Thalberg films and finally down to the uninspired comedies leading to Groucho's dislike of their films, starting with *At the Circus*, was the result of economic considerations and the enforcement of the Production Code.

The Code was the result of longtime social pressure established to restore morality (as defined in those years) to American films. The federal government created Prohibition in the 1920s to curtail vice and degradation in saloons, and the "guardians of civic virtue" monitored morality in motion pictures ever since 1896 with the first on-screen kiss. In 1922, in an effort to overcome negative publicity from off-screen scandals and the Jazz Age departure from Victorian social codes shown on screen, studio executives installed Will Hays, the former postmaster general under President Warren Harding, to lead the Motion Picture Producers and Distributors of America, an industry group that was trying to restore a good reputation to the industry. Still, this moral effort produced little of its intentions as producers and writers managed to sidestep the precepts of the MPPDA. By 1930 the Hays office created the Production Code to give a clearer and more formal definition of the guidelines for the industry "in the new, harsher decade." Finally, in 1934 Hays appointed Joseph Breen, a former newspaperman, to enforce the principles and "particular applications" of the Code. Although MGM and all of the Hollywood studios did not always observe the censorship established by Hays, when given muscle by Breen starting in 1934 they abided by it dogmatically. Breen's tenacious efforts changed movies for some twenty to thirty years thereafter.[35] The current film rating system is an outgrowth of the Code.

Starting with *A Night at the Opera*, released in 1935, the fear brought on by the Breen office affected the producers and writers of the Marx films even though the focus of the comedy in these films was on satire and comment about human, social, and cultural foibles as their major focus rather than sex, crime, immorality, and other moral issues. Concern about these moral issues had been the driving force behind the criticism of films by religious and civic interest groups, yet they affected all feature films, including those of the Marx Brothers. In fact, in *At the Circus*, Groucho makes a wiseguy reference to the Breen office.

Whatever lascivious elements surfaced in the Marx Brothers films, they were mild, ambiguous, and fleeting. Theatrically, they were simply throwaway lines. Often muttered rather than shouted, these slight sexual implications were not the overriding reason why audiences were attracted to Marx Brothers films, unlike some of the other, more explicit pre–Code films. Many of the verbal pseudo-sexual references in the Marx Brothers films came from Groucho's delivery.[36] Groucho could deliver a line to Margaret Dumont or Esther Muir with intonations that made it sound sexually suggestive, but it actually wasn't. As written, it would be an innocent sentence. But with Groucho's verbal treatment and with an added unctuous emphasis, we understand the subtle intimation. Sometimes just a waggling of his eyebrows was all it took to turn an innocent phrase into a steamy sexual invitation. The waggling was sufficient to wiggle the dialogue past Breen's piercing eyes.

Other verbal techniques in Marx Brothers films were more subliminal, and easier to slip past the Breen censors. In fact, an armchair psychoanalyst might parse them as sexual references. In *The Cocoanuts*, Groucho shows Dumont a section of sewer pipe, an obvious phallic symbol that he takes out of his pocket. He describes it as an eight-inch pipe. All prospective property owners for the plots he's going to auction at Cocoanut Manor will be required to vote on the size of their pipe. It's as if he's describing a tribal social ritual and requirement where the size and length of a man's penis is the determining factor in his status in the community.

The shift in Hollywood was so predominant and the power of the Breen Office so forceful that Thalberg and MGM, and all of the Hollywood studios for the next thirty years, worked with strict adherence to the Code's rules. The Code was one of the reasons why American films changed. The studios knew that they had to conform; otherwise they could not release their films and they would lose money.

As well as any moral issues that he had to consider, Thalberg took other steps to insure the success of *Opera*. After the outrage about *Duck Soup* expressed by exhibitors and audiences, Thalberg knew that he had to require that the Marx Brothers' writers lessen the political bite of the films. Once Thalberg released *A Night at the Opera*, and it was a box office success, the tone shifted even more toward audience-pleasing comedy. *A Day at the Races* proved once again that Thalberg's formula could work. After that film, with the Breen Office in full force, there was no longer a need to use the caustic talent, with its subliminal sexuality, of Kaufman, Perelman, Ryskind *et al*. The scriptwriters who followed seemed to use the Marx Brothers' comic antics as a tempering spice. After the two Thalberg productions, these writers added even more alkaline to calm the hydrochloric acid that had been the trademark of the Marx Brothers for more than twenty years.

The Breen Office was so powerful that it wasn't a minor irritation. It was a major consideration in creating movies for theatrical release. And so, the producers and writers of Marx Brothers films began to soften their acrimonious focus, from subjects that were meaningful to those that were minor social irritations, or were simply amusing based on their familiarity to a mass audience. The goal was to produce more crowd-pleasing, morally acceptable fare. The new and younger comedy writers created Marx Brothers films that were still amusing, often funny; but there was less social criticism, and it was infinitely milder, less frenetic. In the hands of this new generation of writers, the Marx Brothers films almost became family sitcoms.

4. You Can Get Stucco

For their first film, the Brothers reprised their stage success *The Cocoanuts*, a vigorous swipe at land speculation and scandal in Florida during the 1920s. The Broadway show had been an easy, almost obvious target for Kaufman and Ryskind, for the Marx Brothers, and subsequently for Ryskind when he adapted the play to the screen. It was understandable that Ryskind was essential to the creation of the film; he had worked on the original stage version of the musical with Kaufman and was experienced in working with the Brothers. That Ryskind was an accomplished and well-known writer with a long résumé as a skit writer for vaudeville acts and writer of comedy for the theatre probably helped to ease the show's transition from stage to film. However, the choice of the film's director was surprising, even astounding. It was the young director, Robert Florey.

Florey, only 29 years old and a former assistant director in Europe, had just a year earlier written and directed the groundbreaking film *The Life and Death of 9413—A Hollywood Extra*. It was the first experimental film made in the United States to show the influence of German expressionism, specifically *The Cabinet of Dr. Caligari*. *The Life and Death*, only one reel long, was noteworthy for its visual creativity with a resourceful use of sets and props made from paper cubes, cigar boxes, tin cans, an erector set and cardboard figures. Florey and his photographer Slavko Vorkapich made their avant-garde film for less than $100 in Vorkapich's kitchen. When completed, it generated so much interest and enthusiasm that it was booked into seven hundred theatres both in the United States and other countries.[1] Serious film students continue to study Vorkapich's camera techniques. Given the fact that sound was in its infancy (there was an aggressive competition for technological improvement and sophistication among the studios in Hollywood), it seems apt that Paramount would take a chance on the relatively unknown Florey. Florey thought that *The Cocoanuts* was an "experimental film"[2] because Paramount filmed it with sound — one of the first feature films with this new technology. As well, it was one of the first musicals that Paramount filmed. (*The*

40

Broadway Melody is usually considered the first feature-length musical. It opened February 1, 1929, just three months before the premiere of *The Cocoanuts*.)[3] There were two directors for the film, Florey and Joseph Santley, who had been a Broadway star, a director and writer. The film credits show Santley before Florey even though the studio hired him just to set up the musical numbers.[4]

The Cocoanuts was a hilarious comment on the kind of boom-and-bust story that makes headlines and has universal appeal in practically any culture at any time in history, with its elements of anticipation, envy, danger, fear, greed, and distrust. The Dutch tulip craze from approximately 1620 to 1637, the South Seas bubble in England between 1711 and 1720, the American stock market crash, the electronics industry meltdown of the early 1960s, the Internet catastrophe at the beginning of the twenty-first century, and a variety of smaller, fraudulent money-making schemes have all become fascinating and memorable events in popular history. And so was the Florida real estate boom.

On December 8, 1925, the Marx Brothers' theatrical version of their musical comedy, *The Cocoanuts*, opened on Broadway during the height of the Florida land boom. The show ran for 275 performances and went on the road for two years after its New York run. Paramount filmed the movie version at their Astoria, New York, studios. Technically, the studio released it after the Florida land boom had run its disreputable course. Nonetheless, the film was a success as a comic and incisive depiction of the hypocrisy and unethical practices engendered by the boom.

After the opening credits, *The Cocoanuts* shows us a montage establishing Florida as a fantasy come true: people at the beach sunbathing, playing ball, ballroom dancing on the sand (some wearing bathrobes!); on a patio overlooking the beach there are other couples dancing. It is a depiction of the fantasy of countless travel brochures. Twenty bathing beauties do rhythmic calisthenics on the beach and finally lie supine doing a leg-crossing form of exercise to a background of Jazz Age music. Three well-dressed women wearing sleek clothing, looking as if they are dressed for afternoon tea at the conclusion of a day of high-priced shopping in the heart of any large city, sit on a patio at the beach. A waiter in a white jacket and black bow tie serves them. There is a five-piece orchestra playing on the patio. The incongruity of the scene is a subtle comment on both the excesses of the Florida boom and the profligate Roaring Twenties in general.

The film cuts to an interior shot, in the lobby of the Hotel de Cocoanut. Groucho enters; there is no romantic, travel-brochure fantasy here. He has his own fantasy to follow. Walking down the steps from the upper floors of the hotel, he appears to be putting on his swallow-tailed coat. Before he reaches the bottom of the stairs, a phalanx of bellhops dressed in stylish uniforms and pillbox hats approaches him. Their uniforms make them look like a foreshadowing of Philip Morris cigarettes' long-running advertising spokesman, "Johnny,"[5] or perhaps their costumes are a comment on the romantic notions of martial efficiency commonly in practice at 1920s movie palaces where ushers were dressed in stylized military-art-deco–influenced uniforms. The bellhops ask Groucho for their pay. His introductory speech, in response to their demands, is both a monologue and a dialogue with them, and is pure Marxian: brash, subversive, argumentative, self-protective, suspicious, hostile, and sprinkled with several cultural and social references. It immediately sets the tone for the film and gives us a clear look at the character that Groucho has played for years and will continue to play for the rest of his film career. He is a fast-talking entrepreneur who will not brook anything that gets in his way. The bellhops, who are both men and women, accost Groucho: "We want our money," they say. Groucho avoids the demand by turning the request around ("You want *your* money?"). They clarify what they mean; they ask to be paid. We begin to see how shifty that Groucho's character is ("Oh, you want *my* money!"). He sounds as if he resents their demand ("Do I want your money?"). Then he asks them two questions, to which there are no real answers ("Suppose George Washington's soldiers had asked for money? Where would this country be today?").

The bellhops ask for their money again. Groucho answers with a pithy homily that appears to have a deeper meaning than it does ("No, my friends. Money will never make you happy, and happy will never make you money"). But Groucho deconstructs his own homespun counsel. In an aside, he says that it may have been a wise crack, but he doubts it.

The bellhops continue to protest; Hammer hasn't paid them for two weeks. Groucho counters this with a reference to socialism. He continues his umbrage as he asks them rhetorically if they want to be wage slaves. When they respond that they don't, Groucho amplifies his train of thought ("What is it that makes wage slaves? Wages!"). Here is Kaufman-Ryskind's calculated attack on popular culture in full bloom in what sounds like hilarious nonsense, but really isn't. Groucho tells the bellhops to throw off the shackles (i.e., wages) that bind them because he wants them to be free. "Remember," he lectures them, "there's nothing like liberty, except *Collier's* and *The Saturday Evening Post*." *Liberty, Collier's,* and *The Saturday Evening Post* were three popular magazines in America at that time.

Groucho reiterates the theme of freedom for the bellhops but with a monologue that once again takes a healthy swipe at convention, with a slight literary reference (The Three Musketeers: "one for all, and all for one"). He reveals his true goal (a *sub rosa* plea for money), adds a hint of a reference to a popular song ("Tea for Two" from the 1925 Broadway musical *No, No,*

Nanette), and at the same time he mimics grocery store merchandising. He doesn't continue his socialistic diatribe; he reverts to the real capitalism that's deep within his character. He expounds on his viewpoint when he says, "Be free, my friends, one for all, and all for me and me for you and three for five and six for a quarter." We feel the rhythm and tone of this sentence. You can almost hear the music of "Tea for Two" without Groucho singing anything. We are ready to accept anything from this mesmerizing huckster.

At the end of this scene, 12 of the female bellhops perform a dance routine on the staircase leading to the second floor. Their performance is a clear visual reference to the Roxyettes, Samuel Rothafel's mid–1920s all-female precision, high-kicking dance line at his Roxy theatre in New York City. Rothafel changed the group's name to the Radio City Rockettes when he moved them to Radio City Music Hall in the early Thirties.

This first scene with Groucho is a skillfully designed clue about the rest of the Marx Brothers clan, a way for the scene to introduce them to a wide audience throughout America who may have never seen them perform, either in their vaudeville tours throughout the country for twenty years, or in musical comedies on Broadway during the five years before making their first film. After seeing and hearing Groucho, we can begin to surmise what we're about to see on the screen. It is a brilliant introduction to social anarchy, Marx Brothers style.

On the Broadway stage the basic plot of *The Cocoanuts* was flimsy at best, as it was with most musical comedies at that time. The film's plot is no different. For the Marx Brothers, the sketchy plot is merely a rickety framework on which to hang the endemic routines that they had tuned to perfect pitch in their years in vaudeville and on the Broadway stage. An interviewer asked Robert Florey when he first met the Brothers. He said that he didn't meet them until the day they began shooting *The Cocoanuts* and that he first met Groucho when he came on the set with Margaret Dumont to shoot a scene: "They did the scene exactly as they had on stage and that was it." Florey realized that he couldn't direct the Marx Brothers in the usual sense; they had performed this show "a thousand times." The finality of it was that "they did what they did and that was that."[6] When they created the original musical comedy, Ryskind knew Kaufman's thinking about not tampering with the Brothers' characters. Their job was to refine the often haphazard direction that the Brothers took, and make it fit into their vision and comments on the Florida land boom. Florey came to the same realization as soon as he saw Groucho and Dumont do their first scene in the film.

The basic story, of course, features Groucho, the ostensible leader of the Marx Band of non-conformists, playing the clearly eponymous Mr. Hammer (Hammer has no first name). He's the manager of the Hotel de Cocoanut, as well as a sleazy land auctioneer. Groucho/Hammer is trying to keep the failing hotel from bankruptcy, so he's planned an auction to sell speculative plots in a proposed residential development that real estate developers seem to have already rejected in toto. He pursues Mrs. Potter (Dumont) romantically, but at the same time laughs at the traditional language of love with demeaning asides. He is George S. Kaufman, anti-sentimentalist.

In a subplot, Bob Adams (Oscar Shaw) is a hotel clerk and striving architect who has created a revolutionary plan to re-design this rejected land. Like Hammer, Bob wants to succeed, too. He hopes to make it attractive for the developers to reconsider and to buy the entire property, and subsequently to hire him as the architect on the project. He's in love with Polly Potter (Mary Eaton). Polly and her mother, Groucho's eternal wealthy dowager and foil, are staying at the hotel. Mrs. Potter thinks that Bob is not an acceptable suitor for Polly because he isn't financially successful. Bob hopes that his ascent as an architect will eliminate his future mother-in-law's objections based on class distinctions.

The Florida land-rush boom attracted unscrupulous human predators, ready to squeeze money from as many people as possible. The Hotel de Cocoanut has its own in-house predators, revealed in a second subplot. Penelope (Kay Francis), a sultry *femme fatale*, approaches Harvey Yates (Cyril Ring), Mrs. Potter's preferred suitor for Polly, with a "plan to take care of both of us" (financially), by stealing Mrs. Potter's $50,000 necklace. When Yates balks, Penelope vaguely refers to his shady past, intimating blackmail, and Yates agrees to Penelope's nefarious plan. Thus, the subplot is established. At its conclusion, the film resolves this simple intrigue.

During Groucho's opening entrance down the stairs confronting the unified protest of his bellhops with his hints of socialism and capitalism almost in one breath, Zeppo makes his first film entrance looking somewhat embarrassed and casting furtive glances at the camera over his right shoulder. His sidelong glances at the camera are our only chance to see his face in this scene because he enters with his back to us.

Several frames later, Dumont enters. We see Groucho and Dumont alone for the first time, and Groucho wastes no time starting his perennial fast-talking verbal attack. Introducing his reorganization plan, Groucho overwhelms Dumont with the features of Cocoanut Beach (and all of Florida) using the same expressed conviction of the state of Florida's boosters of economic development. In the lobby we see a more fully realized example of Groucho as an expert promoter, a role he plays throughout the film. With the rapid growth of the economy in the 1920s, a new sophistication in salesmanship and advertising emerged. Salesmen were encouraged and expected to be more aggressive, much more so than they had to be prior to the war, because business competition had become more intense.[7] So Kaufman and Ryskind made Groucho/Hammer a slick, apparently dishonest, high-pressure salesman exhibiting the boundless optimism of Florida's land speculators. Aggressive is a mild adjective to describe Groucho's machinations.

He makes an anxious sales pitch to Mrs. Potter. Using a delivery that is machine-gun fast, in the manner of goal-driven salesmen, thwarting every attempt by her to speak, he browbeats her into listening to him by telling her that whether she "likes it or not" he's going to tell her about Florida real estate. He starts by citing the rapid growth of property in Florida. His presentation is similar to that which he offered to his bellhops, but the focus here is on the portrayal of untrustworthy salesmen. In true Marxian fashion, Groucho destroys language itself with a dyslexic statement, that "property values have increased 1929 since 1,000 percent." We don't hear the real words; we rely on Hayakawa's "nonsense communication," his definition of how language works. Hayakawa tells us that we shouldn't take some words literally; their actual meaning is subservient to their social surroundings.

Groucho's verbal inversion is a subtle comment on a technique used by disreputable sales people to hide the truth in case anyone questions the intent of the sales pitch. Hammer invites Dumont to the auction of lots in Cocoanut Manor. He tells her that if she doesn't like auctions, "we can play contract," an allusion to the two methods of bidding hands in the card game, bridge. He tells her that there's going to be entertainment, sandwiches and the auction. This was not just a flight of creative imagination, Kaufman and Ryskind were reporting the facts; their description was accurate. Land developers brought real estate auctioneers from California and New York to auction land in Florida, and they lured people to the auctions with the promise of free lunches, prizes, souvenirs, and entertainment.[8]

Hammer is unstoppable in his recitation ("Forty-two hours from Times Square by railroad, sixteen hundred miles as the crow flies...") capped with the inevitable Kaufman-Ryskind wordplay punch line ("...eighteen hundred as the horseflies"). With undisguised loathing toward unscrupulous sales tactics during the Florida bubble, Groucho points out the property that he will auction and says that it glorifies "the American sewer and the Florida sucker." He finally turns to satirical ambiguity by saying it's the most exclusive residential district in Florida ("nobody lives there"). He describes Cocoanut Manor, this area that he is going to auction, as the biggest development since Sophie Tucker.[9] Continuing his dichotomic presentation of Florida real estate, Groucho claims that Florida is the greatest state in the Union, using the alligator pear (not oranges!) as an example of its superior produce. Perhaps the cadence, syllabic complexity, and rhythm of the words "alligator pear" were more comically appealing to Ryskind, than the simpler, and more accurate, "oranges." Groucho asks Dumont if she knows how alligator pears are made. She doesn't, whereupon Groucho insults her with the quick rejoinder "that's because you've never been an alligator. And don't let it happen again." This is the first of several times in their films that he draws a parallel between Dumont and an animal.

Not even pausing for a reaction from her, and continuing this runaway train of thought, he concludes by asking her if she knows how many alligator pears are shipped out of Florida every year ("and told not to come back"). Once more, she doesn't.

But the Florida Marketing Bureau did. They reported that in 1928-29 Florida farmers shipped 114,396 car lots of fruit and vegetables out of state, including five car lots of pears from Santa Rosa County (but not specifically alligator pears; an alligator pear is not a pear; it is another name for avocado, considered to be a fruit not a vegetable). The marketing bureau was proud of the state's achievement. They estimated the total number of car lots there would have been if they had included those consumed in the state and those destroyed by insects, frost, and storms.[10]

The uplifting features of Cocoanut Manor described in Groucho's speech accurately reflect those of Florida's promoters, even if the implied criticism does not. Both private developers and the state of Florida left no stone unturned in extolling the virtues of the state. They appealed to the wealthy, the middle class, the agrarian population, and the working class. A report by the Florida State Hotel Commission, attempting to provide an informative description of the advantages of the state to tourists, expressed a mood of confident optimism about the population increase and the opportunities in the state, for both the resident and the businessman. Groucho's pitch to Dumont about Florida is prescient, accurately reflecting the optimism of the Florida State Hotel Commission's report. His speech is an uncanny prediction of its findings, because the commission published its report in 1930, a year after the release of *The Cocoanuts* and after the bubble had burst. The report gave readers the impression and an assumption that the boom was still on.

Groucho asks Dumont if she knows that the population of Cocoanut Beach has doubled in the last week. She is doubtful and her response implies her doubt. He explains this population surge by saying that "three bulldogs were born. We're expecting a nanny goat in the morning." He not only ridicules the boasts of Florida's enthusiasts, but suggests that Cocoanut Beach is really a sleepy place of no consequence. The real story of the population explosion in Florida centered around runaway land sales on the lower east coast, particularly in the new cities of subtropical Dade County.[11]

In the description of Florida as the "ideal place to live," the Hotel Commission describes the state as a place for entrepreneurs and blue-collar workers, especially in agriculture, citing the growth and shipment of winter vegetables, citrus fruits, tobacco, and live stock.[12] Florida vigorously promoted its cattle raising, suggesting that the state was "beef cattle country" and inferring that the number of cattle was comparable to the giant herds of the "West." Florida cowboys wore sombreros and "six-guns," and had the ability to roll a cigarette with one hand.[13]

Groucho never misses an opportunity to extol Florida, denigrate Mrs. Potter by insinuating that she's a cow, and throw in a wheezy vaudeville gag, using cattle-raising in Florida as a vehicle for making the state more attractive: "I don't mean anything personal," he sneers, "but here is the ideal cattle-raising section. We have longhorns, shorthorns, and shoe horns."

Agricultural accomplishment notwithstanding, the major element of the boom continued to be land speculation. Speculation was easy and feverish. Without ever seeing the land before deciding to buy, many investors purchased lots directly from blueprints, and they had the thrill of seeing "SOLD" stamped on the blue-lined squares representing their lots.[14] Chico ridicules the use of blueprints as a sales tool with the expediency of an unvarnished pun. Groucho shows him a blueprint of the land that he's about to auction to prospective developers; he asks Chico if he knows what a blueprint is. When Chico replies, "Oysters," the pun appears to be superficial word play. But beneath that single streetwise response are Chico's attempts to deflate Groucho's pumped-up enthusiasm. It rebukes, simply and with the decisiveness of a scalpel in the hands of an accomplished surgeon. The widespread use of a mere architectural tool — a blueprint — as the primary reason for a significant investment was outrageous. In reality, for a prospective investor to use a blueprint of a real estate development as the major factor in deciding to buy land — undeveloped land, at that — is naïve at best, and an illustration of the metaphoric real estate tsunami that was engulfing Florida in the 1920s. As such, oysters are an apt piscatorial reference.

The land boom affected all of Florida, not just Miami. It seemed as if real estate developers were dividing the entire strip of coastline from Palm Beach southward into fifty-foot lots.[15] Of course, Groucho/Hammer doesn't let this slip by his eagle eye. He praises the growth of Florida and at the same time, promoting his own land sale, belittles swanky Palm Beach as a coveted destination for well-heeled vacationers and affluent second-home owners. Taking a generational swipe at Mrs. Potter, he suggests that when she's ready to retire, she should choose Cocoanut Beach. He asks her where she'll be when she's 65, which is "only about three months from now" (Margaret Dumont was the same age as Groucho, around 40). Mrs. Potter, drawing herself up to the heights of WASP authority, says that she would prefer Palm

Beach. Groucho counters by describing Palm Beach as "the Atlantic City of yesterday, the slums of tomorrow."

Subdivisions and new towns were established everywhere in the 1920s, and extended deep into the virgin forests. Real estate promoters destroyed numerous orange groves to make room for subdivisions, especially those who came to Florida to gain quick wealth.[16] Quick was an understatement. In October 1924, one real estate developer sold 300 lots within three hours for a total of $1,685,582. Practically all of them were still under water.[17] In *The Cocoanuts*, Groucho explains to Chico how he is going to sell his undeveloped lots at Cocoanut Manor. Cocoanut Manor lies deep in the forest. The next sequence, between Groucho and Chico, is one that matches Groucho's rapier-sharp comments with Chico's innate "stupidity" as an immigrant character. It is a pointed social comment. Several scenes like this one appear in their films, with just Groucho and Chico. The writers designed them to burst the bubble of conventional thought and practice with hilarity.

Groucho asks Chico if he knows what a lot is. Chico tells him that a whole lot is too much. Groucho tries to get Chico to understand by saying that he didn't mean a whole lot, just a little lot with nothing on it. Chico, after listening intently, ridicules the complexity of the entire real estate system, and at the same time, the vagaries of American English, by "explaining" to Groucho what a real estate lot — a "whole lot" — is. Describing the scene cannot convey our enjoyment of the flavor of it. Only by quoting Chico's monologue directly can we see its splendid destruction of logic:

> Any time you got-a too much, you got-a whole lot. Look. I explain it to you. Sometimes-a you no got enough, it's-a too much, you got-a whole lot. Sometimes you got a little bit, you no think it's enough, somebody else maybe think it's-a too much, it's a whole lot, too. Now the whole is-a too much, a-too much is a whole lot, the same thing.

Groucho expresses unqualified confidence in his ability to sell Cocoanut Manor. This aura of confidence among the slick real estate salespeople was the norm. Lots were being sold that were ten, fifteen, even thirty miles outside Miami.[18] Michael Gannon, the Florida historian, noted that in 1925 property that was six and eight miles outside the city limits of Miami was selling for $25,999 an acre.[19] Exuding boundless enthusiasm and fueled with the adrenalin of self-confidence coursing through his veins, Groucho outlines his vision of the future development at Cocoanut Manor to Chico, in a dialogue interspersed with puns and vaudeville gags. Even without the benefit of plans or maps, the usual stock-in-trade of real estate salesmen, Groucho outlines the future building plans for Cocoanut Manor, describing a division called Cocoanut Heights, currently a swamp, and another division "right over here where the road forks" as the future neighborhood of Cocoanut Junction.

Chico counters Groucho's bombast by belittling his description (and thereby hordes of real-life land salesmen). He asks where Cocoanut Custard will be located. Groucho, undaunted by this snide pun, suggests that it will be on one of the forks. Without a contemplative thought, he thrusts his figurative rapier into Chico's tough skin, by saying that he shouldn't be concerned because he probably eats with his knife.

The puns keep coming, without interruption, as Groucho sums up his recitation of the wonders of the future in Cocoanut Manor. He points out the location for a proposed eye and ear hospital: "This is going to be a site for sore eyes." Some of the puns reflect the influence of vaudeville and immigrant humor that was prevalent during the period of great migration of European immigrants from 1880 to 1920. After he describes the site for the eye and ear hospital, Groucho shows Chico the proposed river front, secured by levees. "That's the Jewish neighborhood?" Chico asks. Groucho dismisses his comment with another ethnic reference ("We'll Passover that"). In 1930, if they had never seen a traveling vaudeville show, many of the citizens of rural towns of the Midwest, miles from the ethnic diversity of Chicago, might not understand these two references immediately.

The demand for real estate was so strong that people bought anything in Florida. Not all land sales were honest; the selling frenzy attracted disreputable promoters from all over the country who sometimes sold land that didn't exist. Sales in Florida were frantic, but even throughout the country people bought land blindly, never having seen it, never having been to Florida.[20]

In the defining moment of the film, Groucho auctions Cocoanut Manor, deriding auctioneers, superficial entertainment, and fraudulent land promoters, all in one monologue. The high-pressure salesmen who practically invaded Florida to work for real estate companies subsequently became targets of suspicion for many people. In this auction speech, Groucho's attack is specific, especially when he describes the area as needing "a few finishing touches." Frederick Lewis Allen described the conditions in Florida at that time as being "actual cities of brick and concrete and stucco; unfinished, to be sure ... while prospects stood in line to buy and every square foot within their limits leaped in price."[21]

In addition to its condemnation of disreputable real estate salesmen, the significance of Groucho's auctioneer is that it shows us a portrayal of the traveling salesmen who plied their wares throughout rural America in the nineteenth and early twentieth centuries. Groucho carries on with the tradition. He is the epitome of the classic snake oil salesman, prevalent in the latter half of the nineteenth century. Traveling hucksters would go from small town to small town in Conestoga wagons selling products of dubious quality. Their wares included elixirs, balms, digestives, and ointments (some purportedly manufactured from snake oil, that all-purpose remedy popular in China and used to ease the inflammation and pain of rheumatoid arthritis and bursitis), all "guaranteed" to benefit their users by making them feel better, look better, recapture their youth, or "cure" those incurable annoying physical maladies that plague people in all walks of life: psoriasis, bursitis, male balding, arthritis, acne, general aches and pains, menstrual cramps, and the physical slowdown signaling the approach of old age. In contemporary use, the term snake oil is a metaphor for the marketing of any product or service believed to be fraudulent.

These traveling salesmen sold dreams (of good health). They sold restorative magic. They sold hope. They "sold" religion. And they even sold housewares, dry goods, and clothing. Often, these hucksters were the only "entertainment" available in isolated rural communities throughout the farms, ranches, and mining towns west of the Mississippi River. Frequently they combined entertainment, sometimes with the help of an aide, adding songs, recitations, dance performances, and magic to their sales presentations. They hawked any curative or restorative medications with the solemnity and fervor of evangelists. With products for use in kitchens, they relaxed somewhat, adding the spice of humor to enhance sales. Usually they were just sly, humorous presentations of these culinary wares ("This kitchen knife is so sharp, it can cut a tomato into paper-thin slices, enough to last a family of five for a week"). Today those same marketing and sales techniques are taught at some of the leading graduate business schools because they apply to marketing a range of consumer products, from breakfast cereal to pharmaceuticals and soap, on television, the Internet, print advertising and radio. Turn on your radio and still you will find preachers howling from distant churches, confident market gurus and pitchmen selling herbal remedies and get-rich schemes.[22] Groucho's character in *The Cocoanuts* (and throughout the rest of their films) is an exquisite rendition of these traditional hard-sell salesmen. His auctioneering style makes specific references to salesmen's practices.

Hammer begins his auction by asking the assembled crowd to step in closer (an old technique used by erstwhile Atlantic City boardwalk hucksters selling kitchen tools and small appliances or snake oil salesmen selling pharmaceutical remedies). At the same time, he takes aim at disreputable real estate practices, and insults his audience, too ("All ye suckers who are going to get trimmed, step this way for the big swindle"). He tells them that before the auction begins there will be entertainment ("We're going to have a little entertainment. Very little!"). He includes a caveat by telling the audience that after the entertainment there will be sandwiches, but if there are no lots sold, there won't be any sandwiches. It is an apt portrayal of the huckster's technique that Groucho ridicules in *The Cocoanuts*, offering "entertainment" to induce sales, combined with the suspicious fast-talking presentation of exaggerated claims about the land he's selling. But Kaufman and Ryskind do more than create an intellectual call for reform; they point out public gullibility. It doesn't matter what you say to the buyers, disparaging, insulting, deflating, they still want to buy. With Groucho's auctioneering, he not only tries to sell the land, but he tells his audience that he's going to swindle them and insults them in the same breath. Think of Groucho as W. C. Fields ("Never give a sucker an even break") or Texas Guinan.[23] Groucho offers a prelude to the auction as he introduces Polly Potter, who sings a song. Groucho scornfully proclaims it to be very little entertainment. After the song, he begins the auction:

> Let's get the auction started.... Eight hundred wonderful residences will be built right here. Why, they're as good as up. Better. You can have any kind of home you want to, you can even get stucco. Oh, how you can get stucco! Now is the time to buy while the new boom is on.... And, don't forget the guarantee. If these lots don't double their value in a year, I don't know what you can do about it.

The country had never seen anything like this real estate explosion before, either in oil booms or free-land stampedes. As early as 1915, one of the developers of Miami Beach, Carl Fisher, was offering beach property free to anyone who would move there.[24] With the characteristic of a classic financial boom, investors bought land for speculation, even if only from blueprints, rather than for substantial development and use. A subtext of untold profits awaiting the new owners was the real reward, after a quick buy-and-resell scenario.[25] Gannon reports that "much of what was being sold was not land but paper. A 10 percent down payment would hold a property for 30 days.... Fast-talking hucksters ... swapped paper so rapidly a single lot sometimes changed hands a dozen times a day."[26]

This one speech of Groucho's, the auctioneer's pitch, is the keystone of the film; it satirizes basic persuasive sales techniques: fear ("Now is the time to buy while the new boom is on"), excitement ("Eight hundred wonderful residences will be built right here"), greed ("If these lots don't double their value in a year, I don't know what you can do about it"), and with a heavy infusion of irony ("...you can even get stucco. Oh, how you can get stucco!").

Despite all the optimism and activity, not everyone who went to Florida made a fortune in real estate. A British journalist, Theyre Weigall, wrote of his experiences during the boom. Burton Rascoe, in the introduction to Weigall's book, described how Weigall lost all of his life savings, leaving Florida no richer than he was when he had arrived, except in experience.[27] Groucho describes the same monetary frustration as Weigall had in his 1932 account of the Florida boom. Once again using the same technique of making a contradictory statement during his auction of land, Groucho describes the financial advantages of buying his lots, and at the same time condemns the generally accepted truism of land promoters in the 1920s who limn vast profits for their prospective investors. When Groucho speaks about opportunities for quick riches, he puts this excessive claim for monetary gain in perspective, when he mirrors Weigall's misfortune. (Paramount released *The Cocoanuts* three years before Weigall published his book.) In the lobby of the Hotel de Cocoanut, Groucho tells his bellhops, "Three years ago I came to Florida without a nickel in my pocket. Now, I've got a nickel in my pocket."

When *The Cocoanuts* opened on Broadway in 1925, Florida was still in the throes of the land boom. But by 1927 the boom was over and thousands of people lost their land, their new property, and their money.

Clearly, the film version of *The Cocoanuts* is a satirical comment on the avarice and chicanery of fraudulent real estate transactions in Florida. Spiced with Marxianic comedy it appears to be a simple extension of the antics that were their trademark in vaudeville and on Broadway. The satire is unmistakable as it should be; its attack neatly deflates all things Florida. But it isn't simply an angry rant.

Admittedly, there's a delicate line between pointed satire and sheer anger; to its credit, the film never crosses that line to evolve into a one-note diatribe. It is, after all, a very clever entertainment, and there is a plot, slim as it may be. It's understandable why *The Cocoanuts* is not more hostile. Entertainment and the creating of a successful film were the motivating factors driving the producing of *The Cocoanuts*. The Brothers had been the darlings of Broadway, even with, and perhaps because of, their unpredictable and irreverent behavior on stage.

When Kaufman and Ryskind created the original stage comedy, they understood the frustration that the Brothers had experienced many times before: They were considered by booking agents, even the most powerful and sophisticated, a rough-and-tumble, unmanageable vaudeville act (albeit funny).[28] Kaufman was hesitant about writing the stage play because of the unpredictability of the Marxes. He knew that the ultimate goal of the brothers Marx was to solidify their presence as Broadway (i.e., legitimate theatre) stars, rather than being considered merely a wild-and-woolly vaudeville troupe with a once-in-a-lifetime legitimate theatre hit in 1924, entitled *I'll Say She Is*. The Marx Brothers had to reinforce the rationale of presenting themselves as comedians, not vaudevillians. So, they needed a comedy that would accede to the demands of Broadway. If they could find one, the critics and theatre owners would not only acknowledge their legitimacy, but their future would be more secure on the slippery slope of instability that has always been prominent in the landscape of show business. There is no doubt Kaufman had the ability to write a more incensed satire, but the reality of what Broadway theatre owners and audiences would accept usually established the guidelines. Kaufman knew how to write successfully for Broadway. At that time, unchecked anger was more customary in the productions presented by avant-garde theatre troupes. Kaufman also realized what Broadway audiences came to see, and hear, when they bought tickets for a Marx Brothers performance. The promise of apparently spontaneous horseplay was a strong lure. He had seen *I'll Say She Is* and he deduced that an intricate plot would get in the way of what an audience really wanted from the Brothers.[29] So, along with Ryskind, he interspersed his viewpoint with a more focused refinement of their established characters to create *The Cocoanuts.*

In 1929 on Broadway, the Marx Brothers were hot. They were performing in *Animal Crackers,* another stage success for them. *The Cocoanuts* had been a hit on the stage just three years earlier. Paramount decided to produce a movie version of *The Cocoanuts* with them as the stars, and began filming it in Astoria, Queens, while the Marxes were appearing on Broadway in *Animal Crackers.* The film didn't have the severe anti-political, anti-war irreverence or hostility that *Duck Soup* was to have four years later, it simply focused on the foolishness and futility of the Florida real estate frenzy. But at the same time it introduced and brought the Marx Brothers to their largest audience ever, nationwide. What is also notable about the film is the fact that the Brothers with their manic theatrical routines introduced an outrageous kind of comedy to America via a mass medium, with the latest and the most sought-after technology — sound — to make the package even more appealing. But the film is more important for its satire and casual, but pointed, references.

Beneath the puns, comic routines, and pratfalls in *The Cocoanuts* we start to see a serious layer of meaning. The Marx Brothers were beginning to topple our cultural and social assumptions as no other comedians on film had. Chaplin's silent film humor, as hilarious as it is, simply attacks our social habits with sweet innocence. The Brothers are hardly innocent. They are a modern-day David battling Goliath.

5. Is It Swordfish?

Two of the Marx Brothers Paramount films, *Monkey Business* and *Horse Feathers*, comment on Prohibition as a secondary, but nonetheless important, theme. Written by Perelman and Johnstone, the studio released *Monkey Business* in 1931 and *Horse Feathers* the following year. It's understandable why Prohibition was a significant topic. It had been in effect since 1920 when the Eighteenth Amendment to the Constitution became law. People commonly referred to the various laws associated with the Eighteenth as Prohibition; it held a social prominence in daily life that was exceedingly visible throughout the United States.

Prohibition was one of the more obvious aspects of how living in America had changed since the end of World War I. By the early 1930s the various communal, political, and economic changes were so dramatic that a desire for a drastic social upheaval seemed to be roiling the country. The stock market collapse of 1929 with the ensuing economic depression fomenting a social revolution juxtaposed with the prominence of Prohibition and its concomitant lawlessness — murder, prostitution, gambling, smuggling, symbolically personified by Al Capone in Chicago — was the obvious way of describing the temper of that time. The American population was calling for dissolution of the laws governing Prohibition by 1931 (the federal government repealed the law in 1933). Even though the government was going to repeal Prohibition's laws in the early part of the Thirties, it was still visible enough to be an element in these two Marx Brothers films. Prohibition was so ubiquitous that we continue to remember it as one of two major socio-political facets of America occurring at that time. The other was the Depression and its effects.

The Eighteenth Amendment attempted to control the habits, and the freedom, of Americans everywhere. Striking at the core idea of one of the founding precepts of the Constitution — individual freedom — made the amendment vastly unpopular. This was one of the reasons for Perelman, Johnstone, Kalmar, and Ruby to write *Horse Feathers* with irreverence toward this law.

Prohibition was a massive effort to stop drinking and immoral activity, but it did not halt the sale of liquor. By the end of the decade between 1920 and 1930 there was nearly as much consumption of alcoholic beverages, if not more, than before the Eighteenth Amendment.[1] People could purchase liquor by the drink in what formerly had been saloons, but were called "speakeasies" during that 13-year period. The word "speakeasy" seems to come from Irish immigrant dialect cautioning to "speak easy because the police are at the door."[2]

Authentic liquor was available in two forms. There was liquor smuggled by boat from Canada across Lake Michigan to Chicago, from Western Canada via the Pacific Ocean to the West Coast, from Mexico by land or sea, and from Eastern Canada and the Caribbean to various points along the East Coast. A second form of liquor was the result of attempts by smugglers to increase profits. They would add water to the liquor and rebottle it. According to Frederick Lewis Allen, "one gallon of diverted alcohol, watered down and flavored, was enough to furnish three gallons of bogus liquor, bottled with lovely Scotch labels and described by the bootlegger at the leading citizen's door as 'just off the boat.'"[3]

Horse Feathers shows us an ironic visual that exemplifies the questionable practices of production and bottling of alcoholic beverages purportedly "just off the boat." In one scene, Chico sits in the back room of a speakeasy behind a closed door, and when the phone rings, he answers it and takes an order for "ice." Then he asks the caller, "What kind of ice?" After listening further, he tells his customer, "All right, lady, I'll send them right over." He picks up a gallon jug filled with unidentified liquid, puts funnels into two smaller bottles, and pours from the same gallon jug into each. The labels on the smaller bottles read, respectively, "Scotch" and "Rye."

Very much like many common foods described as "tasting like chicken," the inference is that during Prohibition the taste of all phony liquor was the same.[4] This also suggests that drinkers didn't care how it tasted; they were only interested in the end result.

Disobedience of the Eighteenth Amendment was so pervasive that by the early 1930s it was safe to flout it openly. In *The Cocoanuts*, Harpo and Chico stand at the registration desk in the lobby of the Hotel de Cocoanut. Hennessy, a detective, arrives and questions their status, suspecting vagrancy. At the same time, in a veiled visual threat, he opens his jacket and shows them his police badge, pinned to the inside of the garment. Harpo, undaunted by the authority of the badge, and with a sly look on his beatific face, opens his tattered raincoat and, with blatant irreverence, shows Hennessy a pint of whisky taped to its inside.

Speakeasies in New York City were often on the ground floor of brownstone houses, behind store fronts, or any other innocent-looking establishment. There was often a small, barred window cut into the front door. After a visitor knocked or rang the doorbell, a bodyguard would look out through the window and decide if he would allow the prospective "customer" to enter. Of course, it was impossible for a bodyguard to remember all of the acceptable customers on sight. One method of gaining entrance, of verifying acceptability, was to show a speakeasy "card"—a certificate of membership in that "private club."[5] Another way to enter was to say the speakeasy's "password," a word supposedly known only to select members.[6]

The plot of *Horse Feathers*, in keeping with the usual format of the Brothers' performances, is often secondary to their vaudevillian comic setups. The primary story is critical of colleges and universities that emphasize sports and extra-curricular activities, rather than focus on serious academic study. Lectures and classroom attendance are meaningless. The only discernable plot is flimsy: Huxley College (with Groucho as Professor Quincy Adams Wagstaff, its new president) is trying to win a football game against its rival Darwin College. Of course, this was an opportunity for Perelman to rail against and satirize the shallowness of a university education, just as he did when he was at Brown. As well, it offers opportunities to have the Marx Brothers use some of the material from skits they perfected in their years in vaudeville doing school acts, with Groucho invariably playing the teacher and Chico and Harpo playing the students–class clowns. And so, Prohibition and the availability of speakeasies with their shady moral connotations is a secondary, but noticeable, target for the film.

Groucho tries to recruit better football players for the college team so that they have a better chance to win the annual Thanksgiving Day game against Darwin. He goes to a speakeasy because he's heard that there are a couple of football players who always "hang around there." Chico, the bouncer, i.e., gatekeeper, demands the password from Groucho. (The password is swordfish.) There is the usual Marxian banter where the scene is set up and language is broken down. Chico asks, "Who are you?" and Groucho, not answering the question, and with a knee-jerk response that mocks polite language, says, "I'm fine, thanks, who are you?" This non sequitur doesn't register with Chico as being amiss (nor would it with us, unless we listened carefully; that's the point beneath the mixed-up language that occurs throughout the films). Chico gets right to business and tells Groucho that he can't enter unless he knows the password. When Groucho asks what it is, Chico tells him that he'll give him three guesses, and that it's the name of a fish. Groucho replies with his first guess: "Is it Mary?" Chico replies, "At's-a no fish." "Well, she drinks like one," says Groucho.

This same kind of unexpected wordplay crops up some thirty years later in *A Hard Day's Night,* the first Beatles film. When the film opened in 1964, many critics thought that the Beatles had the frenetic energy and anti-establishment manner, and use of wordplay, prevalent in the Marx Brothers films. In the Beatles film, as usual, they have long hair. This style of wearing long hair was a departure from men's usual hair styles in the United States in the early 1960s. So when a reporter in the film interviews Ringo, he asks what he calls his haircut. Ringo replies, "Arthur." Chico Marx, who died in 1961, would have loved it.

Groucho's reference to the woman who drinks like a fish subtly signals an important change that had occurred in American society. Aside from the heightened place in cultural life that speakeasies assumed in that era, there was more significance in the fact that women unaccompanied by escorts were drinking side by side with men. Women "stood along with men at the speakeasy bar with one foot on the old brass rail."[7] Before Prohibition, the saloon was a man's domain.[8]

The custom of having one foot on the old brass rail while standing at the bar occurs again in *A Night at the Opera,* as a caricature of saloon manners rather than a specific reference to Prohibition. Groucho walks toward the singer, Lassparri, who is lying supine and unconscious on the floor backstage at the opera house. He puts one foot on Lassparri's stomach. Chico enters, stands alongside Groucho, and puts one of *his* feet on Lassparri's stomach. It's an instinctive move. It is a visual intimation of everyday social manners and custom. Men use a bar rail to help ease into friendly saloon conversation. And when Groucho orders two beers (from an imaginary bartender), reality is suspended. Yet, they enter into polite chatter, inquiring about each other's health, commenting on the weather, and remarking on politics and economic conditions. This scene suggests that we can change our environment, and make it imaginary, by simply making an ordinary gesture, such as putting one foot on the imagined bar rail. In real life, we consider a moment such as this strange. In a Marx Brothers film, it's normal.

Groucho is still at the door, still trying to guess the password. He offers the names of several fish, and Chico replies with a series of off-putting and groan-provoking puns (Groucho: "Is it sturgeon?" Chico: "Hey, you crazy. Sturgeon is a doctor!"). After inadvertently revealing the password to Groucho, Chico opens the door and lets him in because Groucho has "guessed" the secret word on the third attempt. But Chico steps outside and accidentally locks himself out. He knocks on the door. Groucho, now the "gatekeeper," asks Chico what he wants, and Chico tells him that he wants to come in. When Groucho asks the password, and Chico smugly tells him "Swordfish," Groucho says no and declares that he was tired of swordfish and changed the password to something else. When Chico asks him for the new password,

Horse Feathers **(1932). The password is swordfish: (from left) Chico, Groucho (Paramount Pictures).**

Groucho says that he's forgotten it. He steps outside to stand with Chico. Now, both of them can't get into the speakeasy. Rational thought would offer that because both of them know the password, it would be a simple matter to say it to the next gatekeeper who guards the entrance. Not with a Marx Brothers script. It is more important — and more pointed — to comment on the inability to enter, even with knowing the password, than it is to be logical.

Harpo arrives. He knocks on the door, and when the gatekeeper asks him for the password, he takes a huge fish with a sword inserted into its mouth from his raincoat. The gatekeeper lets him in, and Chico and Groucho crawl in under Harpo's legs. This leads to Groucho's inevitable comment on drunkenness, common in speakeasies: He tells Chico to stand up because "that's no way to go into a speakeasy. That's the way you come out."

Of greater significance than destruction of verbal logic, we see another example of the Marx Brothers as outsiders, trying to gain entrance to the mainstream of life. Other film comedians have played outsiders: Chaplin, Keaton, Harold Lloyd, Jerry Lewis, Abbott and Costello, Laurel and Hardy, and many others play characters who are on the fringes of society. Try as they might throughout their films, the Marx Brothers can't enter established American society, even though when they attempt to get into the speakeasy they are trying to enter a world that in itself is outside society, and illegal at that. During Prohibition the illegal (the unacceptable) became acceptable (e.g., speakeasies) to many people as places to gather and socialize.

Groucho and Chico stand at the bar and finally Chico remembers the password. "I've got it," he says, "swordfish." Groucho tells him, "Go outside and see if it works." It's as if the password connotes some kind of magic in American society, a sort of "Open, Sesame!" that allows access to a most important place, the secret cave where Ali Baba enters (using the password he inadvertently overheard from the forty thieves) to find a vast fortune waiting to be savored and enjoyed. Speakeasies during Prohibition were that secret cave.

With the emergence of Prohibition came the rise of organized crime with its gangster syndicates. Bootlegging of whiskey from other countries emerged as a major industry in the United States. Prohibition became big business for the underworld in Chicago even before Al Capone's leadership and brilliance at running an efficient organization.[9] His spectacular flamboyance made him a national symbol of the era, and his success was dazzling. In 1927 alone, Capone's personal net income, even after bribes to police and government officials, was $30,000,000.[10] Capone brought to light the profile of the "respectable" criminal, for on the surface he appeared to live as an honest and upstanding businessman might, with a wife and family. He maintained a townhouse in a fashionable residential Chicago neighborhood. His wife and son were never at a loss for all of the comforts a wealthy man could offer.[11] But, the business practices of Capone and his cohorts were not so glamorous. Murder, gambling, loan sharking, bombings, and mass slaying of rival gangs, were common practice in the efforts toward building such a formidable business empire.

Pseudo-respectability and emphasis on family life created the illusion of decency among these vicious gangsters. *Monkey Business* is about the discrepancy between what appears to be and the reality of what is. An unsuccessful gang threatens a wealthy, but retired, gangster because he has refused to grant them a favor. Joe Helton (played by Rockliffe Fellowes), the retired gang leader, is on an ocean liner returning to the United States from Europe with his college-age daughter, Mary (Ruth Hall). They travel in first-class accommodations. Society columns report their movements. Their clothing is understated and expensive-looking. Their home on Long Island, New York, is a suburban mansion suitable for the top echelons of wealthy families. If we didn't know that the underworld was Joe's source of wealth, the impression that he and his daughter exude is one of utmost decorum. They appear to be members of the same social class that Dumont portrays in her roles in the Brothers' films. The irony of Helton's superficial propriety is an obvious comment about the way in which Prohibition gang leaders lived their private lives, as Al Capone did with the comforts associated with the heightened social status that traditionally accompanies the wealthy.

The trappings of wealth displayed by these *arriviste* criminals belie the truth beneath it. No matter how elegant the homes, the clothing, and the tangible rewards of affluence, including education and an envious social life, they were never too far from the environment that produced their affluence. The underworld bosses, no matter how successful and far up the social ladder they climbed, still needed protection from their street-level rivals. So it was common practice during the Prohibition era for rich gang leaders to hire personal bodyguards, usually armed, to ensure their safety. These bodyguards were at a level of notoriety and status in the community as their bosses were. Most people did not know who the crime boss bodyguards were. There were some exceptions. In New York, one of the most famous was Jack "Legs" Diamond, an infamous personality in his own right, who was a bodyguard to the notorious gambler Arnold Rothstein.[12]

In *Monkey Business*, Joe Helton hires Harpo and Chico as bodyguards while they are all traveling on an ocean liner. "Alky" Briggs, Helton's rival, hires Groucho and Zeppo as his bodyguards. The Brothers, penniless stowaways, jump at the opportunity for employment even at these questionable vocations. Their eagerness implies ridicule of the importance of bodyguards to these underworld figures, and suggests the acceptance of gangsters as part of the American social structure. In an expression of how crucial bodyguards are to the underworld, Groucho approaches Joe Helton with an ironic proposition of both defending and attacking him at the same time; that is, like a Cold War spy, a double agent, who works for both the East and the West. Groucho proposes that he should be a double-bodyguard, working for both Alky and Helton at the same time. To persuade Helton he becomes a snake oil salesman once again, using the slick, fast-talking sales pitch as he did in *The Cocoanuts* and would do in other films that followed.

Groucho, in a reflection of Capone and his rise to power as a model of business acumen, offers himself as a bodyguard, but with intimations of more sophisticated and devious business skills. He tries to interest Helton by offering a 20 percent savings, by suggesting that the gangster's "overhead is too high" and his "brow is too low." Groucho makes a plea for, and satirizes, the need of "streamlined efficiency" in big business.[13] Groucho illustrates his irreverent, logically illogical plan when he describes to Helton that there are two fellows trying to attack him (referring to Zeppo and himself) and two trying to defend him (Harpo and Chico). That's a "50 percent waste," says Groucho. Why can't Helton be attacked by his own bodyguards, he asks ("Your life will be saved, and that's a hundred percent waste"). He comes to the conclusion rhetorically by asking what remains. You've got me, says Groucho, and "I'll attack you for nothing." The idea of murder or mayhem at no charge is also in *The Cocoanuts*, when Chico complains to Harpo that they've been in the Hotel de Cocoanut for a short while and they haven't made any money yet. He's so hungry that he'd kill for money. He'd even kill Harpo. No, he concludes with a chuckle, "You're my friend. I'll kill you for nothing."

Helton is confused, and wants a further explanation, but Groucho wants to make the deal. He avoids an explanation and jumps right to the assumption of the acceptance of his deal. He tells Helton that it's all settled and that he is the new bodyguard, with the job of both defending and attacking him. All Helton has to do is to let Groucho know when he wants to be attacked, and Groucho will be there ten minutes later to defend him.

In the first four Marx Brothers films — *The Cocoanuts, Animal Crackers, Monkey Business,* and *Horse Feathers* — there are references to, or criticism of, Prohibition. But it is in the last two that Prohibition is more prominent, even though it was in its dying days. Social and political conservatives who had championed Prohibition hadn't realized that an even more nefarious illegal activity would be born out of the advent of legislated temperance: the growth of the criminal liquor "industry" and the development of the speakeasy. As a result, they became disillusioned with the amendment. In 1932 Americans elected Franklin D. Roosevelt as the country's president partly on a promise of repealing Prohibition. At last, the end clearly was in sight.

But as serious as the issue of temperance was, a more ominous and grim specter had loomed: the Depression and its ensuing economic and social downturn for the entire United States population and, in fact, the entire world.

Because it was truly on everyone's mind, the subject of the Depression began to sneak into the dialogue, and becomes an obvious social comment from Groucho, even though it is only an oblique reference to it. He talks about the need for belt-tightening and savings in business, but with intimations of the personal need for such economy, when he makes light of parsimony by saying that he's come to realize that the saving may only be "a penny here and a penny there." Look at me, he concludes in *Horse Feathers*, I've worked my way up from nothing to a state of extreme poverty. The comment about poverty is a repeat of Groucho's conclusions about financial stability in *The*

Cocoanuts when he talks about having only a nickel in his pocket. Beside the thought about the threat of poverty, a second and concurrent threat during the 1930s was the foreshadowing and build-up toward another, and even more horrible, world war. After the release of *Horse Feathers*, the Marx Brothers took on both of these threats in their next film for Paramount.

6. The Seven-Cent Nickel

They practically ignored it. The Marx Brothers made no films that satirized or had the Great Depression of the 1930s as an overriding theme, yet this devastating economic catastrophe was prominent in the minds of most Americans — in fact, millions of people throughout the world — whose lives were cut apart by its severity for the greater part of that decade. In general, most of the comedies made between 1930 and 1934 did not have the Depression as their main theme. They "tried to pretend that the Depression did not exist."[1] After 1929, movies were more than simple entertainment; they were an escape from the realities of life outside the theatre,[2] often presented to an audience as a double feature to create a few hours of pleasure.

None of the comedies satirized the Depression because the subject was so serious. There were films that referred to it, called for reform, raised social consciousness, and even showed how people were faring, but they were not comedies, not satire. Any references to the Depression in the comedies of the Thirties were casual and almost an afterthought, not really explored in depth as a serious issue. In *My Man Godfrey* (1936), a comedy also written by the co-author of *A Night at the Opera*, Morrie Ryskind, William Powell is a homeless Harvard graduate, a "Forgotten Man," who lives in what appears to be a Hooverville[3] on the banks of the East River in New York City. Powell tells one of the other downtrodden residents not to worry because "prosperity is just around the corner." At best it is an oblique reference to the popular catch phrase that people used during the Thirties to reassure themselves that the Depression was only temporary.

The lesions caused by the Depression were too deep. This widespread downturn in the economy was too profound to be healed with scathing, finger-pointing humor. It didn't matter how smart or sophisticated that humor might be. Neither Chaplin, Keaton, W. C. Fields, nor Mae West, nor any of the other comedians or directors who made films in the 1930s, focused on the Depression as a main comic theme. Not even the so-called screwball comedies that were prominent in the latter part of that decade made it the main subject of their comic viewpoint. There are references to it in the undercurrent of the comedies, usually used as throwaway lines in dialogue, but on the surface, and to the audiences who went to the movies to escape the grinding realities of the Depression for a few hours, those comments were isolated from the evolution of the plots, almost flippant, just as they were in films made in the first few years of the decade. Generally, the comedies of the period were light and frothy. Social commentary was "slipped into the effervescent escapism of backstage musicals, anarchic comedies, and syrupy melodrama."[4]

Of course, the Depression was too debilitating, too severe, and too serious for Kaufman, Ryskind, Perelman, Kalmar, or Ruby to attack head-on with any of the dishes usually offered on their menu of socially and politically deflating humor. It just didn't seem appropriate. This catastrophic economic downturn was so pervasive, so insidious, that it had a profound effect on practically everyone, practically everything; it affected the middle-class and even the super-rich. The major studios in Hollywood earned millions of dollars every year; nonetheless all of them faced bankruptcy except Metro-Goldwyn-Mayer.[5] The studios suffered with declining attendance and, along with it, declining revenue. Given the nature of how business was conducted in Hollywood — the production of each major film was based on loans from banks and other financial sources — if one film or a studio's entire annual output did not succeed at the box office, the producing studio was faced with ongoing debt, and perhaps total bankruptcy. The economic downturn did not seem to affect movie attendance during the early years of the Depression, but by 1933 it was at a "dangerously low level."[6]

So the studios did what they could to fill those seats. They tried to entice audiences showing nudity, pre-marital sex, drug use, alcoholism, and prostitution[7] with dialogue replete with double entendres and sexual innuendo. (In her film *She Done Him Wrong*, when Mae West with her signature nasal drawl, and her depiction of sex as something to be laughed at, says to a man who's coming to visit her at her apartment "Is that a pistol in your pocket, or are you just glad to see me?" she sidesteps the digression of the ambiguous second meaning and gets right to what's on her — and his — mind.) Audiences loved her nasal flaunting of propriety. Her films were titillating enough to accomplish their goal. Who could think about the Depression when laughing along with Mae? Who could think about their hardships when viewing films whose stories included marital infidelity, homosexuality, and debauchery as prominent or simply shocking themes? Most Americans had never seen dramatic scenes such as these before, and thought they were either outrageous attacks on the country's moral fiber, or fascinating glimpses behind the curtains of respectability. But by twenty-first century standards, the depiction of these themes, even by the notoriously bawdy Mae West, was mild.

Logically, if one of the purposes of creating Marx Brothers films was to create entertainment that diverted audiences from thinking about the Depression while sitting in a theatre for an hour or so, then by focusing on the economy satirically would seem to be at odds with that goal. Yes, satire is a raw and unvarnished attempt toward having an effect on social change. But comedy didn't need to remind audiences of the economic problems during their search for the escape that laughter offered them. The illness of the Depression was no laughing matter.

The writers, and the Brothers, did the next best thing. Although they didn't structure an entire film around the Depression, they didn't completely ignore it. They simply made several fleeting references to it and the hard times of the Thirties, just as other comedy films did. They knew where to draw the line between assigning satirical blame and being critical of the menacing economic misfortune that attacked everyone in the country. They didn't want to cross that line so they wrote sly jokes about aspects of the weak economy, but the Depression itself was taboo. The scattered comments about some of these economic and social conditions in the films were clever and muted references to the state of the economy. On the surface they appeared to be passing thoughts. Beneath the surface they were critical outcries.

Startling swings in the economy during the decade before formed the basis of the hard times of the Thirties. The country went from the giddy prosperity of the 1920s, topped by that besotted cocktail party of a wild stock market, to the depths of an economic depression seemingly overnight.

Inflation was the norm in the 1920s, making the dollar worth less than it had been before World War I. In 1917 it would have taken only ninety-four cents to buy goods valued at $1.00 in 1930, but by that latter year, it took $1.17 to buy the same goods.[8] Between 1915 and 1930 the cost of items had nearly doubled.[9] In his usual convoluted language that is logical only in its illogic, Groucho offers a cynical, ironic solution to this rampant inflation.

Analyzing the economics of the day in *Animal Crackers*, Groucho suggests that the nickel isn't worth what it had been fifteen years earlier, and the remedy to this dilemma, and perhaps the cure for America's economic ills, was the seven-cent nickel. He tells us that Americans had been using the five-cent nickel since 1492, and that now is the time to give the seven-cent nickel a chance. If it works out, he says, perhaps the following year we can have an eight-cent nickel. He supports his economic theory with a practical example of the advantages of this altered nickel: You would be able to go to a newsstand, buy a three-cent newspaper and get the same nickel back again as change. He concludes that one nickel "carefully used, would last a family a lifetime." Our approach to established norms of economics had to change in order to survive the Depression, even in Groucho's mind.

The massive swing upward in the economy between 1920 and 1930 was quite dramatic. With the remarkable increase in the cost of living after the First World War, the country was in the midst of a zooming prosperity. People noticed changes in everyday economics, but frequently they ignored them. They assumed that the burgeoning prosperity would negate any fears they had about rising costs. Generally, prices on the stock market had been rising for several years, reflecting the confidence in the overall prosperity of the Twenties. It was not until nearly the decade's end that the stock market gained fame for the frenetic mercurial activity which characterized its "boom." Allen defined this period of feverish speculation starting in March 1928, to September 3, 1929, when market prices reached their highest point.[10] But generally it kept going down until the end of October, when a storm of selling broke in panic fashion. Frightened investors sold stocks at any price, and as quickly as they could sell them. By November 13, the market had reached its low for the year.[11] The downward spiral of General Electric, one of the "blue chip" stocks, is an illustration of that drastic plunge in the market. On September 3, 1929, it closed at 396¼. On November 13, the price was 168⅛.[12]

In *A Night at the Opera*, Harpo holds onto a rope attached to a windlass on an ocean liner's upper deck. Deck hands immerse him in the sea and haul him high aloft as they wind up and lower the rope. It is a comic routine, of course, usually producing peals of laughter from children in a movie theater audience watching Harpo getting dunked and acting silly. But the symbolism is not lost on Groucho. Once again, the deck hands drop Harpo all the way down into the water and as he emerges, Groucho comments: "That's greatest dive I've seen since General Electric went down a hundred points."

By 1930 as the stock market crash sucked the country into a real economic maelstrom, unemployment was a serious problem, and bread lines were a common sight in the big cities. Established by social agencies, lines of unemployed people formed at places where free food or meals were distributed. So many people came for these free meals that the lines frequently spilled out onto the sidewalk and around the block. In some places, conditions were so harsh that the agencies would only distribute bread, and not a full meal, to the people in line.

It was, of course, all tied together, a classic case of the concept of interdependence, a mainstay of college courses in economics. The stock market crash, the loss of jobs and homes, and the conditions of poverty that followed were all connected, each one a result of the other. In *Monkey Business*, as in *A Night at the Opera*, the Brothers are on a passenger ship, but this time, all of them are stowaways. The boys are suffering from extreme hunger, even though the film opens with them hiding in barrels of kippered herring! Chico and Groucho steal into the captain's cabin and brazenly attempt to eat the

Monkey Business (1931). The Brothers as shipboard stowaways (from left) Harpo, Zeppo, Chico, Groucho (Paramount Pictures).

captain's lunch right in front of him. The captain fumes and Chico tells him to calm down, to be quiet and not to be upset, because he and Groucho are big stockholders in the shipping company. The captain, of course, is skeptical, saying that they look like the stowaways that his crew has been chasing. Groucho flavors his throwaway riposte with a Depression-tainted social comment: "Don't forget, my fine fellow, the stockholder of yesteryear is the stowaway of today."

Everyone suffered. Unemployment was a serious problem, for both blue collar and white collar labor. People began to live on a reduced scale; salary cuts had been extensive. In *A Night at the Opera*, Mrs. Claypool (Margaret Dumont) chides Groucho by reminding him that for three months he has promised to put her in society, but he has done nothing except "draw a very handsome salary." Groucho's reply is a rhetorical question, and an apt comment on unemployment: "How many men do you suppose are drawing a handsome salary now days?" At the height of the Depression, in 1933, 25 percent of the labor force was unemployed, some 14 million (the entire U.S. population in 1930 was just 123 million). It was the lowest level of employment for the decade.

The downturn in the economy continued throughout that tortured decade, with only occasional slight improvements referred to with a fleeting comment by Groucho to Chico in *A Night at the Opera*. Harpo has just managed to knock unconscious the Italian opera singer Rudolfo Lassparri, and as he is lying supine, Groucho enters and puts his foot on Lassparri's stomach. Chico enters and stands next to Groucho. He puts his foot on Lasparri, right next to Groucho's. It is as if they are standing at a bar, total strangers, having just met. Then, Groucho starts to make small talk, and refers to the tenuous hope of a receding Depression ("Things seem to be getting better around the country"). Almost as a celebratory gesture, he orders two beers from an imaginary bartender. It is the same whisper of hope that Ryskind repeats in *My Man Godfrey*.

By the 1930s, radio had become a popular source of entertainment. Of all the passive diversions available to Americans, radio was the most dominant; the Depression provided a gigantic audience with plenty of time to listen and no money to pay for much else.[13] Popular entertainment on radio was in great demand. Sophisticated programming such as Toscanini conducting a symphony orchestra, educational and political debates and discussion programs, and news analysis and foreign news, without the apparent touch of bias predominant in newspapers, helped expand the popularity of listening to the radio.[14]

Starting in 1933, President Roosevelt used radio to his advantage. As grim as the Depression was, his platform for election offered hope for a solution; it was a major tenet of his campaign for office. He believed that, and wanted to encourage the public to believe it, too. At the start of his administration, Roosevelt made a demonstrative move, once again, toward encouraging that hope. Eight days after his inauguration he attempted to inspire confidence in the nation, and himself, by beginning a series of radio talks to be broadcast nationwide.[15] These radio appearances were not formal speeches; they were "chats." Roosevelt presented them like the quiet, clear presentation of a "friend or neighbor" who had figured out how to keep the bank from foreclosing on the mortgage.[16] Roosevelt's "fireside chats" began on March 12, 1933, when he explained to the country why he had called for a bank moratorium.[17]

The real significance of Roosevelt's fireside chats was that they were a subtle use of the power of radio as a propaganda tool. With these radio shows he built a following unprecedented in its fervor, as he gained the confidence of Americans in both his personal leadership and his reconstruction programs.

Groucho doesn't let an opportunity to wring a comment about Roosevelt's fireside chats slip by. In *Room Service* he refers to America's "radio president,"[18] a nickname that people used for Roosevelt. Groucho speaks with Leo Davis, a young playwright, trying to convince him to return home to his mother in Maine, rather than to subject himself to living in a New York hotel room. He tries a sentimental, emotional appeal by saying that at that moment she may be sitting at the fireside wringing her hands. Davis tells him that there is no fireside at his mother's house. Groucho is incredulous ("You have no fireside? How to you listen to the president's speeches?").

The advent and growth of commercial radio began in the 1920s. There were many similarities between radio's expansion and the growth of the automobile for widespread use. Both began as playthings for a small segment of the population, and both became necessities for a mass market; with both having social and economic results.[19]

At the end of 1929, nearly one family out of three owned a radio.[20] And that was just the beginning. The demand for radio skyrocketed. Ten years later, 86 percent of the population owned radios.[21] Radio commanded a far larger audience than newspapers, books, or magazines, and was even more important to a vast audience. People listened to the radio ten or twelve hours a day on the average, rather than the shorter time associated with reading.[22]

Other social implications were evident, too. Radio helped to eliminate regional and national cultural barriers, to standardize speech, and to bring an urban outlook to small towns or rural areas. How else could Captain Spaulding sing "Did someone call me Schnorrer?" in *Animal Crackers* with the expectation that audiences would understand that Yiddish word? Radio was a way to exploit popular music, national advertising, and stimulate interest in sports. It helped adult education, if not formally, certainly informally, by expanding sophistication through content. Radio popularized domestic science, reported health information, gave information about scientific farming, and heightened the general interest in current events, both national and international.[23]

When Charles Lindbergh returned to America in 1927 after his solo flight across the Atlantic (the first successful transatlantic solo flight), the city of New York celebrated the event on June 13 with a glittering parade down Fifth Avenue. Radio became a part of the reporting of such public events. Radio informed Americans of current events better than ever. Certainly it reported news faster than newspapers and magazines. A scene in *A Night at the Opera* refers to the broadcasting of such public events. It is an odd scene when, with very little plot transition, there is a hard cut from shipboard to a podium in front of City Hall in New York where the three "heroes of the air," Chico, Harpo, and Ricardo Baroni (Allan Jones), are to receive an award for flying across the Atlantic Ocean. Their assumption of these roles is a ruse to gain entrance to New York without passports because they have been stow-aways on the voyage from Italy. The mayor asks Chico to speak to the radio audience and he makes a wildly comic speech with an improbable comment (in Chico's inimitable style) about their flight ("We get maybe half way across and we ran out of gas so we got-a go back"). Then the mayor asks Harpo to speak to the assembled and to the radio audience! Of course, we get the joke: Harpo never speaks, so how will he be able to speak on the radio? He height-ens the tension by not speaking immediately. As many public speakers do, he drinks water before beginning. He puts down his glass, but almost immedi-ately fills it again. When Harpo finishes drinking, and with the frantic urg-ing of the mayor to begin his speech, he tries to gain more time and fills his glass again, drinking more water than he can possibly consume. He can't swal-low any more so that as he is trying to drink, water from his glass spills onto his beard, and begins to wash the fake whiskers from his face. The authori-ties on the speakers' platform see the subterfuge and the chase after the stow-aways–illegal immigrants begins. It is a repeat of the same chase idea in *Monkey Business* although we don't see any of the hyperactive running that we see in the earlier film.

As we watch any of the Marx Brothers films made during the Depres-sion, we don't get a sense of the catastrophic changes it had wrought through-out the nation. The few references to the Depression are so general that we can assign them to contemporary current events in the twenty-first century and they will continue to be relevant. There are no key scenes about unem-ployment, inflation, or poverty in their films. Everything looks and feels per-fectly normal. But nothing appears normal in the true Marxian world. And that's where the focus on the ills of society enters their lexicon. Logic becomes illogical, and language becomes a predatory jellyfish moving in to create a current, forcing its prey toward its tentacles to hit, sting, and immediately swim away.

Some comedies did more than just toss off a few lines of reference to the economy or its coexistent poverty. Of all of the comedies of that era, the Pre-ston Sturges film *Sullivan's Travels* (1941) comes closest to a more pointed state-ment about poverty during the Depression, but it sidesteps the issue without truly confronting it; it uses a chain gang, whose members are always poverty-stricken even during prosperity, as its illustrative metaphor, rather than depict-ing the effect of poverty on a typical family. *Sullivan's Travels* is more of a call for the elimination of human degradation that was rampant at the work "camps" where chain gang prisoners lived. Sturges's film cries out for relief from such misery rather than make a direct statement about the Depression. The only reason we can ascribe the film to the Depression is coincidental, but not accurate, because it was into production from May to July 1941 just as the country was coming out of the economic doldrums. Nonetheless, there is a point to Sturges's film that applies to the Marx Brothers films. The guards in *Sullivan's Travels* take the downtrodden prisoners to see a movie. The guards have chained them together; the penal system has suppressed every aspect of normal behavior. We observe that the movie they've come to see is a cartoon. The "theatre" is in a small, meager church in the middle of the Georgia swamps. It is a far cry from the Fabulous Fox Theatre in Atlanta. Even in the midst of their misery, the prisoners feel safe as they temporarily escape from their usually dismal lives; they laugh uproariously at the cartoon, as does the assembled audience of parishioners. Sullivan laughs too. Then, he realizes that he's laughing. He can't control his emotions. The scene is cathartic for Sullivan because it allows him to understand that although poverty (and the Depression) is serious, comedy has an important place in our lives even when we are subject to crushing social and economic forces over which we have no individual control. The Marx Brothers knew this lesson, and the seven-cent nickel would save us all.

7. A Job in the Mint

Politically, the United States embraced isolation in the 1930s. People were disillusioned about war after World War I, they were distrustful of the treaties resulting from that war, and were critical of the political jockeying of the world powers that were indifferent to the fate of the rest of the world.[1] Many politicians wanted to recede from international affairs. Let other nations squabble with each other, we should remain apart from such international jockeying, they thought. Many Americans agreed.

This lack of concern with the fate of others in the face of serious political decisions that politicians and diplomats were about to make troubled many people at that time. As such, it is a primary target for the Marxes, especially in *Duck Soup*, the most overtly political of their films. It is more than just a political rant; Allen Eyles suggests that the Marx Brothers dominate this film more than any other because they are not just on the outskirts of the plot, trying to solve another character's problem (the theft of a painting in *Animal Crackers*, the theft of jewels in *The Cocoanuts*, etc.). This time the story revolves around them; they are the driving force behind the story, especially Groucho, who "moves right to the center stage."[2]

The Marxes establish their predominance immediately in the film. Mrs. Teasdale (Margaret Dumont) has twenty million dollars that she could contribute to Freedonia to help that country and its failing treasury. Dumont likes Groucho and believes in him. So, in desperation following a series of unsuccessful political leaders, Groucho is the new president of Freedonia. He has to persuade her to contribute her twenty million to Freedonia's coffers because the country is facing hard times. It is a thinly veiled reference to the shaky economy of the Depression.

Groucho's character is similar to his character in *Horse Feathers*; in that film he is the new president of Huxley College, and is the next in the line of failed administrators. Huxley has had a new president each year since 1888. In *Duck Soup*, Dumont, playing another wealthy dowager, trusts Groucho, so that he is likely to succeed because she is his natural target for fund raising. Groucho, who plays President Rufus T. Firefly, assembles his Cabinet just after the inauguration ceremony to discuss taxes as well as the economic misfortune of the country. The withering economy is a serious problem for Freedonia, as it was for the United States in 1933 when the film opened.

Groucho puts himself at the head of a T-shaped table, in a dominant and authoritarian position, with his Cabinet seated around him. He's dressed in a cutaway and striped trousers, acceptable dress for politicians at that time, and befitting the formality and seriousness of the occasion and the discussion at hand. We know that something's amiss before anyone says a word. Groucho's characters never appeared to be really formal or solemn in the films, but just the opposite. Usually he confronts everything with a lightning stabbed wisecrack.

It is rare that he slows his verbal tempo and speaks sympathetically to or with another character. From the outset — from their first film, *The Cocoanuts*— we notice that the characters that he and his brothers play go to extreme measures to mock formality and pretentiousness with their own style of casual and deprecating humor. But in *A Day at the Races*, Groucho has a brief, kindhearted interlude with Judy Standish, the romantic lead and owner of the sanitarium; in *A Night at the Opera* he is supportive of the two romantic leads, as he is in *The Cocoanuts* with Polly Potter and Bob Adams. For a few minutes in those films he takes a break from being the usually adversarial Groucho — questioning authority, language, and social customs — to become almost an avuncular, compassionate human being. This was Thalberg's concept, defined.

So to appear in *Duck Soup* in such bespoke clothing, well turned-out, is unlike the Groucho we know. It's true that a swallow-tailed coat is usually the main feature of his costume. Such a costume suggests an aura of knowledge, maturity, and leadership. But Groucho's general appearance is just the opposite; his clothing always appears to be rumpled. His brothers wear mismatched clothing, with the exception of Zeppo, who is dressed fashionably in every one of his film appearances, except when he appears in specifically costumed scenes, as at the end of *Duck Soup*, or the engagement dinner scene in *The Cocoanuts*. Groucho's necktie always appears askew or poorly tied. His pants, no matter how intricate a costume he wears, are slightly baggy, implying a reference to the baggy pants of comedians popular during their vaudevillian days. The Brothers' usual costumes, with the exception of Zeppo, are an expression of their disdain for the upper social classes. But this Cabinet meeting scene presents a different Groucho. He appears to have, more than in any other film, a dual personality. Clearly he is President Rufus T. Firefly of Freedonia, suitably dressed and coiffed; there's no doubt about it. But as the camera moves in for a close-up, we see the symbolic truth. It's the old tradition-debunking Groucho.

When he should be calling the meeting to order, he procrastinates (hinting that he wants to exercise his authority over his Cabinet) by playing jacks, a children's tabletop game that emphasizes manual dexterity coupled with fast response, an apt physical metaphor for Groucho's lifelong onstage and offstage verbal habits. Naturally, the rest of the Cabinet must wait for Groucho to finish this game in order to convene the meeting and get started with the real game of the day: running a country.

Absurd? Not really. No more outrageous than President Woodrow Wilson's behavior at one of his Cabinet meetings. Eight days before declaring war with Germany, certainly a most serious and grave action, Wilson took time to indulge in some diversion at the Cabinet meeting of March 30, 1917. First, he told an anecdote or two, and spoke about the message to Congress that he had been writing that day. Then, in a most un-presidential act, he stood up at his end of the table and practiced calisthenics, justifying his childish actions by saying that he had been sitting at his desk writing all morning and was stiff.[3]

Groucho's formal dress, as well as the costumes of the Cabinet members, is surprising, not only because it is unlike the costumes of the other characters he plays throughout the films, but because it is at odds with the usual dress customs practiced in real life. At the White House, just as in the business, academic, and other white collar worlds at that time, men always dressed more formally than they do now, always wearing suits, vests, and neckties. Certain blue collar workers also wore neckties, usually as part of a uniform: Police, gas station attendants, and delivery men, among others, wore ties to work. But in government, men wore more formal wear, top hat, cutaway, and striped pants, and only at state occasions. With some surprise, Josephus Daniels, Secretary of the Navy under Woodrow Wilson, reported that at a meeting of Wilson's Cabinet on April 8, 1913, the president dressed formally for the first time in his Prince Albert, a knee-length coat with a fitted waist designed to make the wearer look thinner. He was dressed properly for an appearance and speech to Congress scheduled to take place later that day. Daniels agreed with some of the other members of the Cabinet who criticized Wilson's dress because it implied that he didn't think that they were important enough to dress up for them habitually, and that meant that he thought more of Congress than his Cabinet.[4] This may appear to be petty bickering, almost child-like behavior among government leaders, but it is common in any society, or in any culture. Groucho's dress and jacks-playing are a suggestion, like so many of the small elements in many of their films, that in order to condemn the unacceptable practices of people in authoritarian positions, whether in government or business, we should establish an element of confusion to ridicule these practices by acting in a variety of unorthodox ways. It is easy for an audience to connect with this behavior, even though it is unspoken, and to accept its subtle, anti-establishment premise.

The dialogue in several of the films repeats this idea, of using language or visual mimicry to confuse. Language is a primary weapon for the Brothers. In *Monkey Business* when Groucho offers his services to Joe Helton as both a bodyguard and an attacker, Helton appears confused. Groucho's twisting of language in his many encounters with Margaret Dumont leaves her face in an expression of bemused perplexity.

Harpo's "language" is mimetic. Verbal wordplay and puns are the basis of its vocabulary. The visual language of Chaplin, Keaton, Harold Lloyd, Fatty Arbuckle, Ben Turpin, and other silent film comedians expressed human emotion and thought in juxtaposition with their use of slapstick. Their lexicon was visual, pure and simple, even pure and complex with only a few scattered dialogue or plot exposition frames to reinforce their messages but at the same time interrupting the action of the films. Harpo's language appears to be simple, but it can be confusing when he's trying to express a complex thought or idea. Frequently he uses Chico to translate aloud what he tries to communicate silently, even though Chico's own language can be a dense thicket of verbal kudzu, in need of translation, too.

Harpo's voluminous overcoat is the warehouse of the props he uses for his visual expression. Filled with a variety of paraphernalia (a blowtorch, a cup of coffee, scissors, an axe, dozens of pieces of cutlery hidden in his sleeves that he allows to cascade to the floor slowly in a cacophonous statement of ridicule), he uses these things to illustrate and clarify his language. But these ordinary objects do more than their intent. They also produce superficial laughter from an audience and they confuse the characters who are the recipients of his prop-laden actions.

Chico's constant puns and attacks on logic are unsettling and supremely confusing. He is easily a doubles partner for Groucho's verbal high-speed serves. In *Animal Crackers*, Groucho asks Chico what his fee is for playing the piano, and finally, exasperated by Chico's circumlocutory answers, he asks, "How much do you get for not playing?" "You couldn't afford it," replies the self-confident Chico. Always the problem-solving salesman, Chico creates his own confusing logic: If there's no house next door, we'll build one (in *Animal Crackers*), or in *Monkey Business* when he tries to sell his grandfather's services as a mousetrap maintenance man to Joe Helton, who declines because there are no mice in his house. Chico counters this argument by saying that there is no problem; his grandfather will bring his own mice to the job.

Groucho's Cabinet meeting starts us on the road to confusion when he espouses corruption in politics with a policy that condones graft and dubious political appointments. Kalmar and Ruby didn't have to look far to see flagrant examples in real life. Although other administrations had been corrupt in earlier periods of American history, corruption in the federal government in the 1920s was noticeably brazen, blackening President Warren Harding's term of office considerably. The most devastating example of corruption, the Teapot Dome scandal, emerged directly from the president's Cabinet, involving Secretary of the Interior Albert Fall and Secretary of the Navy Edwin Denby.

Other scandals involved the director of the Veterans' Bureau, who was involved in the corrupt sale of government property, liquor, and narcotics, culminating in a prison term for him. The alien property custodian was dismissed from office and convicted of criminal conspiracy to defraud the government; the United States attorney general, Harry Daugherty, was dismissed for misconduct involving the illegal sale of liquor permits (during Prohibition).[5]

It was more than mere coincidence that scandal was rife. When Harding took office, he appointed his political friends from Ohio, his home state, to prominent government positions. Called the "Ohio Gang," these political appointees drew widespread criticism for their corrupt activities. Nonetheless, they had their way in national politics. Harry Daugherty was one of them.[6]

In local politics, Kalmar and Ruby only had to look to the Seabury investigation of New York Mayor Jimmy Walker, with its report of the city's corrupt spoils system summarizing, "[M]any city positions are filled by political appointees who have neither the training or [sic] qualifications for their jobs."[7]

Reflecting this national and local predilection toward corruption, Kalmar and Ruby have Groucho dispensing his political largess in the form of a naïve and crass political appointment. Groucho offers a job to Chico, whose actual "job" is that of a peanut vendor. He tries to entice Chico by asking him if he wants to be a public nuisance (or, if that's certainly to be his title, The Public Nuisance). All Chico wants to know is how much the Nuisance job pays. But then Groucho gets down to the real business of politics. He contends that if Chico gives up his "silly peanut stand," he'll get him a soft government job. "How would you like a job in the Mint?" asks Groucho. Chico declines because he doesn't like mint, and asks what other flavor Groucho can offer. Groucho begins interviewing Chico for another job, with his usual destruction of the techniques of job interviews and of the language associated with them. Groucho's sarcasm doesn't deflate Chico. In fact, Chico reverses the interview so that he's asking Groucho the questions. Groucho finally gets it and tells Chico that as retaliation for this switching of roles, Chico isn't going to get the job he has in mind, after all. Chico asks him what job it is. Groucho tells him that he had intended to offer him an appointment as Secretary of War, but has changed his mind after hearing how Chico has twisted the interview in a bizarre role reversal. But Chico ignores Groucho's decision and closes the deal anyway. "All right," he says, "I'll take it." "Sold," says Groucho. They shake hands to consummate the absurd deal. The frivolous and corrupt form of political appointment, a clear reference to the Harding and Walker administrations, is apparent. The Seabury Investigation of Walker concluded that his appointees were both untrained and unqualified for their positions. Chico, a peanut vendor, is certainly not qualified to handle the job of Cabinet member, let alone the often intricate responsibilities of war secretary. Because of his ability to avoid answering questions that were not cogent anyway, Groucho appoints him to be Secretary of War. His ability to deflect questions with challenging and illogical answers makes him perfect for the job. It is absurd, critical, and an apt condemnation of the political climate of the Harding and Walker administrations.

Warren Harding seemed to have been personally innocent of participation in the oil scandals during his administration even though his government was rife with misconduct. Morison and Commager speculate that Harding was aware of the corruption.[8] By virtue of Harding's position as president, he was involved, perhaps not blatantly, but indirectly, in the oil scandals. *Duck Soup* does not tread lightly on the high wire of gentlemanly avoidance of responsibility, by merely depicting Harding's role as "being involved" or "participating" in the scandal. Symbolically, Firefly points his finger directly at Harding and the rampant corruption in his administration when he sings a song that clearly implies that the Harding administration was directly responsible for the deterioration of the country. Always at odds with authority, the Marxist anarchistic viewpoint ran throughout *Duck Soup*. Thomas Doherty suggests that the film barely conceals its attack on Harding; Groucho/Firefly is crystal clear in his condemnation of Harding's administration.[9]

However, there is an underlying greater issue. *Duck Soup* is really about how people in authority ultimately abuse power and fall prey to its seductive handmaiden, Mademoiselle Corruption. More than mere intellectual exercise, in this film the Marxes are a metaphoric vehicle employed to create an antiwar environment by reversing generally accepted logic and practice. They espouse antiwar sentiments by actually starting a war — born from the union of chaos and mistrust of repugnant political and social traditions (as in the slap across an opponent's face with a glove to call for a duel).

Corruption in government was only one facet of the problem in the Twenties and Thirties. The United States became a creditor nation rather than a debtor nation, as it was prior to the war. American debt to the world in 1914 had been $3,000,000,000. In 1921 the countries of the world owed the United States $4,000,000,000, not counting war debts.[10] War debts amounted to an additional $10,000,000,000, with an added $4,000,000,000 in private investments owed to the country.[11] The interest on these debts totaled approximately $6,500,000,000 in the ten-year period after the war.[12] As serious as it was, it was not a simple tally of numbers, an IOU written on a piece of notepaper. It was more complicated and more sober than that.

War debts and international loans became a complex and confusing issue for the American economy given the fact that foreign nations entered upon a system of inter-allied debts; Great Britain lent money to other countries, while France and Italy had entered upon similar agreements.[13] Added to these economic maneuvers was the problem of Germany's payment of reparations after the war. The debtor countries hoped to repay their loans from the United States with the money received from German reparations; however, Germany had trouble meeting the scheduled reparation payments and had to borrow money from the United States to make their payments to other countries.[14] As a result of these financial tactics, Americans became highly skeptical of international loans and confused about their structure and their significance to the country. Finally people reached a level of intolerance. The average American, aware of the inability of foreign countries to pay debts they incurred during the war, became angry and disillusioned. Loans between international countries were then lent to other countries, so the system became complex, exacerbated with default and unkept promises.

Firefly comments on these worthless promises when he asks for a loan of twenty million dollars from Sylvania, Freedonia's neighboring country, rather than, or perhaps in addition to, approaching Margaret Dumont for the loan. Sylvania's ambassador says he has to discuss the loan with his minister of finance; Groucho counters that by asking for a personal loan of twelve dollars until the next payday, suggesting that there was nothing to fear because he would tender an IOU for ninety days. And "if it isn't paid by then, you can keep the note," says Groucho, implying that his promissory note is worthless. Of course, his IOU is really worth nothing, and acts as a reference to the lack of validity of foreign nations to pay their debts. His comment about the instability of finances as a cause of frustration is similar to his auction of building lots in *The Cocoanuts*, when he promises prospective buyers that they will double their money, but if they don't he doesn't know what they can do about it.

There is a polarization of thought from critics of any Marx Brothers film in discussing the meaning of their nihilistic comedy. Is it an attempt to overturn the existing hierarchy? An identification of the confusion in politics? Or, are the films a mere satiric attempt to illustrate the foibles of the entrenched social and political order? The answer is that they are comedies, but not simple. They are serious comedies. Doherty describes the Brothers as "skulking about the mansions of the rich and spraying insults and seltzer water at officials in formal wear" and he further describes them as guerilla comedians, a truly subversive force of disorder.[15] The Marx Brothers films are not documentaries exposing the ills of society and meant to be a call for direct and immediate action. They were not selling anything. Their first films with their condemnation of American politics and social structure represent a reflection of both the expressed and subliminal thoughts of audiences everywhere in those years. What Groucho and his brothers were offering in *Duck Soup* in 1933 was a collective *geschrai* against a world that appeared to be boiling away, with the ducks in the audience everywhere in the United States all in the same soup pot as the Brothers.

8. A Standing Army

If the sinking economy was uppermost in everyone's mind in 1933, the distrust of domestic and international politics completed the picture of America nearing disarray. Groucho, as President Rufus T. Firefly, exudes the confidence of the peace-loving and rational leader of Freedonia in *Duck Soup*. But it doesn't take much to ruffle his feathers. Margaret Dumont tells him that she's taken the liberty of inviting the ambassador of Sylvania to visit for a friendly conference with a goal of settling their problems peacefully. Groucho digresses, pedantically. He corrects Dumont's pronunciation of the word "either" in a comment on social class distinctions defined by how words are pronounced. Groucho's nit-picking comment was perhaps the inspiration for George and Ira Gershwin's ironic 1937 love song entitled, "Let's Call the Whole Thing Off." The Gershwin brothers wrote about these same class distinctions in their clever lyrics when they phonetically illustrated social class differences in pronunciation of the words either and neither (ee-ther and eye-ther, nee-ther and ny-ther).

However, Groucho seems to appreciate Dumont's gesture toward détente and he reinforces it with a banal observation. He says that he would be unworthy of the trust placed in him to keep their beloved country at peace with the world. He tells her that he will be happy to meet Ambassador Trentino to offer him "the right hand of good fellowship." Then, paranoia creeps in when Groucho wonders if Trentino might not accept his friendly gesture. Groucho expands on his fears by expressing hostility at this imagined outcome. He is the leader of the country, and an ambassador is going to snub him? He describes his feelings of embarrassment, in front of the people of Freedonia, caused by his speculation that there will be a diplomatic gaffe.

Firefly's feelings have come full circle in one speech; in less than a minute he evolves from expressing cooperation to conveying paranoiac distrust ("I hold out my hand and that hyena refuses to accept it.... He'll never get away with it!"). He has gone from willingness to collaborate with Trentino toward creating peace, to one of complete hatred, built upon fantasies of persecution and inferiority. When Trentino arrives, Groucho has already decided that there will be no peaceful gestures between them. Before Trentino has a chance to say anything, Groucho verbalizes his paranoia when he accuses Trentino of refusing to shake hands with him. With this he slaps Trentino in the face, the traditional extreme insult between gentlemen, and Trentino can do nothing else but insist on war.

Groucho's expressions of mistrust are a significant comment on diplomatic relations. Paranoia in international diplomacy and political planning lurk just beneath the expressions of cooperation between nations. Richard Hofstader maintains that American politics and diplomacy have the paranoid qualities of "heated exaggeration, suspiciousness, and conspiratorial fantasy."[1]

Many countries maintain military forces even during peacetime. Are they for their own protection or are they just expressions of paranoia in international diplomacy? Sidney Fay thinks that militarism and its competition was one of the basic causes of World War I. Standing armies and navies were part of the militarism and hostility between two groups of world powers, both of whom became increasingly suspicious and paranoid about each other as military spending grew.[2] After Groucho appoints Chico as Freedonia's war secretary, Chico states his attitude toward military reserves, with another pun, in his inimitable style, that balances the need for military spending with fiscal prudence, naturally a demanding requirement in the 1930s. Groucho asks Chico what kind of army he thinks Freedonia should have. Chico replies that Freedonia should have a standing army. Groucho asks him why and Chico tells him that with a standing army, Freedonia would "save money on chairs."

Having a standing army adds to the aura of suspicion, fear, and hatred between nations, leading to a paranoid competition for an increase in armaments. If a country increases its army, builds new battleships, and adds to its war materiel, its fearful neighbors are frightened into doing the same.[3] This paranoid fear seeps into the thinking of a country's statesmen who, while they publicly declaim against the horrors of war, propose armament.[4] Woodrow Wilson, in a statement of gross inconsistency, declared in 1916 that he was so eager to achieve peace that he would be willing to go to war for it.[5]

The fear of espionage from foreign spies is part of the mass paranoia that can grip an insecure country.[6] But espionage — treason — can come not only from foreign agents, but from intricate plots created by major statesmen.[7] In a plot idea similar to *Monkey Business* when Groucho suggests to Joe Helton that he's willing to work for him, and ergo, as a double agent, Trentino of Sylvania hires Chico and Harpo to spy on Groucho. Chico, of course, is the new Cabinet member, the secretary of war. Harpo is Firefly's presidential chauffeur (he drives him to destinations on the presidential motorcycle with Groucho sitting in a sidecar).

The first thing Chico and Harpo do in their job as spies is to explore disguises as a visual comment on the importance of appearances in spying. Superficial elements are more important than action in role-playing. They place more meaning on how they look rather than what they plan to do; perception is more persuasive than accomplishment. When they enter Trentino's office, Harpo wears a false beard and false face, onto which is attached spectacles with the lenses spinning in concentric circles. He walks in backwards with Chico, and we realize that he has attached his mask to the back of his head when he turns around to reveal his real face. Chico wears a false beard, too. Trentino asks them for a report on their spying activities. Chico responds in a monologue that is reminiscent of his illogical reasoning in *A Night at the Opera* when (again wearing a false beard) he describes how as one of the "heroes of the air," he flew across the ocean. He tells Trentino that they watched Firefly's house all day Monday, but he wasn't home. Tuesday, Harpo and he went to a baseball game, but Firefly fooled them and didn't show up. He continues working his way through the rest of the week, culminating on Friday ("[T]here was no ballgame, so we stayed home and listened to it over the radio").

Chico faces charges of treason against Freedonia; after all, he is the country's secretary of war, and he's been moonlighting as a spy for Trentino and Sylvania. The widespread paranoia about spies in our midst, in a time of national crisis, results in the discovery of treason in high places in government, whether those accusations are true or not.[8] Freedonia puts Chico on trial, and the validity of such trials with their dubious legal procedures comes under attack. Groucho is the plaintiff. When the prosecutor defines the meaning of the trial to Chico, he tells him that if he's found guilty he'll face a firing squad. Chico objects and the prosecutor asks him why he raised an objection. "I couldn't think of anything else to say," remarks Chico.

Courtroom procedure is often confusing, and Groucho and Chico turn the system into a verbal shambles. Groucho decides to help Chico and actually becomes his defense attorney as well as continuing to be the plaintiff. As defense attorney he pleads for clemency for his new client, asking the court to send him back to the open arms of his father and brothers. He suggests a reduced sentence of ten years in Leavenworth or eleven years in Twelveworth. Almost before we understand Groucho's joke about federal prisons with melodic use of rhythmic syllables (Leavenworth, Twelveworth), Chico makes a counter offer, invoking the name of one of America's mass marketers with parallel rhythmic emphasis ("I'll tell you what I'll do, I'll take five and ten at Woolworth").[9] It is more than silly; it is an anti-establishment slam.

Chico's trial is not about any espionage that he has committed. It's about the fear of espionage. Chico hasn't carried out Trentino's orders; he has done nothing. It doesn't matter whether or not Chico is a spy; the trial was the important aspect in assuaging any fear of treason based on Firefly's suspicion of Sylvania's motives.

Here, in an open courtroom, Groucho takes the opportunity not only to plead for clemency for Chico, but to cast off his heretofore public denial of the preparation for war. He declares war with Sylvania with a joyous fervor, and right in the courtroom the entire cast breaks into a musical parody of Broadway and vaudeville shows, with a subtext that ridicules the naïve patriotism that ignores the horrible realities of war. As early as 1933, anyone who took Hitler's rise to power seriously believed that war was coming. It was just a matter of time, no matter how isolationist the United States had become. It was inevitable that America was to be involved in World War II because the nation had rejected all responsibility for maintaining peace.[10] With Groucho's announcement of war, there is almost a sigh of relief among the assembled Freedonians. The entire cast — judges, prosecutors, secretaries, even Chico — joins in the spirit of this patriotic musical outburst. They all sing, with the conclusion repeated in the lyrics by Zeppo and Chico that, irrevocably, war is imminent. The song builds to a nationalistic frenzy. In a final burst of jingoism, the chorus sings in a style that's a parody of the Negro spiritual song, "All God's Chillun' Got Wings."

By the mid–30s, America was preparing for war once again, even though its politicians denied it.[11] Together with the rejection of responsibility, the movement toward isolation became stronger, backed by an attitude of moral superiority and leading toward totalitarianism in the countries that had suffered defeat in World War I.[12] The official stance of the United States in the Thirties was isolationist. It was a return to Wilson's pre–World War I pronouncements. Nonetheless, the nation was ready to prepare for war. Wilson had preached a moral attitude toward war: War was a moral issue not related to actual political conditions in America.[13] No matter how much moral opposition there might be to war prior to its declaration, there develops among those same peace-loving people who opposed the war a frenzy of patriotic excitement; a complete turnaround to their prewar philosophy.[14] *Duck Soup* reflected this turnabout when we see Freedonians caught up in the passion of this courtroom-musical parody.

Just as Wilson declared in 1916, Ambassador Trentino expresses his desire for peace ("I'll do anything to prevent this war"). But Groucho tells him that the situation is unalterable ("I've already paid a month's rent on the battlefield"). Hofstader believes that war seen as an inevitable facet of international politics, results in a rigid diplomatic policy. Once begun, "complete victory" is the only goal.[15]

According to Hofstader, war itself is in great part "a comedy of errors and a museum of incompetence."[16] *Duck Soup* shows us the extent of such incompetence. Firefly is a verbal manipulator; he is not educated in military ways. After his declaration of war, he takes an active part as both a soldier and as the country's president, the commander-in-chief of its military forces. The war itself takes place in one wildly comic scene that takes us to the end of the film. We see Groucho and his army: Harpo, Chico, Zeppo, and, improbably, Dumont, along with some staff, at battlefield headquarters. Their war is interspersed with rear-screen projections of tanks, a herd of elephants, a troop of monkeys, and a congregation of crocodiles, all coming to the rescue ("Help is on the way") like the cavalry arriving to save an embattled pioneer wagon train during an Indian attack, often depicted in movie Westerns. As a comment on the incompetence of officers, Groucho sticks a machine gun out the window and fires it in a short burst. He's proud of the results ("Look at them run.... They're fleeing like rats"). He decides to award himself the Firefly medal for his military success. Zeppo corrects him. He tells Firefly that he's been shooting his own men.

Aside from the incompetence involved, modern technology increased the destructiveness of war that lifts such incompetence from being a human error to become a horror. War in the eighteenth and nineteenth centuries was a "contest" to settle a country's objectives that could not have been settled through diplomatic channels.[17] These wars proceeded according to rules, and they lasted only a few months of the year. They were frequently "no bloodier, in proportion to the time consumed and the men engaged, than our football matches."[18] But by the beginning of World War I, new technology had changed war drastically, with the power to eliminate a large number of enemies through one single operation with machine guns and bombs, and the skill to effect these operations over great distances.[19]

Advanced military technology made shelters ineffective in modern warfare. With the ability to destroy entire cities with a single bomb attack, can a shelter be effective? Groucho doesn't think so. In *Duck Soup* a live shell enters through a window in his field headquarters, passes through, and sails out through another window. Groucho doesn't say a word, but he jumps up and goes to the window that the shell entered and pulls down a window shade to prevent other shells from entering. This simple, absurd gesture tells us that there can be no effective protection against bombs, mortars, and mines, all common horrors of modern warfare. War had become so horrible that thoughts of desertion during World War I increased dramatically. Soldiers who revolted against unfair military authority and the unreasonableness of war itself tried to find "an easy way out" by surrendering to the enemy and perhaps spending the rest of the war in a prison camp.[20]

Chico enters the officer's headquarters and punches a time clock. His commanding officer, Groucho, scolds him for being late and tells him that the Freedonian army is facing defeat. Because Chico is the secretary of war, Groucho wants to know what he intends to do about the impending downfall. Chico tells him that he's already solved the problem; he has joined the other side. When Groucho asks him why he's come back to Freedonian headquarters if he deserted, Chico tells him that "the food is better over here."

World War I shattered all idealistic notions about war. It was no longer a "contest" between nations, but an ugly, demeaning, horrible and dangerous experience, especially for enlisted men. Soldiers often thought that the military treated them as second-class people, and they resented it. Food, clothing, and living quarters were all inferior to those provided for officers. It was a common gripe of ordinary soldiers during World War I that "generals die in bed" while the foot soldier is sent out to the muddy trenches to be killed. This division of classes, the caste system, dates to feudal times when there was a wide social gap between fighting lords and the menials who served them. In the armies of absolute monarchs, officers came from nobility, while officers treated ordinary soldiers as the scum of humanity.[21]

To keep morale up, officers give orders to enlisted men using patriotic words. In their attempt to end the war, Groucho, Chico, Zeppo, and Harpo draw lots to see who is, in Groucho's sarcastic words, "going to have the rare privilege of sacrificing his life for his country." Chico manages to control this lot-drawing so that Harpo "wins." Groucho makes a speech to Harpo, the manipulated "volunteer." The hidden subject of his speech illustrates the caste system where officers are privileged non-participants in the war, and the foot soldiers merely carry out their killing orders. Groucho offers an inspirational and pessimistic speech to Harpo that clearly defines the film's stance on the absurdities of war. He tells him to break through enemy lines and while he's out there risking his life they'll all stay safely behind thinking what a sucker he is. Harpo has his revenge. Groucho's head is stuck in an upside-down vase that covers his face and extends down to his shoulders. Harpo removes the vase and eliminates Groucho's physical discomfort by lighting and sliding a stick of dynamite up into the vase and blowing it apart. It is a bizarre look at a surrealist's illogic; the dynamite blows apart the vase but doesn't blow up Groucho's head.

But war is illogical and bizarre; its glory is an illusion. The Marx Brothers try to tell us that war is not limited to soldiers trying to kill each other, but it includes the hostile absurdity of officers who remain in safety behind the front lines as they order their troops to go into trenches in the middle of hopeless battles with predictable outcomes; they know that they will be killed. William Faulkner expressed his anger at officers who sat in the comfort of their headquarters and gave unreasonable orders to enlisted men. Addressing students at the United States Military Academy at West Point, Faulkner referred to the end of one of his antiwar stories that described the brassbound stupidity of the generals and admirals sitting safe in the dugouts telling the young men to go there and do that.[22]

The absurdity of military uniforms in *Duck Soup* is another surrealistic offering. In their films, the Brothers never adhere to conventional dress of their day. Their costumes are usually casual and uncoordinated. They wear mismatched jackets and pants, sport shirts with (or without) neckties, half-formal wear, half sportswear; for Harpo, it was the ubiquitous bathrobe-overcoat-raincoat garment that he wore everywhere. It was their comment on the dynamics of fashion as a superficial tradition associated with upper social classes in America. In the climactic battle scene in *Duck Soup*, shells flying through Freedonian headquarters, rear screen projections, inconsistent uniforms, and a general chaos reinforce the point of view about the absurdity of war.

Throughout all of the Brothers' films, Harpo wears the least coordinated costumes — a collection of mismatched clothing, the antithesis of sartorial

Duck Soup (1933). Freedonia's army: (from left) Chico, Zeppo, Groucho, Harpo (Paramount Pictures).

poise and taste. But in this climactic battle scene he is not alone. The Brothers wear an outrageous pastiche of military uniforms that completes the antiwar attitude of the dialogue. Each Brother wears several different uniforms, from several different armies and from different periods in history. Even Zeppo, the usually fastidious dresser, gets into the spirit of the irregular uniforms, adding to the complete absurdity of the scene and to war itself. The costume changes appear to take place within a few seconds, of course, they don't because the sequence is a series of jump cuts.

As the scene begins Firefly wears a colonial soldier's coat and an American Civil War foot soldier's cap. His various aides are dressed like World War I French army soldiers. At the next cut, Zeppo wears a World War I uniform, Harpo wears an eighteenth-century tricorn, Groucho is dressed as a Civil War Grand Army of the Republic officer, and Chico is dressed as a French soldier. At the next cut, Groucho is dressed as a World War I British army officer. Next, Groucho appears to be wearing a fifteenth-century hussar's uniform, complete with busby and featuring decorative frogs on the front of his coat. Next, Groucho wears a coonskin hat, Zeppo wears contemporary jodhpurs, undershirt, and a World War I helmet, and Chico wears a torn shirt and a World War I helmet. Harpo wears a colonial soldier's hat and what appears to be a movie theatre usher's jacket. The absurdity of the rapid change of costumes reinforces the pointlessness of war. We can't trust our political leaders (Firefly is ready to allow Harpo to be killed), and loyalty has eroded to the point where it doesn't exist (Chico deserts and returns because the food is better in the Freedonian army).

This portion of the battle scene begins the denouement of *Duck Soup*. It takes place in Freedonia's headquarters, presumably near the battlefield; we hear bombs bursting and machine gun fire in the background. Groucho is pacing rapidly across the room, with four of his military aides accompanying him. He tells his radio operator to send a wire asking for immediate reinforcements, but to send the wire "collect." One of his aides asserts that the men need trenches. Groucho tells him that there's no time to dig trenches. Instead, he wants to buy them ready-made. He takes some money from his pocket and hands it to the aide, ordering him to run out and buy some trenches. Zeppo enters with a message from the front whereupon Groucho tells him that he's sick of messages from the front ("Don't we ever get a message from the side?"). When Zeppo reports a gas attack, Groucho's solution is a teaspoon of bicarbonate of soda in half a glass of water. Groucho asks the radio operator if there is an answer to his message. The operator says there isn't, and Groucho says that if that's the case, don't send it. It is the usual illogical reasoning that he and Chico display frequently in several of the films.

If Leo McCarey, the director of *Duck Soup*, had thought of the film as a way to call for change and for caution against ignoring the growing nationalism in Germany, Italy, and Japan, leading to another world war, then he achieved only a modest success. In America, on its first release, audiences missed the point, thinking that the film was denigrating Roosevelt's attempt to solve the nation's economic problems. But the film hit its real target, if not in America, in Europe. Benito Mussolini, Italy's Fascist dictator, and future partner with Adolph Hitler during World War II, was so angry at *Duck Soup* that he banned the showing of it in Italy, calling the Marx Brothers "exemplars of the full flower of anti–Fascist culture."[23] Mussolini's reign as Italy's wartime dictator was short-lived. *Duck Soup* and the rest of the Brothers' films have lasted much longer. In April 1945, Italy's defeat by the Allies was imminent. Mussolini attempted to flee to Switzerland but Italian partisans captured him; they displayed his body publicly, hanging upside down, at his execution. What the Marx Brothers executed in *Duck Soup* was an attempt to turn our naïve thinking upside down.

9. Dear Old Ivy

The inauguration of the new college president before the assembled student body is a ceremony and custom of importance at universities throughout America. It represents the culmination of a search for this new president after what might have taken the board of trustees several months of intensive work. *Horse Feathers* makes a pointed comment on the inauguration of college presidents, with Groucho as Professor Quincy Adams Wagstaff, the president-elect of Huxley College, in his inaugural speech, ridiculing the ceremony itself and its dullness. Groucho introduces his remarks in the manner of the traditional speaker, addressing the faculty, the students of Huxley and Huxley students, and emphasizing the dullness of other faculty members' speeches when he hears another speaker at the ceremony. Groucho says that he thought his razor was dull until he heard that speech. At the time, many people thought that college teachers and college presidents were especially dull speakers.[1]

Wagstaff isn't, especially when seeded with typical Marxian humor that sounds like it comes from Perelman. Once again taking on his role as auctioneer–snake oil salesman as he did in *The Cocoanuts*, and similar to his bodyguard proposal to Joe Helton in *Monkey Business*, Groucho punctures the serious intent of his presentation by quickly assuming high pressure sales techniques to present his ideas to the assembled audience at Huxley. In the middle of his speech, increasing the speed of his delivery, he asks the audience if they have any questions, or any answers, any rags, bones, or bottles. Then he starts his auction with a rap of his gavel on the podium, slipping into the monotone and nasality of an old-time North Carolina tobacco auctioneer. He segues into the quintessential pitchman, trying to sell American history to students. "Who'll say 76?" he asks. "Who'll say 17.76? That's the spirit," he concludes: 1776.

Huxley's retiring president asks Wagstaff to outline his plans for the college to the trustees and the students as part of his inaugural address. Dexter Keezer, who had been appointed president of Reed College in 1935, thought that the traditional custom for the incoming president to state quite definitely the program that would be followed during his tenure was impossible and an unfair request.[2]

Wagstaff never answers the question, nor takes the challenge. Instead, he attacks the dullness of academic speeches and conversation by implying that scholars are too wordy. It is a rant at the obsession with talk and lack of practical ability or action by professors. That's the trouble around here, says Wagstaff, talk, talk, talk. Whicker suggests that college teachers present material to their students that is nothing but "words, words, words" while not being able to give any more than a wordy, meaningless abstraction to any lecture.[3]

Often, the president of a college must act without listening to the careful analysis of his faculty who want to maintain the status quo. John Tunis's ironic short story "College President" makes this point. The story is about a progressive college president who had to ignore the advice of his faculty in order to execute his own plans. He was careful, intelligent, flexible, and honest, yet he could not maintain control over his faculty, who were rigid in their ways.[4] Wagstaff ridicules the suggestions of the board of trustees, calling for severe reform at Huxley when he sings the obviously nihilistic song, "I'm Against It," written by Bert Kalmar and Harry Ruby. Once again, Groucho is in the role of a school teacher. But this time he's openly against the educational system. In vaudeville, doing their school act, the Brothers hid their animosity toward education under a barrage of schoolroom jokes, puns, and slapstick. Now, the ridicule is more pointed, more mature, and clearly a more sophisticated statement. Completely rejecting the suggestions of the trustees is the viewpoint that their decisions and pronouncements make no difference. No matter what they say, Groucho is opposed to it.

But nihilism is not satire, even though the call for reform in the song came at a time when "academic freedom" and self-determination of colleges was a burning issue.[5] Harold Laski suggests that because the president is the most influential man in the forming of university policy, that faculties should have some voice in the selection of their president. However, although there is a danger of "academic inbreeding" (that is, a man who is a "local boy made good"), the president should be a man who is able to make executive decisions.[6] He should be of his own mind, not bound by tradition for sake of tradition.[7] Although Eyles suggests that "I'm Against It" satirizes the element of tradition in education, showing how "farcical the education system is,"[8] we can see a greater significance to the lyrics. This espousal of nihilism is not just about the educational system, it is a description of Groucho and his brothers' behavior in all of their films.

Confronting the age-old issue of the sources of revenue for American colleges was the criticism of income from intercollegiate football during the

1920s and 1930s. Broadcasting football games on radio made the sport more admirable because radio brought the games directly to thousands of listeners, and among them might be a wealthy donor. Radio helped make college sports more accessible, more enjoyable, and more popular. Graham McNamee, one of the most popular sports announcers in the Twenties and Thirties, was able to project the atmosphere of events with his on-the-scene announcing. Along with Philip Carlin, he covered most of the important sports events of the decade.[9]

With its growing popularity, college football presented a disparity between the demands of commerce versus the purity of education. Many colleges and universities offered money to students in order to attract them to play on their teams. In those two decades between World War I and II, universities built huge stadiums. Football became a significant means of supporting not only other intercollegiate sports but a range of non-sports collegiate expenses.[10] With such emphasis on building these stadiums, many colleges went into debt voluntarily, even cutting back funds for academic departments in order to build the stadiums.[11] Critics argued that because the players were paid, the college teams were actually professional, not merely a youthful amateurs playing for the love of it. Universities claimed that football financed further improvement of their physical plant with the ultimate goal of improving the academic offerings of the institution. Even so, there was audible criticism of their football programs. And the criticism was harsh and severe. But not all colleges and universities ignored this issue. President Lowell of Harvard agreed with the criticism. He thought that intercollegiate sports were overemphasized.[12] At the University of Pennsylvania, because of the national denunciation of football as big business, all athletics were de-emphasized. Football was just another college "activity."[13]

The conflict between scholarship and sports was a real one with educators and they responded in various ways.[14] President Keezer of Reed tried to handle a discussion of the role of college athletics to a group of alumni by suggesting facetiously that football players should be paid between $70 and $100 a month, plus having a special faculty hired to tutor the football team in order to keep the players eligible to play under the academic standards maintained by the college. He teased the issue even more by saying that "such an arrangement would have the great virtue of making a contribution to the relief of the grave unemployment in the ranks of teachers" during the Depression.[15] Keezer had his tongue lodged firmly in his cheek when he proposed that colleges stop "hidden" subsidies and offer the best money in America to openly hire athletes and coaches. Athletes and coaches took him seriously, and besieged him with applications.[16] Even with the added emphasis on football and its transformation from a collegiate sport to big business, receipts began to slip during the Depression. Students, who were serious about their studies rather than being obsessed with athletic importance, took less interest in the game. The stadiums built in the previous decade, financed by large bond issues, were now causing financial problems for universities. Colleges and universities were facing hard times just as businesses were, and so there was an added intensity about finances in higher education. When the revenue from football receded drastically in those Depression years, universities could hardly meet the interest on the building loans.[17]

Perelman, Johnstone *et al.* thought that the athletics vs. academics issue was so prominent in American cultural debate that, more than just taking a swipe at it in *Horse Feathers*, they made it a major theme of the movie. Stepping out of his usual role as "yes man," Zeppo introduces the two viewpoints when he suggests to Groucho that Huxley needs something more than education to help cure its financial problems ("What this college needs is a good football team"). Groucho/Wagstaff, who expresses mock naïveté when he asks where Huxley can get good football players, lets us know that he's aware of what's really going on when he questions Zeppo about the propriety of buying good football players at a speakeasy. Isn't that against the law?, he asks. In fact, his "innocent" query is ironic because both things are illegal: selling football players, and going to a speakeasy. Many people accepted both of these activities without question, creating a greater paradox: the buying of football players and completing the transaction in a speakeasy, while at the same time ignoring the even more illegal act of selling alcoholic beverages. Groucho/Wagstaff is so eager to create a winning football team that he completely rejects the legal issues, asking for the address of the speakeasy where "two of the greatest football players in the country hang out." Groucho's interest in going to the speakeasy to recruit the football players is a comment on the lack of ethics prevalent at some the universities at that time.

Erroneously thinking that Chico and Harpo are the two "greatest football players," Groucho approaches Chico in the speakeasy, raising the possibility of a deal for them to play for Huxley. "What would you fellows want to play football?" asks Groucho. Chico tells him that the first thing they want is a football. The conversation between Groucho and Chico is similar in tone and feel as their vy-a-duck sequence in *The Cocoanuts* and the details of hiring Chico to provide music in *Animal Crackers*. The ethical dilemma of hiring freelance football players was a reflection of what was occurring in real life at campuses across the nation. John R. Tunis thought that any deal was possible as long as no one discovered it. The level of ethics was such that it did not make any difference whether colleges or universities bought or "endowed" players for a few years. He suggested that everyone knew about these illegal deals, but looked the other way.[18]

The controversy between those who thought the emphasis should be on scholarship and those who argued for emphasis on sports leads Wagstaff to take drastic, and facetious, measures. Wagstaff asks two of the trustees if Huxley has a stadium. Yes, they answer. And does Huxley have a college?, he asks. Yes, they reply. "Well, we can't support both. Tomorrow we start tearing down the college," rejoins Wagstaff. Objecting, the trustees ask if the college is demolished, where will the students sleep? "Where they always sleep: in the classroom," says Groucho. If Groucho tears down the college, except for the stadium, there will be no classrooms for student sleeping. The logic of his joke is erroneous, but it introduces other thoughts. We don't know if this is a slip by Perelman or if it is another example of deconstructed logic that often crops up in the Marx Brothers films. More likely we can assume, simply, that Perelman ignored logic to make way for a gag.

The faculty offers no refute to Groucho's proposal to demolish Huxley; they had to keep their jobs. Job security was a threatening dark shadow constantly hovering over the teaching profession. During the Depression there were few new teaching jobs available at colleges and universities and there were salary cutbacks for existing faculty members. It looked like it would be a long time before there would be a change in salary policies at universities.[19] The enforced cutbacks brought on by the Depression made the customary problem of low salaries for teachers even more serious. One critic cites the fact that her husband had to take a cut in salary during the Depression, making his normally "meager" income substandard.[20] Many schools did not pay their teachers and had to close their doors, while others shortened the school year with salaries sinking to levels lower than ever.[21]

Not really laughing at the matter, nor laughing with it, the Marxian sense of absurdity kicks in. Reminiscent of the futile sense of the importance of money in *Animal Crackers* when Groucho interviews Chico about his charge for not playing the piano, Groucho asks the faculty at Huxley, how much the college is paying them. "Five thousand a year, but we've never been paid," they reply. "In that case," says Wagstaff, "I raise you to eight thousand and a bonus." In 1932, $5,000 was considerably more than the median salary for college professors. A full professor could expect only a median of $4,114; an associate professor, $3,228; while an assistant professor made only $2,725.[22] The exception to this schedule was football coaches. Generally, colleges and universities paid them handsomely, well exceeding normal professorial salaries.[23]

But it was a broader issue that annoyed the critics of college curricula. During the 1920s, enrollment at institutions of higher learning grew rapidly. A greater percentage of young men and women were finishing high school, the number of junior colleges had grown, and there were more than a thousand colleges and professional schools by the end of that decade.[24] The number of Ph.D. degrees granted by graduate schools during the Twenties had tripled by the end of those ten years. However, critics complained that graduate schools were often not preparing students for teaching, but rather for pure research.[25]

Students were critical, too. With few jobs available and facing an uncertain future, college students focused their criticism on practical matters, even though there was a growth in the number of professional and business schools in the Thirties. This criticism stemmed from a universal debate about whether college education was too classical and set apart from reality, or whether they were focusing too much attention on practical education.[26] The emphasis on vocational education, business courses, agriculture schools, home economics training, and trade education had grown, with a decline in liberal arts courses. This growth in practical, business-oriented courses was the result of an emphasis on job hunting during this bleak period of almost non-existent employment.[27] In 1935 James R. Angell, president of Yale, took the side of those who favored the practical, suggesting that the curriculum at American universities should prepare students to face the complexities of the real world, rather than to school students in the classic disciplines which may provide a philosophical and cultural foundation, but not necessarily prepare a student for contemporary life.[28]

Many students stayed in school — colleges, graduate schools, vocational and professional schools — if they could afford it, continuing their academic years to avoid having to face the despair of enforced idleness caused by the lack of jobs. High school enrollment continued to grow, too, because there were so few jobs for students who would have ordinarily halted their education to enter the workforce.[29] Because of the growth in attendance and the demand for more practical education, availabilities for expanded courses suffered as a result of the cutback in funds, declining endowments, and the cut in teachers' salaries, all overshadowed by the presence of the Depression.[30]

Critics of college athletics had another complaint about these programs. They thought that this emphasis on athletics rather than education was part of a growing anti-intellectualism in American education: not the training of intellect, but of physical skills or citizenship or "almost anything except creativeness."[31]

Students often wanted practical education rather than courses aimed at encouraging the intellectual process and reasoned thinking. They balked at dull lectures that presented information not really applicable to their needs for job hunting after graduation at the start of their careers. Criticism of the mind-numbing dullness of lectures was prominent in the debate. *Horse Feathers* is lucid about dull and pedantic lectures as Groucho/Wagstaff visits an anatomy class and listens to a lecture, then completely disrupts the professor ("Is this stuff on the level, or are you just making it up as you go along?"). Critics said that good teachers make dull subjects interesting, while bad teachers "can barge their way through dynamite without setting it off."[32] Abstract language is one of the culprits, a prominent theme in many of the Marx Brothers films, not just *Horse Feathers*. Wordy abstractions which appear to be erudite can make students resent a college curriculum.

When Wagstaff disrupts the professor of anatomy, wordy abstractions are the target ("Psychopathetically, the duodenum is in inverse ratio to the coordination of the planephas"). College students were dismayed that abstract language and thought was "the substance of every lecture, and the content of any course from the arts to the sciences."[33] Tweaking the system, Groucho takes over for the anatomy professor, using a wall chart that shows the upper part of a human body. He uses the professor's long-handled pointer as he talks. It's the Marx Brothers school act of 1912, revisited, as Groucho asks Chico a question ("What is a corpuscle?") and Chico replies with a hoary pun, followed by wilder puns by Groucho ("We now find ourselves among the Alps. Beyond the Alps lie more Alps, and the Lord Alps those that Alps themselves"). Never missing a chance to destroy language itself, Groucho refers to the Alps as "a very simple people" living on a diet of rice and old shoes.

Illustrating his lecture with his pointer, Groucho indicates various parts of the human anatomy as he speaks about the Alps, rice, and old shoes. He illustrates that the technique of dull lecturers is not only awkward, but passé, as he points to "an unusual organ" and that the "organ will play a solo immediately after the picture." *Horse Feathers* implies that traditional college professors with their dull lectures have become obsolete, and to make education more attractive we need a little more life in the classroom. Edgar J. Goodspeed wrote an ironic article suggesting that colleges replace their professors with film and books, since "having put all they know into their books, [they] have made themselves superfluous." He continued by saying that all a student needed to do was to obtain a syllabus for a course, read through the reading list, and take the final examination.[34]

In another plea for educational reform, Groucho teaches anatomy and history when he sings "Lydia the Tattooed Lady" for the circus performers on their train in *At the Circus*. The lyrics imply that college professors can make the usual methods of presenting historical, geographical, cultural, and socioeconomic facts more palatable than their traditional point-at-the-chart lectures. In the song, Groucho traces Lydia's "anatomy." But he has no anatomical wall chart as he does in *Horse Feathers*. Instead, he points to parts of his own body as he sings and dances to emphasize the anatomical points in the song. At the same time the lyrics tell us how Lydia's tattoos illustrate scenes that range from world history and geography, to current (in 1939) American social and historical events: Grover Whalen and the New York World's Fair of 1939, an exposition in California at Treasure Island in San Francisco, and the American Social Security system. Lydia's tattooed body is a graphic encyclopedia. As well, she has eyes that people adore so and a torso they adore even more so with its graphic overview and wide-ranging knowl- edge.[35] The song is a resounding whack at dull, professorial lectures.

Horse Feathers is not merely four Jewish fellows shouting to an indiffer- ent audience, it is also the quintessence of Perelman: a return to his short- lived undergraduate editorial tenure on the student newspaper at Brown, railing against the narrowness of the administration (university faculty) and, at the same time, chastising the student body for its lack of intellectual curios- ity. Perelman's role as editor-in-chief of the *Brown Jug* was a real-life blue- print for his future role as author of *Horse Feathers*.

10. A Coed with Two Pair of Pants

References to, and intimations of, sex were always just beneath the surface in all Marx Brothers films. From those eyebrow-waggling suggestions by Groucho, direct invitations from Chico in ersatz broken Italian-English, to the silent, mad dashes of Harpo chasing after one, two, or more pretty young women in and out of the scenes, sex was never far from the scripts for the Marx Brothers. Sex bubbles up once again in *Horse Feathers* as a critical comment on the social habits of college students. Groucho tells Chico to go to college where he can meet all the beautiful girls. Get yourself a coed, he tells Chico. Chico's first response is, as usual, with a nose-wrinkling pun ("Last week for $18 I got a coed with two pair of pants"). Play on words aside, the real point is that there was no more pretense about college women: They were more open about their sexual activities than were the coeds from the previous decade. Chico's response is ambiguous but sexually evocative. Was the co-ed wearing two pair of pants as a type of chastity belt, or did Chico offer two pair of pants to her as enticement for sex? The reference could be just a simple joke based on imprecise language. Groucho makes a similarly ambiguous joke in *Animal Crackers* when he tells us he shot an elephant in his pajamas ("How he got in my pajamas, I'll never know").

Chico's coed having, or wearing, two pair of pants suggests the duality of what appears on the surface as the virginal youthful ideal, often espoused by parents, and the reality of the post–World War I, post–Twenties, modern world. The outlook toward premarital sex, especially among the youth of America, had changed considerably after the war: There was a greater freedom of expression, a continuing lessening of parental and social repression, and a more relaxed attitude among young people. However, many young people were still bound by the tenets of their parents' day: that premarital sexual relations, even as innocent as hand-holding, kissing, or walking along in a public place with any show of affection, was in bad taste.[1] As well, boys did not "respect" girls who were free with their show of affection.[2] And girls wondered if perhaps they should indulge in sexual petting to achieve a level of "popularity" with their male peers.[3]

Clearly a comment on the change in these restrictive sexual rules that parents and communities impose, *Monkey Business* ridicules their naïveté when Alky Briggs threatens Groucho with his pistol. Briggs discovers Groucho with his wife, Lucille, in their ocean liner stateroom. About to shoot Groucho, Briggs asks if Groucho has any last words. Groucho mocks the mores of the day that preached the homily that boys think less of a girl if she allows him to kiss her on a date. But Groucho is Groucho. He not only pierces this smug social sermon but he reverses the sexual roles. He asks Briggs if he thinks that girls think less of a boy if he lets her kiss him.

The flaunting of the social norms in marriage itself came from the economic changes in American society after World War I, leading to a growth in illegitimate marital unions. In the 1920s, Ben Lindsey, a judge in Denver, suggested and championed "companionate marriage," that quickly erupted into a controversial social issue. In a reply to the controversy, Lindsey advocated a "provision by which, through legalized birth control, marriage might be made practical for thousands of young people who are delaying marriage for economic reasons produced by this industrial age."[4]

Critics of Lindsey's plan often misinterpreted his concepts. They thought that he was advocating "free love." Kathleen Norris thought that companionate marriage made it possible for "impecunious youngsters of high school age" to be joined in companionate marriage to merely "legitimize relationships that already exist." Once the couple agreed to a companionate marriage, they would be "free to live together as man and wife, supported presumably by their parents ... in their old homes."[5]

Lindsey's plea for this drastic change in societal norms embroiled such debate that it is a pointed satirical reference in *Animal Crackers*. Groucho's Captain Spaulding proposes marriage to two women, Mrs. Whitehead and Mrs. Rittenhouse. Whitehead protests, calling it bigamy, setting up Spaulding with his usual pun ("Yes, and it's big o' me, too"). He carries the thought further when he suggests that we should change conventional marriages because one woman and one man "was good enough for your grandmother," but that was a different time. Groucho emphasizes that we should change. This leads to the inevitable sexual subtext. Groucho imagines a *ménage à trois* honeymoon with his two "wives," that would be strictly private, of course. "I wouldn't let another woman in on this. Well, maybe one or two, but no men," promises Groucho. The other woman, Mrs. Rittenhouse (Margaret Dumont), is almost indignant, as she protests by asking with a sly smile playing across her face if Groucho is proposing companionate marriage. Groucho outlines the advantages, saying that Dumont could live with her folks, and he could live with her folks, too. Groucho tells Mrs. Whitehead that instead of living with Rittenhouse's parents she could sell Fuller brushes.[6]

This more relaxed outlook about premarital sex among American youth had changed considerably after the war toward a greater freedom of expression. Young people were more open about their sexual practices. One of the changes in the social customs that helped foster this freedom was the growth of dating as a social innovation. The automobile and the distance one could travel in it helped make dating a commonplace activity.[7] By 1927, when Henry Ford ended production of the popular Model T, his company had manufactured more than 15 million Tin Lizzies, as they called them.[8] The automobile was a perfect mean of escaping, even if temporarily, the supervision of parents and chaperons, or the influence of the opinions of neighbors. A couple could drive a car to and park in a country lane, day or night, with some degree of freedom for its occupants.[9]

The critics of Judge Lindsey's plan for companionate marriage thought that he was asking for a modification of prior concepts of romantic love. The Marxian view in their films asks for this reform with no strings attached to it. The Brothers, even before their ascendance as social gadflies in their Broadway musicals and their films, simply wanted to take the starch out of the stiff-necked guardians of the old social order. They discovered they could, and liked to, topple the old social rules in Nacogdoches before World War I. They scoffed at formal social precepts in all of their films. And, by inference, the depiction of romantic notions in American films between 1920 and 1950, and in those romantic ideas expressed in plays of the Victorian era such as *East Lynne* and *Romance*. They thought that these romantic ideas were quaint, as did many young people in America.

Victorian romantic and sentimental films presented plots in an atmosphere of passion that had little to do with the realities of love and marriage. When Groucho/Captain Spaulding speaks to Margaret Dumont in *Animal Crackers* about his love for her, he does so in "poetic" simile, with a slight hint of sexually suggestive double entendre, in what appears to be a reference to his penis, posing as a poetic symbol for an invitation to a tryst. He tells her that something has been "throbbing" within himself ("Oh, it's been beating like the incessant tom-tom in the primitive jungle"). But he lightens his monologue, and laughs at the romantic myth, by turning language around ("Ever since I met you I've swept you off my feet"). He continues to pierce the ideal when he brings us down to the realities of love and marriage, something diametrically opposed to the attitude of romantic love expressed by romantic poems, plays, and films of the earlier age ("Would you wash out a pair of socks for me?"). Dumont tells him that she's surprised at this domestic request. Groucho tells her that asking her for this mundane domestic favor is simply his way of telling her that he loves her.

Groucho's outward espousal of the romantic myth is akin to romantic literature of the twelfth century, when poetry began to express the myth of passionate love.[10] The romantic myth as a leitmotif is still popular in films. These films portray romance as the "dream of having a miraculous love affair."[11] Traditional courtly love, romantic love, was profoundly rhetorical, based on perpetual dissatisfaction: a man stating his plaint in poetic terms and a fair lady who continuously rejects him.[12] This little sequence between Captain Spaulding and Mrs. Rittenhouse in *Animal Crackers* is a direct reference to this definition of traditional courtly love. In fact, an analysis of the dialogue between Groucho and Dumont and his other intended paramours, extramarital or not, in all of the Marx Brothers films, shows a repeated presentation of the plaint/rejection of the romantic ideal. It is a conclusion with no contest.

To make sure that there is no doubt about this disdain for romantic love, Groucho alludes to Shakespeare in *A Day at the Races* when he tells Emily Upjohn (Dumont) that he loves her. And Emily starts to soften. Once again, not taking romance seriously, he upsets the tenderness of the scene when he describes his emotional outburst by drawing a parallel with Romeo and Juliet and changing it from a literary to a geographic reference with a lowbrow joke. He depicts his expression of love as a time-honored story ("Boy meets girl, Romeo and Juliet, Minneapolis and St. Paul").

The presentation of passionate love stories in films was always a durable theme. Max Lerner suggests that the emphasis on passionate love stems from the medieval reaction against the anti-erotic strain in Christianity and the cult of virginity. The idea of romantic love, traveling through the ages, "reached its most intense form ... in American culture, with its novels about romantic love, its slick-paper magazine stories, its Hollywood formula movies, and its radio 'daytime serials.'" Lerner believes that Americans make a cult of love more than any other people.[13]

Zeppo, stepping out of his role as a straight man to his brothers, pierces established romantic customs in modern society. He always appears as a well-dressed romantic lead, so in *Monkey Business* as a ship's stowaway he tries to elude the crew, who are in pursuit, in a way suited to his character. He catches up with, and walks briskly alongside a pretty girl on the promenade deck, making conversation with her, giving the impression that he has been with her all along, and thus is able to hide from his pursuers in plain sight. He destroys a pickup line as he points to the ocean and says, "Mighty pretty country around here." Eventually, he expresses genuine romantic interest in the young woman; he tells her how much she means to him, promising never to leave her, but immediately runs off as some of the crew arrives on the scene searching for him.

Kaufman's lifelong personal and professional dislike of expressed sentiments, especially of romance, and perhaps to a lesser extent, Perelman's derision of romance, was a theme that ran throughout all of the Marx Brothers' films, even after the both of them were no longer writing the scripts. The call for a shattering of attitudes toward the romantic ideal, expressed openly and broadly, not only came from the minds of these caustic dramatists and screenplay writers, whose thoughts were brought to life by the Marx Brothers and others during the Twenties. In general, after World War I the attitude toward sex changed; the open expression of adolescent interest in sex was widespread. With it came an "accent on youth." It was a dramatic change, a revolution in thought and social practice that adults expressed in their actions, too. Matrons and middle-aged adults imitated youthful ways — the flapper, cigarettes, bobbed hair, short skirts, use of cosmetics, cocktail parties, necking — all changes in the social and cultural patterns and customs of Americans that occurred after the war.[14] So life-altering were these social reforms that they continued in the Thirties and beyond: far beyond, and with a greater scope, than expressed by the Brothers.

The Marx Brothers were not the only comics skewering the sentimentality of romantic love. Mae West's attitude toward the romantic ideal called for freedom in sexual relations with a straightforward and clear presentation of what was on her mind. There were few subtleties of meaning in her comments. Although she used double entendres, she's more memorable for her ability to twist commonplace truisms into language that oozed sex, and deflated the idea of romantic love, getting right to the point ("A hard man is good to find"). Doherty calls this the single entendre.[15]

But the Marx Brothers thrust their swords to pierce romance in a multitude of ways. Primarily, they expressed their antipathy through language. Right from the outset in *The Cocoanuts*, Groucho turns around romantic notions by deflating their clichéd similes ("I mean your eyes, your eyes! They shine like the pants of a blue serge suit"). Harpo offers an endless, frenzied chasing of pretty women in several of the films, or lambastes tender, loving emotion when he tries to break Thelma Todd's leg in *Horse Feathers*. Chico destroys soft and alluring romantic piano playing as he rolls an apple over the keys (as he does in *Go West*) or "shoots" them with his outstretched forefinger with his right hand shaped like a pistol, to complete an arpeggio.

Mae West and the Marx Brothers remain as impregnable icons in American film, who told us that "the times they are a-changin'" as Bob Dylan would sing thirty years later. But the Marx Brothers didn't need to tell us. They show us. They take off their pants, and let us come to our own conclusions.

11. The Whole Wig

Coinciding with the abhorrence of romantic love sprayed throughout the films, the Brothers laugh at banal expressions of physical beauty. Literature often presented physical beauty in classic poetic superlatives: Men were "the strongest," women were "the most beautiful." Nearly all of the comments about romantic love come from Groucho, rather than his brothers, because the criticism is verbal rather than visual. He is their mouthpiece, and naturally the messenger of their writers' opinions.

Transcending the ordinary, traditional romantic love often characterizes a man and a woman in love as a knight and princess.[1] In *The Big Store*, surprisingly, and seemingly without sarcastic bias, Groucho tells Margaret Dumont, in the romantic style, about her physical beauty and of his love for her ("How can I keep from telling the world of you and your beauty?"). As soft, gentle music plays in the background, Groucho quotes the poetry of Byron ("She walks in beauty like the night/Of cloudless climes and starry skies") and Dumont answers his recitation with a passage of love poetry from Shelley. Can this really be Groucho Marx and Margaret Dumont? They are gentle lovebirds, cooing and billing. Don't bet on it. Wasting no time, Groucho comes up with the usual devastating punch line when he offers more "poetry," in the form of a rhyming singsong verse, modeled on a unique American advertising campaign. Dumont, still flattered, and apparently with no understanding of the reference, asks him where he learned to write such "beautiful poetry." He destroys their tender love scene with their poetic, romantic sentiments when he answers by telling her that he worked for Burma Shave for five years.

The reference to Burma Shave offers both a comment on romantic poetry and on the memorable advertising campaign for a man's shaving soap that was literally part of the American landscape from 1925 to 1963. The Burma-Vita Company of Minneapolis erected road signs, in sets of four, five, or six. They painted one line of a humorous jingle on each, and they placed the signs in sequence along the highway spaced far enough apart so that as a car drove by, its passengers could read the consecutive lines of the jingle. The signs were small (each measured one foot high by three and one-half feet wide) and they were usually in rural areas. The first Burma Shave road signs were erected in Minnesota.[2] The lines rhymed, and the final sign, the end of the doggerel — a punch line and corporate identification at the same time — always said, simply: Burma Shave.

Of course, nothing is sacred to the Brothers. In *Go West*, Lulu Belle, the saloon entertainer, sings a love song and, while humming a musical interlude, *sotto voce*, Groucho, in the romantic manner, ruminates on love ("It's madness, this thing that's happened to us. It can never be; we come from different stock"). It is a scene that he plays as he does in *Animal Crackers* when he speaks directly to the camera in soulful tones during the "Strange Interlude" sequence. As he continues in counterpoint to Lulu Belle, his soliloquy apes the maudlin parting of traditional romantic lovers after a marital spat, ending with the usual Marxian deconstructive pre-symbolic and dyslexic syntax ("Someday this bitter hate shall part, my sweet. Time wounds all heels"). In spite of knocking down the stability of time-worn epigrams, Groucho mocks the French romantics and their excuses for the partings of lovers (the self-conscious pretexts of marriage and honor, social duty, virtue and the lover's melancholy or religious scruple) as reasons for parting. This "melancholy of parting" is a refusal to consummate the love urge. Like Tristan and Iseult, Groucho's speeches in *Go West* signify that he does not love a woman for herself, but for the love of love that her beauty mirrors for him.[3]

Every generation forms a standard notion of beauty, and often in the romantic ideal, one lover seeks a symbol — a talisman — in order to remember or symbolically represent the other.[4] In medieval days it was a scarf that a knight would carry into battle with him; in the generation before and during the 1930s, it was often a lock of hair. Groucho asks Dumont for a lock of hair when he professes his love for her in *Duck Soup*. She's surprised and astounded by his unusual show of heartfelt emotion, but he doesn't disappoint her, or us. He suggests that his softness is really letting her off easy, because he had intended to ask for the whole wig.

All through their films, Groucho's expression of the romantic ideal is a departure for him. Usually his characters do not love women for themselves, but rather they are mercenary fantasies that he pronounces with an underlying theme stressing the financial gains that he may make from a marriage. The incompatibility of romance and marriage is the incompatibility of the romantic ideal and the realities of marriage. In the medieval romantic ideal, passion was a substitute for love, and therefore was irreconcilable with the elements of a good marriage.[5] Two people in love must plan for the realities of home and family no matter how much of the emotional, romantic love there is between them, otherwise the marriage will fail.[6] The difference between romantic love in medieval times and the idea of romantic love in modern marriages is that the medieval concept of romantic love was hostile to the institution of marriage. In medieval cultures, women viewed romantic love as a "frill to embroider the institution of chivalry and a make-believe ritual under whose cover the women of the knightly order could get release from the bleakness of [medieval] marriage." Modern Americans rely on courtship and expect a great deal from marriage, as a romantic ideal, so that when the idyllic does not occur, there evolves a disillusion which appears in the form of conflict. In contemporary America, people "associate the idea of romantic love only with the pre-marriage years: afterward they are likely to speak of love ironically as of a deflated ideal or of a pleasant but foolish dream."[7] Bitter arguments in marriage often occur after the romantic courtship has come to an end. Groucho "referees" such a marital spat between Alky and Lucille Briggs in *Monkey Business* by standing between them listening closely to follow the ebb and flow of their argument. He turns his head toward each speaker as one might follow a tennis match.

Alky and Lucille's marital problem is based on a misunderstanding of motivation and desires. There is no logical solution to their constant and antagonistic serve and volley. As usual, Groucho's solution is an illogical pun, when Lucille catalogs her discontent by describing her marriage by saying that she's suffered four years neglect, four years of battling, and four years of heartbreak ("That makes twelve years. You must have been married in rompers. Mighty pretty country around there"). His pun about Yonkers (New York) must have worked well on the Broadway stage, but likely did not when the movie version played in small-town, rural America to audiences who were not familiar with the geography of New York.

At the same time, Groucho and Lucille overhear another couple who have come out to a veranda to speak of extramarital love. Groucho is offered a bribe to keep quiet about his discovery ("Sir, are you trying to offer me a bribe? How much?"). Instead, he takes the opportunity to comment on extramarital relations and divorce — no longer socially shocking events in America after World War I.[8] In fact, the divorce rate had increased from twelve per one hundred in 1920 to twenty per one hundred in 1940.[9] When the woman explains that she's not happy with her husband, and that he should have married a little housewife, Groucho berates her and her lover. He turns his admonishment into the usual Groucho-as-an-auctioneer sales pitch once again, taking a ring out of his pocket, offering it to them for "a buck and a half." Suddenly he drops the price to one dollar, then fifty cents. Finally, as he does in *The Cocoanuts, Horse Feathers,* and *Animal Crackers,* he starts an auction ("Now, my friends, what am I offered for this fine French piece [*sic*] of bric-a-brac?").

The quest for romantic love is unending, even if the realities of marriage have cooled the passion of romance. The need for divorce and a subsequent romantic entanglement is the need for men to possess women as symbols of the romantic myth. But the actual possession, in the form of marriage, is not as delightful as the pulse-increasing quest. The chase is more exciting than the result. For a man, to win the chase and finally have the woman is to lose her, romantically.[10] The quest for passion is a vicious circle, a deliberate effort to renew the search for the romantic ideal; once won, it is lost. The relationship between the quest for romantic love and divorce comes up when Groucho offers romantic love to Lucille Briggs (blonde beauty Thelma Todd) in *Monkey Business.* He approaches her on a veranda, crawling along the railing and meowing like a concupiscent cat, speaking of love in a heavy, romantic style ("Ah, 'tis midsummer madness. The music is in my temple. The hot blood of youth.... Let us hear of love"). They do a comic waltz. Groucho continues his verbal lovemaking, while Lucille expresses anxiety about being caught at extramarital love. She fears that if her husband, Alky, finds out, he will "wallop" her. Groucho alters the subject as he attempts to heighten his romantic efforts. He offers an erotic, sadistic response ("Couldn't I wallop you just as well?"). It is a classic S. J. Perelman send-up as he suggests that they go away together and "lodge with my fleas in the hills. I mean, flee to my lodge in the hills." Lucille protests and Groucho destroys the mood by saying that she shouldn't be afraid because she can join the lodge for just a few pennies and no physical examination is required, unless she insists on one. Even without seeing the scene, we can imagine his eyebrows arching up and waggling down in a suggestion of sexual groping. Lucille continues to complain about her domestic squabbles with Alky. Groucho further notes the prominence of squabbles as part of marital adjustment that occurs during the initial period after the honeymoon when he is hired by Alky as a member of his gang ("Of course, the first year we might have our little squabbles, but that's inevitable").

Other kinds of problems creep into romance, especially those associated with money. A man trying to attract a rich woman and a woman trying to find a rich husband has always been a motivation for "romance" that has resulted in a heightened concern for caution among the wealthy or well-off. The concern of wealthy widows was more than just a potential suitor's quest for riches. It was an intrusion upon social and economic class distinctions. But no matter how cautious a wealthy widow might be, often she could not avoid falling prey to these wily male "fortune hunters." Often the successful ones were well-dressed and well-mannered, with a great deal of charm as part of their personalities.[11] Groucho uses the technique of romantic advance by fortune hunters with the ability for suave lovemaking in several of the films. He turns romance into a negotiated business deal.

Invariably these scenes include Dumont playing the dowager, with Groucho making a blatant economic and romantic statement almost in the same breath as he combines a quest for money with an expression of romantic love. As insulting as Groucho is to Dumont, she always seems to think that his approach is charming. She often falls victim to his lovemaking and marriage proposals even though they're usually based on his desire for money. Of course, he protests to the contrary. In *A Night at the Opera* Mrs. Claypool (Dumont) talks about her dead husband who has left her alone with eight million dollars. Groucho fends off the advances of another rival for her — another money-motivated suitor — by saying that if she wants to marry a fortune hunter, she has him. As a matter of fact, he's not really a fortune hunter because when he first proposed to her he thought she only had seven million, so the extra million has never interfered with his feelings toward her.

But the confluence of love and money is never far from Groucho's mind. He is never more open about his quest for money as part of a romantic liaison than in *Duck Soup* when he discovers that Dumont's husband is dead. Almost immediately he proposes marriage ("Will you marry me? Did he leave you any money? Answer the second question first"). Succinctly presented, this is the essence of the romantic intentions of the characters played by Groucho in all the films.

In *Animal Crackers* Mrs. Rittenhouse regards Groucho's insults as charming. Groucho makes romantic comments to both Mrs. Rittenhouse (Dumont) and Mrs. Whitehead, at the same time expressing his interest in money overshadowing any future emotional relationship. He peppers his romantic statements with a wise guy's subordinate clauses when he compliments both of them that he loves their eyes. He's never seen four more beautiful eyes in all his life: "Well, three anyway." Describing what he likes about them in flattering terms, he concludes by saying that they have beauty, charm, and money. After this inquiry into their financial worth, he insults them by implying that he would no longer love them if they were poor. If they don't have money we can quit right now, he says. Mrs. Whitehead still thinks he's charming. Dumont concurs.

Groucho is not just an ordinary fortune hunter, with a vague idea of his financially secured life after such a marriage. He knows how much he needs from Dumont as she plays another dowager (Mrs. Dukesberry) in *At the Circus*. He's going to be quite specific.

At first, Dumont doesn't want to listen to his romantic appeals. She threatens to scream for the servants if Groucho doesn't leave her room because they must respect social conventions. Groucho is not rebuffed as he offers a sexually suggestive rejoinder by asking if the two of them could be simply "a man and a woman." But Groucho is a professional exploiter of women, as were some fortune hunters in real life. Ignoring Dumont's plea for propriety, he gets right down to business; he starts to define exactly how much he wants from her, while at the same time making a mockery of smooth and sophisticated fortune hunters who never reveal their secret ambitions. He tells her that he doesn't need her millions. He'll be happy to write down how much he needs. But he asks if he may borrow a pencil from her because he has left his typewriter in his other pants.

A professional exploiter uses a technique that flatters women. The subtlety of their flattery is tempered with the intelligence of their prey; the more intelligent the woman, the more subtle the man must be.[12] In *The Big Store* Groucho offers not a smooth and subtle idyllic presentation, but a display of gross flattery coupled with a repeated reference to finances. Groucho insists that the Phelps Department Store should fire the unctuous Mr. Grover, the store's manager. Played by the always-villainous Douglass Dumbrille, Grover tries to dilute Groucho's insistence by saying that he would rather resign, except that Martha Phelps (Dumont), the owner of the store, is his fiancée. Groucho confronts Dumont with flattery, expresses his interest in her money, and belittles Grover at the same time ("You mean that a woman of your culture and money and beauty and money and wealth and money would, would marry that imposter?").

The subtlety of the professional exploiter does not exist in Groucho's role in *The Cocoanuts* as he makes a direct appeal to Dumont. She suspects that Groucho might only be interested in her wealth, and she questions his motives when she tells him that she thinks that he wouldn't love her if she were poor. Groucho protests by saying that he might still love her if she were poor, but he wouldn't say so, he would keep his mouth shut. Groucho compounds the fracture to Dumont's vanity by insulting her. She protests, saying that she'll leave, and Groucho begs her to stay. He tries to keep her there by putting his arms around her in a romantic gesture, but she asks him to keep his hands away from her. Groucho, discarding any sense of subtlety, assumes the stance of a wrestler. He insults her girth by describing her as being three times larger than she is. He tells her that he'll play one more game with her. Come on, he says, the three of you. The reference, although somewhat different, is the similarity between Groucho wrestling with Dumont and the custom of American Indians entering into a wrestling match in order to win a squaw as a future bride. This custom was common among ancient savages, too.[13] The difference is that Groucho offers to wrestle *with* the woman he professes to love rather than wrestling *for* her as the young braves did in competition with other male tribe members.

Groucho is a master of the well-placed insult, and he uses it as a way of deflating the romantic ideal as he contrasts romantic prose with cutting slurs.

The Big Store (1941). A woman of culture and money and beauty and money and wealth and money. Groucho and Margaret Dumont (Metro-Goldwyn-Mayer).

He doesn't mean to aim the insult at the person, but rather at the romantic myth and its relation to modern society. After World War I, with the change in attitude about many social customs, the use of flowery, romantic language became an outdated custom. When Groucho describes a date to Mrs. Potter in *The Cocoanuts*, he tells her that he imagines them together under a romantic moon. But he cautions her to wear a necktie so that he would recognize her and not mistake her for the moon.

Domestic tranquility and happiness in marriage are not defined in glowing terms, but in destruction of amorous thought usually associated with descriptions of the bliss to follow the wedding. When Harry Ruby and Bert Kalmar wrote *Duck Soup* they gave Groucho the opportunity to wipe out any acceptance of domesticity by letting him hurl a demeaning insult aimed at physical appearance. He tells Gloria Teasdale that he can envision her in the kitchen bending over a hot stove, but he can't see the stove. Surprisingly, this scene of domestic tranquility is not disturbing to Dumont, as Groucho outlines it, even though he has implied that her girth is large enough to hide some of the kitchen equipment.

However, Dumont is suspicious, and she asks Groucho what he is thinking. He makes a sly reference to the new president, Franklin D. Roosevelt, by trying to sublimate the sexual implications of his focus on her rear ("I was just thinking of all the years I wasted collecting stamps"). Roosevelt, an avid stamp collector starting when he was eight years old, continued his passion for philately all his life, as a way to assuage his temperament during the pain and frustration of his severe illness (polio), or to ease the pressures of his political career.[14]

Still, nothing is sacrosanct. In *The Cocoanuts* Groucho aims at domestic tranquility and the romantic approach to marriage when he proposes to Mrs. Potter and uses the clichés expressed in Victorian drama by newly married couples who are planning to settle down, raise a family, and have a home. Such plays as Mrs. Henry Wood's *East Lynne* and Edward Sheldon's *Romance* are prime examples of such formulaic middle-class ideas. In *Romance* the husband tells his wife that they will follow each other "side by side, shoulder to shoulder, making all the good things seem a little better."[15] Groucho, as a contrarian, completely demolishes the tone of the Victorian playwrights as he outlines the domestic future to Mrs. Potter in *The Cocoanuts* as part of his marriage proposal. He wonders if they could find a little bungalow — a nice, little empty bungalow — just for the two of them. He's confident that they might be able to find one, but pessimistic at the same time. He's not sure whether the present inhabitants would leave. Like two lovebirds they could bill and coo, except that he makes a mistake and says bill and cow, then corrects himself and stammers making another mistake when he says that they could bull and cow. He offers a stuttering description of their future romantic life together, sounding as if he is nervous and unsure of himself in any amorous setting. Could this be a reference to an upcoming awkward wedding night? Not from our dear, jaded Groucho. He paints a picture of Dumont inside this cozy bungalow while he stands outside "trying to get in, or inside trying to get out."

He continues to mix up sentences. He can't seem to say what he means, and confuses Dumont. But he really does say what he means. We see three conclusions. The most apparent is his stammering of this "trying to get in" sentence, another clue that Groucho and his Brothers are the quintessential immigrants always on the outside of American society, constantly trying to gain acceptance. Or, it could simply be a way to mask another sexual reference to make it acceptable to the Hays office. And when he stumbles over "bull and cow," once again he destroys language by showing the possibilities that come with twisting words around. Exasperated by tripping over his tongue, he finally gives up by saying that if she doesn't hear from him by the following Friday, "the whole thing's off." Eyles thinks there's only one meaning to this speech: He thinks that Groucho has made romantic love completely vulgar, linking "the idea of love to crude animal sex."[16] But viewed from a different vantage point, we should consider the importance of these three levels of intent: immigrants' place in American society, side-stepping of the Hays office, and destruction of language (Groucho destroys language in the same way with Thelma Todd when he asks her to "come lodge with my fleas in the hills").

Dumont says that she doesn't understand Groucho's stammering and mixed-up speech. It is then that he finds his old self-assured voice. So, he tries to clarify his intentions with a romantic description of her eyes. Just as Dumont thinks that he's softened and become human, he changes gear immediately and discontinues this romantic portrayal of her eyes. He doesn't want us to think that he's actually expressing sentiment. Not Groucho. He tells her that her eyes "shine like the pants of a blue serge suit" and he immediately qualifies his comment by saying "it's not a reflection on you, it's on the pants." We can conclude that he hasn't aimed his taunts at her, but at the conventional romantic ideal of another age, or perhaps another level of society. He starts to describe the environment in which they would have sex, but then he digresses. Instead, he offers her a marriage of convenience, with no pretense of romance. He tells her that because she's going to be at the Hotel de Cocoanut all winter anyway, she should marry him until she "can make other arrangements."

Groucho's affronts toward Dumont and his other romantic liaisons in the films frequently connect the women with animals. Throughout the films he relates her size to that of animals: a whale, an alligator (*The Cocoanuts*), a baboon (*Animal Crackers*), and in *A Day at the Races*, a horse ("Marry me and I'll never look at another horse"). He also refers to Esther Muir's Flo Marlowe, the big sultry blonde, as a horse. Perhaps this comes from George S. Kaufman's inability and refusal to write tender love scenes, but the intent is to satirize traditional romantic language, rather than a chauvinist's expression of arrogance. Kaufman did not work on *A Day at the Races*, but the sneer at romantic language was completely Kaufman-like. In *At the Circus*, Groucho speaks with Dumont/Mrs. Dukesberry to recall some romantic past history between them, and offers an anatomical insult by describing the size of her feet. He reminds her that he remembers romantic evenings on the Riviera when they sat outside along the Mediterranean Sea with the moonlight shining down on them. He recalls drinking champagne from her slipper: two quarts. It would have held more, he tells her, but she was wearing inner soles.

At the Circus (1939). Finally, Groucho gets the girl. J. Cheever Loophole (Groucho) and Mrs. Dukesbury (Margaret Dumont) are happy together. Groucho and Dumont (Metro-Goldwyn-Mayer).

Verbal hostility between two suitors for a rich woman is akin to the wrestling of American Indian braves to win a squaw. As Groucho tries to claim Mrs. Claypool's affections in *A Night at the Opera*, he concurrently tries to nullify the attempt by another man to attract her. He introduces Mrs. Claypool to Herman Gottlieb, director of the New York Opera Company. Gottlieb invites Mrs. Claypool, a dowager with an interest in being a patron of the opera, to his opera box in Milan to see "the greatest tenor in the world." Groucho warns Gottlieb and at the same offers an insulting jab. He tells Gottlieb not to try to get romantic with her because he saw her first, or rather her mother saw her first, but there's no need to bring the Civil War into the discussion.

In all of the films, Groucho's insults are not really expressions of animosity toward his various women; sometimes the films include a typical "Hollywood ending" success for him and he gets the girl. Not in *Duck Soup*. The end of the film shows all the Marxes throwing apples at Dumont to end the war. No matter how one interprets it, Dumont is not the apple of Groucho's eye. Depending on the vagaries of plot, the fact that Groucho is seen at the end of some of the films with the women he has grappled with in his unique way of making amorous overtures is an indication that his tossed insults in romantic dialogue are satirical of courtly, sentimental expressions of love rather than reflecting a personal attack on any of the women individually.

We can view hostility in different ways. Hostile language can attack a person, groups of people, or institutions, whether corporate, educational, religious, or political. As well, it can be an inimical rebuff of a society and its practices. If we call hostility a rebuff, it sounds like a gentle, polite way of explaining it. As Groucho hurls hostile insults in the Marx Brothers films, we think beyond their superficiality, and about how they fit in with Molière's stated purpose of satire: a way to "correct the ills of society." It is this more sophisticated definition that makes the Marx Brothers films more interesting. We remember them as an emblazoned strike against the affectations of romantic literature and social practices. They are more than just a mere lock of hair. They are the whole wig.

12. It's Tough on My Suspenders

When we look at the Marx Brothers films, there is a danger of falling into a critical trap. To go beneath jokes and puns and horseplay to see the satirical referential significance of the films leads us to think that their films may be monotonous in their attacks on society. We think that the Marx Brothers are just playing one repetitive note — attack, attack, attack — in what should be a fully formed, complex symphony of social criticism. On the surface it appears that absolutely nothing is out of bounds for the Brothers, or to their writers, especially the formal social conventions and customs of an earlier age that continue to stay alive, even though they may be anachronistic. It's easy to think that the Brothers simply want to destroy all the flourishes of social civility. But if we peel away the hostile patina of their actions, we see that they are taking us away from a formal and stilted social order and really bringing us into the modern world, where we must maintain civility, albeit in a more streamlined, more casual style. There is no doubt that informality is their style. It is also the American style.

In the United States, some social customs are so formal that they we consider them amusing and quaint, even though their purpose is to maintain a gentle graciousness as part of the acceptable social etiquette. Kissing another person's hand as a show of respect was traditionally part of the ritual of introduction between two people, and has its antecedents in European societies, especially in Mediterranean cultures. Upon being introduced, or simply meeting once again, men would kiss women's or other men's hands. This gesture has practically vanished in America. Europeans still use the ritual, although it is not in commonplace use as it was in the eighteenth and nineteenth centuries. It is a sign of a well-bred person. Between men and women, when hand kissing is called for, the woman is usually at the same or higher level of society than the man. The upper classes of society still make this gesture occasionally. Most visibly, when men or women meet royalty or the Pope, we see them kiss their hand as a sign of respect. The prerequisite introductory custom was to kiss the ring on the Pope's hand. It is customary to bow slightly and kiss the ring even today. Although it is rare, some European men still kiss women's hands as part of the everyday ritual of personal, social introduction rather than offering handshakes as they would to men. According to the strict rules of etiquette, hand-kissing was still acceptable in certain social circles as recently as the 1950s, especially if the woman was still married, European, and extended her hand first.[1] Otis Driftwood (Groucho) introduces Herman Gottlieb to Mrs. Claypool (Dumont) in *A Night at the Opera.* Gottlieb bows slightly and takes Mrs. Claypool's hand, palm down, and kisses it at the knuckles. Trying to disparage Gottlieb's motives and character, Groucho takes her hand and examines it closely, saying that he just wants to see if her rings are still in place.

Introductions have always been a delicate balance between knowing the acceptable social rules and wanting to complete the ritual in a society that continues to demand equal balance between the sexes. Groucho and his brothers called for sexual equality even in something as simple as social introduction. But they don't completely trust the imbedded social customs of polite society, or the people who practice them. Following the hand kiss, men would offer a slight, polite bow or handshake, depending on the custom or formality of the occasion. We should always introduce men to women.[2] Usually there is no handshaking unless she offers her hand to initiate the gesture. People are often confused about the mechanics of the custom. They are not sure what to do, whether to kiss, shake hands, bow, or all three. When Gottlieb makes his entrance to the scene, he bows to Groucho, and Groucho bows back. He introduces Gottlieb to Mrs. Claypool by simply saying their names ("Mr. Gottlieb, Mrs. Claypool") and bows at each mention of their names, acting like a toy canary repeatedly bobbing up and down, dipping its beak into water for a drink. He increases the speed of the repetition of their names, and after a several seconds of this he tells them he could continue bowing all night, but "it's tough on my suspenders." Finally, even though he has just said that he's going to stop, he continues repeating their names in a short singsong cadence: a coda-like denouement to introducing them to each other, as he begins to dance a few steps of the Charleston to the rhythm of his singsong. He's not only wearing out his suspenders, but there is no doubt that he considers such formal bowing a rote, meaningless social nicety.

To be polite, we learn to say "thank you" as an expression of gratitude for any offer or performance of help. The normal and acceptable response to "thank you" is "you're welcome." But Groucho overdoes it, and in the process shows us a ludicrous version of this standard vocal civility. In *A Day at the Races,* he prepares for a tryst with Esther Muir in his room at the Standish

Sanitarium. He wears a paisley robe and dances around the room to Viennese waltz music while preening and brushing lint off his robe. When Flo Marlowe (Muir) knocks on the door he sprays the room with perfume before she enters. He opens the door for her and as she walks in she says, "Oh, doctor, thank you." Groucho replies by saying, "Thank you." He invites her to sit down and he holds the chair for her. She says, "Thank you," and his reply, almost on top of her words, is "Thank you." They repeat the "thank you" "thank you" mimicry seven times in six minutes, each time Groucho offers help or a compliment. The words of gratitude become meaningless when used incessantly; they become nonsense words.

Completely confusing the etiquette of introductions, Groucho introduces himself several times in the same speech in *Animal Crackers* when he talks to Roscoe W. Chandler. After introducing himself twice, he concludes that he has heard of Chandler and that Chandler has heard of him, the great Captain Spaulding, so they dispense with the formality of introductions and get to business. But it's not to be, as he introduces himself again and Chandler introduces himself. Groucho introduces himself again ("I am Jeffery T. Spaulding"), and we think that they could go on introducing themselves to each other until the end of the film, without moving the conversation further. Finally, Groucho turns to business, and asks Chandler to finance a scientific expedition. After chatting awhile, they end their conversation by rising and shaking hands. Spaulding introduces himself all over again, telling Chandler that he has always wanted to meet him. He changes the subject from introductions and asks Chandler what he thinks of the traffic problem. Without waiting for an answer, he asks him what he thinks of the marriage problem, and what he thinks of at night when he goes to bed. This simple overturning of a simple means of human communication not only points out the farce of introductions, but it also comments on "nonsense communication."

Nonsense communication is what the semanticist S. I. Hayakawa calls pre-symbolic language. He defines it as a vocal equivalent of an expressive gesture. Often, we do not take words literally, but rather for the meaning of the sounds involved, either friendly or hostile.[3] Groucho turns introductions and the nonsense language associated with them into a competitive game. Margaret Dumont introduces Groucho to Mrs. Whitehead in *Animal Crackers* and the usual nonsense language follows as she says, "How are you?" He responds without replying by asking her the same question. She says she's fine and then asks him the same question. He asks her again, and then tallies the score. That leaves you one up, he says.

A more telling example of pre-symbolic language occurs in *Horse Feathers* when Chico is the designated bouncer at a speakeasy and he asks Groucho/Wagstaff to identify himself before he admits him. "Who are you?" Chico asks. Wagstaff replies by saying, "I'm fine, thanks." The actual meaning of what they are saying doesn't matter; the tone of the conversation communicates the meaning. It doesn't matter what the words really mean, it's what they seem to mean: In fact, property values *have* increased 1929 since 1,000 percent.

The Brothers thought that handshaking itself was a nicety that was passé, even before they began making films. In their films, they ridiculed it in several ways at various times. In *The Cocoanuts* Groucho and Zeppo are behind the desk at the hotel when Chico and Harpo make their entrance. The four of them walk toward each other rapidly with outstretched right arms, ready to shake hands, but they completely miss (by the way, this is the first time all four Brothers appear on screen at the same time). Trying to connect, they walk over a centrally placed two-sided sofa. Groucho gets close enough to Harpo and extends his hand for Harpo to shake it, but Harpo's hand is open so that Groucho inadvertently slaps it. Harpo responds by slapping Groucho's face. Harpo eventually starts to shake hands with Groucho but instead he revives one of his standby comic bits of stage business with a routine that he used in their vaudeville and Broadway career — to tell us that the intricate scenario of the ritual, not the custom, of shaking hands should be disrupted. When someone attempts to shake hands with him, he substitutes his leg for his hand, putting the thigh of his leg in the other person's outstretched hand. In this scene, when Groucho is about to shake his hand, he puts the bulb of his Klaxon-style car horn in his hand so that when he squeezes it inadvertently, it makes its bleating sound. Groucho and Zeppo turn and run; Groucho hides behind the reception desk, and Zeppo leaves the room, running out a door behind the desk. In *Animal Crackers*, Hives, the butler, introduces Harpo to Margaret Dumont. Harpo repeats the bulb-in-hand routine with her. It's as if Harpo wants to blow this horn to alert us that assigning an almost holy importance to handshaking is silly. These little visual gestures that he does several times throughout their films are a simple comment. He's giving us his opinion that we should not take the rite of handshaking too seriously every time.

Sometimes the Brothers aim at a specific group with their call for the reorder of the importance of ceremonious introductions. Introductions and how we make them are sometimes just an indication of other obnoxious dimensions in society. In *A Day at the Races*, just by illustrating the social hierarchy of introductions, the Brothers tell us that physicians are often pompous and self-important. The Standish Sanitarium hires Groucho to be its director. Of course he does not have the requisite medical degree. Actually he is a veterinarian, an occupation he defined for himself once before in *Monkey Business*. Just as in *Duck Soup*, Groucho is to be a savior. But he is the quintessential outsider looking in, hoping to garner Margaret Dumont's millions as financial support. The Standish Sanitarium is facing the real possibility of closing because its financial advisor is trying to force it to go out of business so that his sleazy business associate can redevelop the property to be a casino as an adjunct to his already existing racetrack. The Standish medical staff has concluded that there is nothing wrong with Emily Upjohn (Dumont), but she is so trusting of Groucho that it doesn't matter if he *is* a veterinarian; she wants the Standish medical team to listen to his medical opinion. When Groucho arrives, Dumont introduces him to the staff of doctors who respond pompously, clicking their heels, and bowing, reciting their résumés by merely mentioning where they earned their medical degrees. It is a perfect opportunity for Groucho to attack the formality of introductions among members of a professional group. Dumont presents Groucho to the staff by telling him that she would like him to meet his new associates. Each doctor presents himself quite formally. The first doctor says: Jackson, Savior Hospital, 1918; the second: Franko, Johns Hopkins, '32; the third: Wilmerding, Mayo Brothers, '24. We know what's coming next. Groucho's self-presentation is the expected punch line that deflates their pomposity: Dodge Brothers, late '29.

Social ballroom dancing was popular in the Twenties and Thirties in the United States. So popular was it that dancing schools for nonprofessionals were overcrowded.[4] The rumba and the tango, dances with Latin American origins, were especially popular as novelty dances. Groucho mimics comic versions of these south-of-the-border dances with references to their identifiable steps. With the growing popularity of ballroom dancing, many people still felt awkward about doing these Latin American dances. As a verbal way of blowing up the social importance ascribed to dancing, on an ocean liner during dinner in *A Night at the Opera* Groucho asks a woman to dance. He asks her if she can rumba. Flattered by the appearance of an invitation to dance, the woman responds by saying that she does. Groucho makes a sarcastic and ego-destroying comment on this social ritual ("Well, take a rumba from one to ten").

Arthur Murray, one of the most successful American dance teachers, even taught dancing by mail order.[5] Critical of the social dancing craze, Groucho sets his sights on the impossible idea of teaching dancing by mail. He speaks with Julie Randall, the female lead in *At the Circus*, as an interruptive train whistle appears to frighten him. He tells her that he used to take rumba lessons by mail and that every time he hears a whistle he thinks it's the mailman delivering another lesson.

The tango was just as popular as the rumba, with many men and women clamoring to learn the dance. They could no longer evade dancing it. The tango was so prevalent that they thought that they would miss half an evening's social dancing if they had made no effort to learn it.[6] Groucho does a comic version of the tango in *Monkey Business, A Day at the Races,* and in *Duck Soup*; in the latter, Groucho dances the tango and at the same time makes a comment about the attitude of Americans toward dance halls, implying that they are places where one goes to find unattached women. By the beginning of the twentieth century and through World War I, dance halls were places where working classes could go to escape the dreariness of working in factories, whereas middle and upper classes danced at their homes. Some of the dance halls were in unsavory neighborhoods. For example, in Chicago the more notorious dance halls were in so-called vice districts, where gambling and prostitution were rampant. Typical was Freiberg's Dance Hall, with its long bar, a hall with small tables, an orchestra in the balcony, female performers, and prostitutes who pushed liquor and sex.[7]

Dumont introduces Groucho to Vera Marcal, the "famous dancer," and he does a little dance asking her if she knows how to do it. He shows her another dance identifying it as one that he picked up in a dance hall. Pointing to Mrs. Teasdale (Dumont), he describes her ("Here's another one I picked up in a dance hall"). The implication is that Mrs. Teasdale, the dowager who is singly supporting the entire country of Freedonia with the millions left by her deceased husband, is a low-class dance hall girl. However, Groucho must do whatever he can to be successful. He dances with Mrs. Teasdale, perhaps as a means to get additional financial support for Freedonia, because good dancing, in addition to promoting the social graces, was an excellent way for a man to become popular with dowagers.[8]

People of all economic and social classes were encouraged to display courteous manners and proper etiquette, and adhere to traditional societal graces in the 1930s. But some of those traditions had changed, and were changing as a result of the Great Depression. Things that used to matter no longer did. The emphasis on rigid formality in society was less important when people had to face the realities of a drastically changed world. The Brothers had been pushing for a lessening of formality ever since their epiphany in Nacogdoches with its metaphoric runaway mule. The mule simply wanted to escape from the restrictions of his harness. Groucho tells us twenty years later that he wants to escape from a similar social rigidity as he suggests that he wants to eliminate the restrictions imposed by a formal society, because they are tough on his suspenders. But by 1935 when MGM released *A Night at the Opera,* fewer men were wearing suspenders.

13. Three Hardboiled Eggs

International travel on ocean liners was at its height in the Twenties and Thirties because airplanes were not acceptable to most people, nor passengers' comfort assured, to make them appealing for mass travel.[1] Engine noises and restricted seating space made for uncomfortable travel. Bad weather, even the slightest rainstorms, made flying unpredictable. Ocean liners were different. They were comfortable and elegant, offering relatively fast, luxurious transoceanic passage, compared to the wind-powered sailing ships of the mid–nineteenth century. Innovative maritime design continued to improve crossing times, and in 1933 the Italian liner SS *Rex* was able to cross the Atlantic in four days and thirteen hours.[2]

Shipping lines were able to attract wealthy and socially prominent passengers who wanted to be able to travel in style. They brought their social code of etiquette with them, from large, socially structured metropolitan areas to the compressed version of the social world on shipboard. So pervasive were these social niceties, that Kaufman, Ryskind, Perelman, and Johnstone eagerly included a deflating send-up of the social structure throughout their scripts for *Monkey Business* and *A Night at the Opera*. The underlying message perpetuated by the shipping lines was that ocean travel was not just a quest for speed and comfort, but it was a time for fun. It was party time, and the revelry started before a ship left port, with bon voyage parties. In *Opera* at the bon voyage scene on deck, where passengers are waving goodbye to their families and friends on the dock, Harpo starts to kiss people goodbye. Caught up in the rhythm of his actions, he frantically kisses everyone in sight. He kisses men, women, children, total strangers, and even some of the crew assembled at the gangplank, all in manic succession. He crazily jumps into people's arms and kisses them before they have a chance to prevent him from this frenzied outburst.

Among the visibly prominent people to travel regally by ship in the Twenties and Thirties were actors and other show business personalities.[3] But the crews of ocean liners imagined their own social status to be superior to the passengers' social standing no matter how famous or wealthy these passengers might be.

In *Monkey Business*, Groucho belittles this imagined social status of luxury liner crews when he "interviews" an opera singer who is about to debark in New York. Actually, the press interviews her. It is a legitimate opportunity for her to get some free publicity, but Groucho interrupts. He takes over and dominates the interview. He begins to ask her hostile questions. She demands that he stop, and if he doesn't she threatens to call the captain. Groucho sounds indignant and accuses her of being infatuated with a pretty uniform, saying that "ordinary" people don't count, because she prefers an officer even after "we've given you the best years of our lives." It was common for illustrious passengers to be friendly with the ship's crew, from the lower ranking officers right up to the captain. The chief steward of the *Berengaria* supposedly had a "larger nodding acquaintance with great Englishmen than anyone in the United Kingdom."[4]

Ocean liners often carried the socially prominent, too, and these ships pandered to their wishes and whims. One Cunard captain thought that "everybody on the *Berengaria*, even the dogs, were socially prominent."[5]

The ship captain in *Monkey Business* is the target of Groucho's disdain. Groucho ridicules the captain directly by attacking his naval and executive abilities when he tells him that he doesn't like the way he's running the boat, and he suggests that the captain should get in the back seat for a while and let his wife drive the ship. The captain counters this accusation with the self-importance of an unsuccessful business executive, citing meaningless "evidence" to protect his job. He tells Groucho that as proof of his abilities, he's been captain of the ship for twenty-two years. But longevity does not equate with ability and Groucho isn't convinced. So, he continues to put down the captain's vocational and professional sluggishness as an indication of his ineffective command. He tells him that if he were a man, he'd go into business for himself after all those years. He illustrates his point by saying that he knows a fellow who started only the year before with just a canoe, and now he's got more women than he can shake a stick at ("if that's your idea of a good time"). Groucho's non sequitur is funny, as is, but its meaning is ambiguous. If we read between the lines, we could think that he implies that the captain could be a successful pimp or even a gigolo; after all, his friend has all those women in his canoes. Why women? Why not men and women (passengers)? Or cargo? So, Groucho is offering a concealed taunt in his criticism; he suggests that being a pimp or gigolo is a better job than just being a captain of an ocean liner.

Ocean liners offered luxury accommodations to its well-paying passengers, and everyone knew that by simply reading travel brochures produced by the shipping companies for their ocean-going fleets. The famous stateroom scene in *A Night at the Opera* is a visual jab at such luxurious living accommodations — living accommodations that in some instances included reproductions of great masterpieces of art on the walls, Byzantine chapels, Pompeian swimming pools, and dining rooms styled like those at the palace at Versailles.[6]

Enter Groucho sitting on top of his steamer trunk as the porter pushes his "cargo" along a passageway. When the porter accidentally hits the wall of the passageway, he bumps Groucho off the trunk. Groucho accuses the porter of being a hit-and-run driver. He examines his trunk and describes the damage, then threatens the porter by saying that he has to pay for it. He asks the porter if he has insurance. When the porter says that he doesn't, Groucho assumes his familiar role as salesman–con man. He pulls from his pocket his hotel bill from Milan and makes believe it's an accident insurance policy. Describing the features of the policy, he says that the insurance will protect the porter absolutely, no matter what happens ("If you lose a leg, we'll help you look for it"). After seeing a one dollar bill in the porter's pocket, he tells him that the entire cost of the policy is $1.00. He hands the porter the hotel bill (for $540).

Groucho enters his "suite" with his steamer trunk. Our simple glance at his "stateroom" is the first swipe at the lavishness of first class travel by ocean liner. The cabin is the antithesis of opulence. Groucho notices immediately how small and sparsely furnished it is. He describes it as a birdcage, the size of a telephone booth. He's just come from Dumont's suite and it is, in contrast, lavish — the stateroom of a wealthy woman, comfortably furnished. What happens in Groucho's cabin is the crux of the social comment about the amount of stateroom space, social privileges, and leisure class comforts enjoyed in ocean travel. Groucho opens his trunk to unpack, and discovers Chico and Ricardo hiding in it. He finds Harpo asleep in one of the trunk's drawers. The three refugees from Italy are stowaways; it is *Monkey Business* revisited, but only three stowaways this time. Groucho tells them that they have to leave because he has a date with a lady (Dumont) in a few minutes. Chico counters that by saying that he and his fellow stowaways are hungry, and they won't leave until they have something to eat. Groucho acquiesces and goes out into the passage way to call a steward and order a meal.

Groucho orders abundantly, requesting one of everything the steward offers, as well as two fried eggs, two poached eggs, two scrambled eggs, and two medium boiled eggs. We hear Chico's voice adding two hardboiled eggs to the order, with his request filtered through the closed door of Groucho's cabin. Immediately, we hear Harpo's horn honk once. Groucho adds, "Make that three hardboiled eggs." With the next segment of Groucho's order, Chico adds two hardboiled eggs, and Harpo amends it by blowing his horn, and

Groucho translates it as a request for an additional hard boiled egg. The sound of Harpo's air horn honking is like a nonverbal comment on the selfish and demanding excesses of wealthy shipboard passengers.

Next comes the stateroom scene, made famous over the years by critics and writers. Some of them think it's the most memorable scene in the entire Marx Brothers' work. That accolade is debatable, but certainly understandable; it is a hilarious scene on its own, even without considering its social reference and significance. Explaining a punch line is usually a death knell to any joke, but a thorough look at this frenetic scene reveals the classic intelligence of its writing. It is a lyrical comedic routine, building and flowing, with its tempo and pitch rising to a crescendo equal to the heightened ending of a musical composition. The parallel to music composition makes it a metaphor for the drama we often see in grand opera and it is especially apt in a film created pointedly with a background of opera. On the surface, its obvious comment is about ocean travel. Beneath the surface is its comment on the accommodations afforded to socially prominent passengers on transatlantic crossings. Even if Boasberg didn't write this dual-edged scene alone and it was the result of a group effort, it is a tiny masterpiece. Its pace is reminiscent of that of Keaton, Chaplin, W.C. Fields, Harold Lloyd, and Laurel and Hardy, all masters of comic timing in their own films.

The scene: Groucho/Driftwood returns to his room and starts a conversation with Chico. There is a knock on the door, and two cleaning women enter to make the bed and clean the room. The cabin is just large enough for a single cot, and there is hardly enough room for the two women, even without Driftwood and the three stowaways. But a multitude of people are jammed into it during the course of the scene. One after another, people knock on the door and enter; each knock on the door occurs in less time than its previous knock, and thus increases the pace and introduces an environment of hysteria to the room. Each new entrant is on a different mission and the room is jammed full: two cleaning ladies, a scrubwoman, a plumber, his assistant, a woman looking for her Aunt Minnie, a manicurist, Chico, Groucho, Ricardo Baroni, and Harpo. The chaos builds when Harpo lunges horizontally toward the food order carried by four waiters who have just entered carrying trays. Dumont arrives, knocks, and opens the door from the passageway. All the occupants of the room, squeezed and squashed together, come cascading out into the passageway, like some great dam bursting from the strength of a tidal wave, and bowling over Dumont in the passageway before she's able to step into the room.

Once a ship arrives at its destination, the process of passengers leaving had its own rituals. When the Brothers attempt to disembark in *Monkey Business*, they are still stowaways, without passports. The ritual of verifying identity and stamping passports was more time-consuming than it is today. To save time, customs officials would check passports and identities on shipboard before they allowed passengers to exit the ship. Still, it was a slow procedure; there were no computers then, and they scrutinized each passenger's passport thoroughly. The officials in *Monkey Business* sit behind a long table on the deck, their backs to the camera. They check each passenger's documents against the ship's manifest and their passports are verified. There is a long line of anxious passengers waiting their turn. Chico, Zeppo, and Harpo push their way to the front of the line and attempt to get through the passport check with a ruse of impersonating Maurice Chevalier. They had stolen his passport and each brother sings Chevalier's "If a Nightingale Could Sing Like You," in Chevalier's manner, in support of their claim to their false identities. Harpo, who performs last, but without singing of course, offers the most accurate imitation. He has a miniature hand-cranked record player strapped to his back, playing a Chevalier recording of the song. But within a minute the "power" has run its course, and when the record starts to revolve more slowly, Chevalier's voice slows with it. The officials realize Harpo's fraud. It is obvious immediately to the customs officers that the other Brothers, who have performed bad imitations of Chevalier, are not what they pretend to be, either. When discovered, the Brothers are chagrined. Not Harpo. He goes berserk, completely destroying the setting. He stamps the bald head of a customs officer with the official's rubber stamp, throws papers around, jumps up onto the officials' table, and disrupts and disturbs other passengers in line. He overpowers the scene, calling attention to the formality of the officials. He regards it as a ritual worthy of reform. Harpo's visual condemnation is similar to Chaplin's "mad burst of comedy" in some of the scenes in *The Gold Rush*.[7]

Part of the unwritten code of conduct aboard ocean-going liners is that passengers are expected to offer tips to the crew for just about every service offered, but just as it is in other forms of social etiquette, there were no specific rules or guidelines: the extremes of offering a tip ranged from paucity to extravagance, depending on the circumstances surrounding the service offered. Groucho's intentions are perfectly clear. He orders a meal delivered to his stateroom in *A Night at the Opera* and asks the steward if he will accept a tip. The steward expectantly says that he can. Groucho, setting him up for a fall, asks him if he has two five dollar bills. Yes, says the steward, about to reach into his pocket for change for the presumed tip. Groucho uses the steward's expected answer to justify his niggardliness ("Well, then, you won't need the ten cents I was going to give you"). The scene is a direct reference to tipping the steward for a meal served in a passenger's cabin. In 1935 it was standard procedure to offer five dollars to the steward, and not any less, for serving a meal in your cabin.[8]

Groucho seems to offer ten cents as his standard tip, no matter what the circumstances. In *Go West* he enters a train station followed by an entourage of attendants pushing steamer trunks, carrying luggage, and schlepping assorted impediments. All of them belong to Groucho. In the same way, but as a variation of his approach toward tipping in *Opera*, he asks if any of the baggage handlers have change of ten cents, suggesting that he's about to offer a tip. In unison, they reply that they don't. Groucho says, "Well, keep the baggage." He takes another look at tipping when he offers a tip to someone who would not usually qualify for one. In *A Night at the Opera*, he sits in a box at the opera and accidentally knocks his top hat over the rail. He asks another member of the audience, sitting in the orchestra section below him and who is dressed in formal white tie and tails, too, to pick up his hat. Groucho offers him a dime so he can "buy a good cigar."

It is socially correct to give a tip to a servant when one is a guest at someone's home.[9] Groucho uses the opportunity to offer a tip in an embarrassing way of dismissing the servant, rather than rewarding him. It is a tacky way of ridiculing the social custom of tipping. In *At the Circus*, at the home of Mrs. Dukesbury (Dumont), a servant enters to announce that the dinner party and entertainment for the evening have been arranged, amplifying his announcement by saying that the maestro for the orchestra will arrive on time. Groucho replies, unnecessarily, "That's fine. Here's a dime, get yourself a clean shirt."

The separation of social classes on an ocean liner was most apparent when comparing the number of passengers traveling in steerage with those traveling in more comfortable surroundings, i.e., "above decks." But steerage fares were profitable for shipping lines, requiring a minimum expense for them, whereas the accommodations and services mandatory to attract passengers in luxurious accommodations often meant a thin or even nonexistent profit. Two thousand passengers might be traveling in steerage on a ship with 2,600 passengers.[10]

In *A Night at the Opera*, Harpo, Chico, and Ricardo come upon a group of steerage passengers; they appear to be Italian peasants. These are not typical steerage passengers traveling to America, "yearning to be free." They are a happy lot in a party atmosphere — singing, dancing, laughing, and playing music. The peasants look like they are enjoying life. There is no evidence of the miserable conditions, sparse, crude, and unhealthy, usually experienced by steerage passengers during the great waves of immigration from Europe to the United States between the end of the nineteenth century and 1921 when open immigration laws ended.[11]

For our three stowaways, this serendipitous discovery is a bonanza: friendly people and no disdainful social stigma attached to their dress, their looks, their education, or their vocations that is prevalent in the rigid social environment above decks. It is a sequence, in its entirety, that offers a visual comment on the vast differences in the usual shipboard caste system.

At first Harpo seems to be wary of their good fortune and the welcoming atmosphere. The steerage passengers make three stowaways feel quite comfortable and accept them without provision. Any fear of discovery by the crew melts away rapidly, and the three of them realize that there is no need to be furtive about their presence among this earthy group. Quite the opposite. The ship's crew serves dinner, buffet style, and the boys go to the line of people waiting for their meal. The ship's crew works behind long, open tables distributing piles of spaghetti, meats, bread, and wine, and offers them more than enough to satisfy their ravenous hunger. Of course, Harpo, his eyes ablaze with his good fortune, piles enough food on his plate alone to feed his accomplices and himself, and probably enough to feed several more people. They enjoy their gastronomic good fortune as they sit on a stairwell and dig in.

A group of dancers among the steerage passengers perform the 1930s Hollywood version of an Italian folk dance. This turns into an opportunity for Chico, Harpo, and Ricardo to contribute to the entertainment. Ricardo sings a romantic love song. It's as if he is singing for his supper, even though he's already eaten it. Chico and Harpo play their usual musical interludes after filling their bellies with the free meal (we see Harpo gleefully wiping his overstocked plate clean with a last hunk of bread). Once fed, their fear of discovery has completely disappeared. Chico and Harpo are sated, their obsession with trying to eat no longer their focus, dulling their usual sunny disposition. They are alive again and back in mischievous form.

Chico plays "All I Do Is Dream of You" with some of the peasant children clustered at the piano near at his left elbow. In his usual fashion he strokes or shoots the keys with his right index finger pointed like a pistol toward the upper registers of the keyboard. After a little comic business at the piano to further entertain the children, Harpo settles into a serious and enjoyable harp solo. Everyone appears happy and boisterous. In real life, the adversities of makeshift and unsanitary below-decks accommodations in steerage tempered such expressed joy. We will see a similar joyous scene in the middle of adverse conditions in *A Day at the Races*, when Harpo comes upon a party of poor families who work and live at the racetrack. In the racetrack stable is another festive dance number, performed by Whitey's Lindy Hoppers. Their dancing is a form of modern American folk dance: a vigorous and free-flowing Lindy Hop, predecessor to the popular 1940s Jitterbug.

We can identify with this group of steerage passengers in *Opera*. As comfortable as they make it for the three stowaways in this brief scene, their presumably spontaneous partying is comforting to us, too. This interlude in the film offers a relief from the rigid social structure above decks. Dumont's provincial code of social conduct, Lassparri's villainous striving for success, and even Groucho's venomous ripostes — accurate as they may be — fade and disappear into insignificance. The steerage sequence is more than visible evidence of Thalberg's plan to take Harpo and Chico's popular musical performances and re-insert them into the framework of their films. The way this scene is staged and directed illustrates another significant step toward friendlier, story-oriented movies and characters acceptable to people everywhere, in contrast with the stark cynicism and Marxian absurdity of *Animal Crackers, Duck Soup, The Cocoanuts, and Horse Feathers*. No matter what their ethnic or cultural origin, the dance and musical numbers in *A Night at the Opera* and *A Day at the Races* delighted movie theatre audiences, especially Chico's comic piano playing and Harpo's lyrical, quasi-classical harp solos.

Music and songs play an important part in many of the films, often as satire. In the first five Marx Brothers films, with the exception of *Duck Soup* where there were no instrumental performances by Harpo and Chico, the musical interludes are the relief we need from the ongoing Marxian madness just as they were in the Brothers' vaudeville shows. Usually there is little or no reaction to these musical interludes from the audience within the films, if there is actually an audience for their performances. Chico and Harpo normally perform in limbo, except in *The Cocoanuts* at the end of the film at Dumont's party, and in *Animal Crackers* in the party sequence. In *A Night at the Opera* there is a genuine reaction from the audience: those children in steerage. Entertained by Chico and Harpo, they are quite happy. With the added fillip of the on-screen audience being entertained, the music represents another softening to the hard-edged, wisecracking Marx Brothers. Earlier, when Groucho orders three hardboiled eggs, he may have been simply describing himself and his two brothers. After placing his order, and for the rest of their films, the eggs just became a little softer.

14. Ice Water in 318

Hotels are frequently locations for filmed scenes, and with the introduction of sound in movies, a fully realized depiction of hotels and their social practices became possible. The Marx Brothers films are no exception to using hotels as backgrounds. Rather than just showing the rituals and practices of hotels, the Brothers' scripts point to these social conventions and with their figurative extended forefinger, just as Chico shoots the piano keys with his forefinger/pistol, poke holes in these conventional ideas.

No matter what type of guests a hotel caters to, whether they are industrial tycoons who park their private railroad cars on the Atlantic Coast Line spurs just east of the hotels in Belleair, Florida,[1] or ordinary public guests at unexceptional hotels, everybody has to register whether or not they have reservations. When Chico and Harpo enter the lobby of the Hotel de Cocoanut in *The Cocoanuts* and make their film debut, with the over-the-top introduction of the Brothers' characters to each other with their pugnacious handshaking routine, it is also the figurative introduction of the four Brothers *en masse* to the expectant audience in the movie theatre. Imagine the reaction of someone in the audience who had never seen the Brothers on stage when, without hesitation or time to get a feel for their characters, their first appearance together is simply raucous, uprooting the polite tradition of handshaking, by turning it into a rowdy, high-spirited affair that gets right to its satirical message. It is comparable to a four-piece bebop jazz combo, or a chamber music quartet, starting to play the rapid-tempo main theme without the standard four- or eight-bar *andante* introduction to ease us into it.

After this introductory scene, Groucho assumes his role as the hotel's manager–reservation clerk and asks Harpo and Chico what they want. Chico tells him that they want to take a room. Groucho asks them what kind of room they want ("Would you like a suite on the third floor?"). Given a slurred pronunciation, suite sounds like "Swede," and Chico, reflecting the vaudevillian practice of laughing at each ethnic wave of "greenhorn" immigrants with a verbal baptism of fire, replies, "No. I'll take a Polock in the basement."[2]

The Cocoanuts (1929). Lobby of the Hotel de Cocoanut. The first appearance of the Brothers on screen in the same frame: (from left) Zeppo, Groucho, Chico, Harpo (Paramount Pictures).

Exasperated, Groucho asks them if they want a single room and Chico says that they want to double up. "Eat some green apples" is Groucho's quicksilver-fast reply. It is pure Kaufman and Ryskind.

Harpo eats a sponge on the desk, drinks ink from the inkwell (really Coca-Cola), and starts to eat the telephone (in reality, made from chocolate). Groucho offers him a vase filled with flowers, as if he's daring him to try an exotic dish on a gastronomic tasting menu. Harpo takes it in stride; he eats one. We're not sure if the flowers are fresh or silk imitations, but it doesn't matter to Harpo. He's doesn't care what they taste like, he just wants to make a point about cleaning up the clutter of front-desk décor.

Groucho asks the boys to register. Harpo picks up a pen from the registration desk and we think he's going to sign the register. Instead, he throws it at the wall as if it were a dart, and Groucho and Chico turn the scene into that of a carnival midway, offering a carnival's hard-sell nasal patter to drum up and enhance excitement ("Step this way, folks"). Each time Harpo throws a new pen from the selection on the desk, Groucho rings the service bell to imply that Harpo has tallied a score. Finally, he offers Harpo his reward for his cumulative score ("And the boy wins the gold cigar"). Harpo, motivated by the excitement of the moment, picks up the telephone to throw it but Groucho stops him ("Hey, don't throw that, that's only for long distance"). Harpo goes behind the registration desk and starts taking mail out of the guests' cubby holes, earnestly tearing up each envelope. When a delivery boy enters with a telegram, Harpo rips it in half, too. Groucho decides to help him. He hands Harpo pieces of mail from the cubby holes to make his job easier; they are a two-man postal censorship team.

Hotels have their own set of social rules about registration and checking in. Traditionally, hotels frowned upon unmarried couples registering as guests sharing the same room, but in practice nearly every hotel has allowed it, often unwittingly. Unless these guests do not conduct themselves with decorum, a hotel will not ask for a marriage license.[3] If a couple is well-dressed and decently mannered, a room clerk is not liable to ask whether or not a couple has a marriage license, because that is considered insulting.[4]

But insult is a hand-lettered invitation for Groucho. In *A Night in Casablanca*, a distinguished middle-aged couple enters the Hotel Casablanca wanting to rent a suite. Groucho questions their marital status, even though they appear to be perfectly respectable ("Your wife, eh? Have you any baggage?"). When the prospective guest answers by saying that their luggage is on the way from the airport, Groucho remains suspicious and tells him that for all the years he's been in the hotel business, that "story" is the phoniest he's ever heard. His continues to be skeptical, with a touch of sarcasm ("I suppose your name is Smith"). The man corrects Groucho and says that his name is Smyth, spelled with a "y." Groucho is even more disbelieving ("Mr. and Mrs. Smyth and no baggage. Let me see your marriage license"). Outraged, the man tries to establish his credibility when he describes himself as president of the East African Telephone Company. Groucho will hear none of it ("I'll bet your baggage is full of telephone books"). The implication is that their baggage, filled with telephone books making it weighty, will make the couple appear to be legitimate. Groucho attacks three of the standard ploys of illicit hotel registration in this one sequence: the lack of luggage, the use of a pseudonym such as Smith or Smyth, and the use of weighted luggage to give the appearance of legitimacy as a ruse to gain entry.[5]

This same ruse appears in *The Cocoanuts* when Groucho orders a bellhop to carry Chico and Harpo's one piece of luggage. There is a brief tussle over the bag because the boys don't want anyone touching it. During this struggle, the bag pops open and we see that there's nothing inside. Groucho asks if Chico knows that it's empty, implying that it shouldn't be. But Chico, always prepared, has an answer ("That's all right. We'll fill it up before we leave").

Aside from its furnishings, the more elegant a hotel is the better its services are supposed to be. In Florida during the land boom, even though many of the practices of selling real estate were questionable, elegance and service at hotels were pursued with vigor.[6] Kaufman and Ryskind's comment on such emphasis on service has Groucho answering a call from one of the rooms with his typical pun to deflate the social arrogance of the request for service ("Ice water in 318? Is that so, where did you get it? Get some onions, that'll make your ice water"). James Feibleman suggests that we have a habit of telephoning for service in a hotel in a laconic and demanding manner. We pick up the phone in our hotel room, and like a rude business executive making a demand to his secretary, we say, "Ice water in 318." It is not a sentence, not a request, just an order barked into the phone.[7]

Feibleman's conclusions are correct. However, there are other things to consider. We should include the societal implications of this terse demand for ice water. Groucho is not belittling the guest's request for service, but rather the way in which people use language in order to intimidate those in the "servant" class, or, in the greater world, the landed gentry's haughty attitude toward recent émigrés, the working class, and others less privileged than they are. That supercilious attitude is the real target of Groucho's curare-tipped arrows.

The entire staff is supposed to offer fast and efficient service to its guests. The method of calling bellhops to the registration desk used to be simple and effortless, especially at small hotels. The registration clerk would just ring the desk bell and yell "Front!" and a bellhop would appear, ready to carry out orders. It was the traditional call for service. At the Hotel de Cocoanut, when Groucho taps his desk bell and commands "Front!" there is no response. He repeats his request, and still no response. Eventually he stoops down and puts his head out from behind the desk, almost at floor level, and calls, "Here, Front! Here, Front! Here, Front, Front, Front, Front. Front. Front. Front." He looks like he's calling the family dog, suggesting that there is really little importance to customer service at hotels, even though the hotels insist otherwise.

Naturally, Harpo and Chico discover another use for the service bell at the registration desk. It is their version of the most important personal service they can request at a hotel. Both of them are behind the desk, and in his controlled madness, Harpo accidentally taps the service bell that's sitting on the desk. One of the female bellhops appears, looking fresh and pert, standing at attention, waiting for a command. Harpo rapidly makes the connection between ringing the bell and the quick appearance of a pretty young woman. He rings the bell again, and another bellhop appears. It's magic. Enlisting Chico's aid, they ring the bell a multitude of times and ten pretty young bellhops are there to satisfy their every wish. Of course, this is a cue for Harpo's satirical chase of pretty women (now including his aide, Chico) throughout the set, not only in this film, but in most of their films. The attitude toward fawning hotel and restaurant service is clearly Kaufman's. He had no patience with waiters and other servants who would annoy him with their efforts.

Room service at hotels, especially ordering in-room meals and the etiquette of eating, come under fire in *Room Service*. The Brothers sit at a dining table in their room and Harpo begins to devour dinner, disregarding the usual standards of etiquette. He stuffs food in his mouth without pause to chew or swallow. With the same frenetic speed, he steals food from everyone's plate. When Chico superstitiously throws salt over his shoulder, Harpo, without pause, quickly catches it in mid-air and licks off his palm without losing the rhythm of his hyperactive dining motions.

In *A Night at the Opera*, Groucho orders breakfast, served in his hotel suite, for Harpo, Chico, Ricardo, and himself. When Harpo arrives, he immediately piles pancakes on his plate and pours syrup on them. Calmly, he pours ketchup on top of the syrup. He puts a coffee cup between two pancakes and starts to eat it as if it were a sandwich. He offers some to Chico, and Chico rejects the offer ("Naw. I no like cupcakes"). Harpo puts Groucho's cigar on top of another pancake, folds the edges around the cigar to create a taco, and starts to eat it. He cuts off a piece of Chico's necktie and puts it between two pancakes to make another kind of sandwich. Finally, he takes the top from the sugar bowl and uses it as if it were a small hand-held mirror. Using another pancake as a "powder puff," he dips the pancake into the sugar bowl and powders his nose with the sugar. He puts his little finger in the ketchup bottle and applies the ketchup on his finger as lipstick. To complete the female social ritual, he takes the top from a vinegar cruet and dabs it behind his ears as if he's adding a hint of perfume. He takes a rubber glove from his pocket, blows into it, inflating the fingers, and "milks" the fingers into Groucho and Chico's coffee cups. Harpo is doing what children love to do: "play" with their food (and maybe this is why children in movie theatre audiences love him). He is acting out, and getting away with, what we all wanted to do when we were kids. Of course the difference is that this isn't mere playing to avoid food that he doesn't like. His playfulness is more of an ad lib comment of etiquette and the emphasis that women put on makeup and fashion. The playing with food as a visual ad lib is reminiscent of Chaplin's "Oceana Roll" in *The Gold Rush*, and carried to a modern version in Billy Crystal's audition scene with Ron Silver in *Mr. Saturday Night*.

The business of paying, or evading, hotel bills is never far from the mind
in the Marxes' standard operating procedure. With their economic status
always questionable, we wonder how Chico and Harpo are going to pay for
their room at the Hotel de Cocoanut; they have no money and no posses-
sions of any value. And in *A Night at the Opera* Groucho manages to check
out of his hotel in Milan with just an invoice for his hotel charges. Management has extended credit to him, and assumes that he will pay it. Not slippery Groucho. He passes the bill along to a steward on shipboard.

In *Room Service* the Brothers don't get away with avoiding payment so
easily. Groucho is an indigent, struggling theatrical producer. Chico and
Harpo are his assistants. The hotel is holding them in their room with the
cast and playwright of Groucho's latest production. They are unable to pay
their bill, and unable to leave until they pay the bill. They try to leave by
dressing in their entire wardrobes to avoid having to carry their luggage
through the lobby and taking the chance of hotel management stopping and
questioning them. Professional hotel confidence men check into hotels, eat
all their meals there for five or six days, and then depart wearing all the clothing in their luggage beneath an oversize raincoat. The hotel is left "holding
the bag."[8]

The art and science of the stowaway's techniques extend from shipboard
to hotel room in *A Night at the Opera*. Groucho's hotel suite in New York
includes Chico, Harpo, and Ricardo as its illegal occupants. Before taking
residence at the hotel, Groucho and his three stowaways engineered an illegal entry into the United States by having the three of them posing as celebrities. They make a fast getaway after city officials discover that they are
imposters when they make a public appearance at city hall. Henderson, a
detective, played to the hilt by Robert Emmett O'Connor as a beefy, prim
Irish cop in the manner of Pat O'Brien, comes to Groucho's hotel suite to
question him about the whereabouts of the other three. Although he is not
the hotel "house detective," his role is similar. You remember me, he says to
Groucho, I'm a plain clothes man. Groucho makes light of Henderson's visit
("You look like an old clothes man to me"). When Henderson asks him if he
lives in the suite alone, Groucho describes a solitary existence, saying that he
lives quite alone ("Yes, just me and my memories. I'm practically a hermit").
Henderson takes Groucho literally and is disbelieving. He tells Groucho that
he couldn't be a hermit; he notices that the table is set for four. That's nothing, says Groucho, my alarm clock is set for eight.

After asking more questions, Henderson is still determined to find out
if Groucho is hiding the three imposters in his suite. In a fast-moving scene
reminiscent of a George Feydeau farce, with its foreshadowing of the theatre
of the absurd, Groucho, Harpo, Chico, and Ricardo move the furniture from

one room to another, practically in front of Henderson. This completely confuses him. The pace of the scene is fast and uses a split screen in the manner of a split set on stage, frequently used in bedroom farces. In the final cut of the scene the Marx Brothers form a tableau to throw Henderson off the track. Chico stoops and they throw a sheet over him. Groucho sits in an easy chair reading a newspaper and wears a false beard and handlebar moustache. Harpo puts a shawl around his shoulders, a doily on his head, and sits in Chico's lap. He rocks back and forth to make it look like Chico is actually a rocking chair, while Harpo uses a spoon and fork as if they were knitting needles and he is an old lady knitting a sweater. They appear to be a Victorian family in a *tableau vivant.* Henderson enters from the other room and, completely confused and embarrassed, apologizes for his intrusion into what appears to be an evening of familial bliss. The ruse is accomplished, and we have a blackout. The scene is complete, they fooled the dim-witted detective, and we have a pristine comment on hotel security and the fiendish ways that con men evade discovery.

The traditional question often lurking in the minds of security personnel in "family" hotels is: "Do you have a woman in your room?" No one in hotel management trying to find out if a man has taken a woman to his room for sex asks that question, bluntly.[9] And the practice of having a house detective burst into a room, unannounced, to ask if there is a woman present is no longer practiced. More subtle means are used. Usually, an assistant manager will call the room and ask politely if the occupant is "entertaining" a woman. If so, the management asks for an additional fee for a second person occupying the room.[10]

Still infatuated with house detectives and their methods of unannounced intrusion, *A Day at the Races* has the wonderful scene where Groucho entertains the seductress, Flo Marlowe (Esther Muir), in his room at Standish Sanitarium. Chico bursts in. He wears an oversize moustache and impersonates a house detective as a ruse to warn Groucho of impending danger, not related to the possible tryst. Chico asks if Groucho has a woman in his room, but he denies it ("If I haven't, I've wasted thirty minutes of valuable time"). Chico calls in Harpo, his assistant. Harpo wears a deerstalker hat and carries a large magnifying glass. He is the comic book version of Sherlock Holmes. Harpo has two bloodhounds with him, on leashes. He examines one of Flo's arms with his magnifying glass, prompting Groucho to comment about his "scientific" investigation ("If you're looking for fingerprints, you're a little early"). Once more, Groucho treats us to a hilarious sexual allusion, but slight enough to pass the restrictions of censorship as, at the same time, he ridicules detectives and their methods of crime detection.

The increased sophistication of scientific crime detection in the 1920s is the target of the Marx Brothers' jabs in *Animal Crackers*. Detectives use many methods of gathering facts for intelligent solution of crimes: investigating fingerprints and footprints, using photographs, and an awareness of criminal habits. Good common sense and an analytical mind are important in solving most any case.[11] Chico explains to Groucho how he is going to solve the mystery of the stolen Beaugard painting, using contemporary methods of crime investigation. Of course, he doesn't quite understand deductive reasoning as we see him trying to analyze the events leading to the theft. He tells Groucho that the first thing a detective must do is to ask himself, "What happened?" The answer is automatic, says Chico, and he continues asking himself easy questions and giving the right answers. He compliments himself on his progress, citing that so far, he's right. Groucho is skeptical ("Well, it's pretty hard to be wrong if you keep answering yourself all the time"). Chico puts together all the "clues" and comes to some naïve conclusions: Someone, either a guest or staff member at Margaret Dumont's mansion, has stolen the painting. To find it, all he has to do is go to everyone in the house and ask them if they took it. Groucho's response to this is more realistic. He wants to know what Chico will do if no one in the house took the painting. Chico never lets logic interfere with his reasoning: If no one in the house has stolen the painting, they can ask at the house next door. And if there is no house next door?, Groucho asks. Chico is relieved because he has an expedient answer ("Then we gotta build one"). Unsophisticated as it may be, many people thought that people who solved crimes were mysterious individuals with occult and supernatural powers with a complete knowledge of people and events, in the past, present, and future.[12]

Chico makes another attempt at deductive reasoning in *At the Circus* when he joins forces with Harpo to try to discover who stole $10,000 from the circus. How to find the thief? He tells Harpo that all they have to do is reconstruct the crime just as detectives do. Harpo, taking Chico literally, wants to hit Chico on the head to illustrate how the thief attacked the bearer of the money. Groucho joins them in their attempt at deductive reasoning to solve the crime. They try to trap the circus midget into revealing himself as the thief because someone found a cigar at the scene of the crime and the midget is a habitual cigar smoker. They plan to have the midget smoke one of his cigars and they will compare smells, theorizing that if the smells are alike, then the midget is guilty. They visit the midget and Groucho asks him for a cigar, explaining that he doesn't have any of his own with him. Chico interrupts and offers Groucho a cigar from his own pocket. Groucho tries with the midget again, and Chico offers another cigar. This happens several times. Groucho is unable to trap the midget because of Chico's stupidity. It is a repeat of the auction scene in *The Cocoanuts* when Groucho hires Chico to be his shill, and Chico, not quite understanding how this scenario works, repeatedly outbids himself, and the other bidders, frustrating Groucho's efforts and upsetting the auction by destroying their devious plan and its reason for being. Chico focuses on the technique of what he has to do without knowing or understanding the overall goals of his actions. In that sense, he is stupid. Maybe not. Once he has an idea or a goal, he pursues it unwaveringly, either alone or with his brothers.

In hotels, their hyperactivity, verbal or physical, in chase scenes (think of Harpo chasing blondes constantly off and on the set) and in the hurly-burly kinetics of classic farce (in various hotel rooms, on shipboard, in the operating room at the Standish Sanitarium, and elsewhere) probably has resulted in the Marx Brothers being worn-out and perspiring somewhat. They can use some of that ice water for 318 themselves, but not necessarily for drinking. They simply want to splash it onto our faces to wake us from our ill-conceived notions of the social pecking order.

15. The Main Hungerdunger

In many of the Marx films there is a sequence where Groucho and Chico appear together in close-up shots as they criticize business practices. Groucho usually assumes the role of a high-pressure salesman, while Chico regularly takes the simplest concepts of business, both legitimate and unscrupulous, and enacts them with an exaggerated stupidity that might make even an unsophisticated audience groan at his clumsy behavior. In *Animal Crackers*, Groucho's inclination toward the techniques of high-pressure salesmen first surfaces when he makes his sales pitch to Mrs. Rittenhouse. Captain Spaulding arrives at Dumont's home, Rittenhouse Manor, for a weekend of social activities, and upon his entrance to this lavish home he "sells" the idea of home improvement, as if she lives in and runs a boarding house instead of a grand mansion. He tells her that she's letting the house run down, and as a result she's not getting the class of people that she did at one time. He promises that he can make some dramatic changes, i.e., erecting a sign that tells everyone that her place is under new management and then altering the menu ("We'll set up a seventy-five cent meal that'll knock their eyes out"). He tells her that after she knocks their eyes out, she can charge them anything she wants.

After asking for a down payment for the renovations, he changes the sales pitch to that of an insurance salesman, a technique that he will use in their next film, *Monkey Business*. True to form, he insults her. He tells her that the insurance policy that he's selling her will provide generously for her children and her old age which "will be here in a couple of weeks now, if I'm any judge of horseflesh." As he has done in *The Cocoanuts* and will do repeatedly with Dumont and other women, he pictures her as an animal. This emphasis on salesmen's techniques reflects the change in business practices and fierce competition among sales people during the Twenties. Companies required their salesmen to do more than merely recommend products in modest and explicit terms. They expected them to "break down consumer resistance."[1]

More than just face-to-face salesmanship, *The Big Store* reflects the steps taken by department stores to promote their merchandise. In the bedding department at the Phelps Department Store, Harpo and Chico meet an Italian immigrant and his wife, who are shopping for a bed. The rest of their family, a large contingent of children, is with them. There are no beds visible. It is a comment on frivolous retail marketing, circa 1941. The department store, following the current style of retail merchandising, hides them within walls or as part of other furniture. They actually hide one behind a fireplace. The beds work electrically, appearing and disappearing by simply pushing a button. The children scurry around the display, pushing buttons, jumping into beds, and disappearing into walls, behind fireplaces, and various other caches that hide the beds. They seem to be "lost" to their dumbfounded parents. This is a cue for Harpo and Chico. They frantically push buttons, too, hoping to find the lost children, meanwhile creating further havoc as some of the children are "found" while others continue to be "lost" during this frenzy of button-pushing. It looks like a bedroom farce with no rooms, only the beds. Can any department store survive Harpo and Chico's child-like fascination with modern department store merchandising? Can any department store merchandising survive Harpo and Chico?

Department stores went to extremes in merchandising, sometimes illogically and unrealistically. Tony Martin plays the male romantic lead and sings a song in the music department at the special request of a passing shopper, and at the same time recording the song for the customer to purchase. That such a service could be performed, let alone with any fidelity, is a pure whimsy, and deserves to act as an illustration of the absurd fantasy about modern-day marketing created by department stores and Hollywood.

More absurd fantasy is evident in the sequence that presents the merchandising of women's high fashion. Groucho presides over a runway show of models while he recites rhymed descriptions of their clothing, accompanied by romantic background music. More than the attack on verbal presentations by emcees at runway shows, the incongruity of haute couture clothing is the major point as the models wear grotesque distortions of high fashion; most of them are simply impractical for any woman to wear for any event in real life. Newsreels in the Forties usually would present a segment showing bizarre clothing as a comic relief to their reportage of the serious events of the war, and as a way of reassuring audiences that "normal" life continues.

The emphasis on high fashion was just a small part of the changes in American business to come under attack with Marxian japes. In *Animal Crackers* Captain Spaulding makes reference to the Industrial Revolution of the eighteenth and nineteenth centuries and its influence on socioeconomic and cultural changes in present-day society. He talks about how American living habits had changed ("We're away past tents. We're living in bungalows now. This is the Mechanical Age, of course"). Mass production and mass consumption were aspects of normal American life by the 1920s. Machines were no longer mechanical wonders. Most Americans thought that they lived better, had more power, and had more comfort and leisure time than they had ever experienced because of the role of the machine in contemporary life.[2]

By 1930, in nearly every American city and town, local service clubs had become a phenomenon. These service clubs — the Rotary, the Lions, the Elks, the Knights of Pythias — were composed of groups of middle-class business-men who joined together for a combination of noisy good fellowship and the promotion of social "good."[3] Through the years the reputation of the clubs became tarnished; along with their good deeds came conventions where the emphasis seemed to be on parties and wild drinking. Groucho comments about liquor consumption by businessmen in *Animal Crackers* during his speech describing his adventures in Africa. He talks about hunting big game, and says that elks live in the hills and in spring they come down to gather around a water hole for their annual convention ("You should see them run when they find that it's only a water hole. What they are looking for is an elk-ohol"). The idea of businessmen and boozy parties was a main theme of Laurel and Hardy's *Sons of the Desert*, released in 1933 and directed by William Seiter who went on to direct the Brothers in *Room Service*.

Business practices, and especially letter writing, deserve the attention they receive in *Animal Crackers*. Captain Spaulding asks Zeppo to take a let-ter to his lawyers: Hungerdunger, Hungerdunger, Hungerdunger, Hunger-dunger, and McCormick. When he asks Zeppo what he has so far, Zeppo reads the list of addressees back to him, listing only three Hungerdungers. Groucho scolds him repetitively, becoming indignant and claiming that he left out the main Hungerdunger at the firm. But, in fact, at this law firm one Hungerdunger is indistinguishable from another: No Hungerdunger seems to have a first name, and the letter's salutation is vague and surreal ("Gentle-men, question mark"). Groucho decides to dictate the letter anyway, with-out including the invisible main Hungerdunger. He dictates a letter full of clichéd Victorian phrases and jargon. There is no meaning to it; the letter makes no sense. Groucho's letter is composed entirely of stock phrases — *In re* yours of the fifth inst., yours to hand and beg to rep brackets, i.e. to wit e.g., in lieu that despite, we received an *ipso facto* — many of the things that the critic Maurice Weseen cautions against. As an added gesture, Groucho closes with the standard Victorian ending ("Hoping this finds you, I beg to remain"). Zeppo questions the ending by asking Groucho where he hopes the letter finds him. This kind of dangling phrase is a holdover from the Victo-rian ideal. Critics opposed such "participial and hackneyed balderdash" rather than a conversational tone in both the body of a letter and the ending.[4]

Specifically, critics at that time lobbied for the elimination of jargon and stock phrases in business writing.[5] Reminiscent of the flowery, Victorian style of writing, these formulaic devices were still considered acceptable by less sophisticated letter writers up to the first third of the twentieth century, and were exemplified by a suggested list of Latin, French, and Italian words as well as a list of form letters, in at least one handbook for use in social, business, and legal letter writing.[6] Although less flowery, the practice continues to this day. For Kaufman, a superb stylist, the jumble of Latinate phrases commonly used in business letters touched a raw nerve, making him scream in pain symbolically, with enough anger to prompt him to write this letter-writing scene in *Animal Crackers*. When Groucho asks Zeppo to read the letter he has dictated to him, Zeppo just reads the first sentence and then omits all the phrases that Groucho has dictated because he didn't think they were important. Groucho sounds incensed, accusing him of leaving out the body of the letter. However, always flexible, he relents ("All right, send it that way and tell them the body will follow"). Zeppo asks Groucho if he wants to put the body in brackets. Groucho declines, saying that it will never get there in brackets; he should just put it in a box. Finally Groucho congratulates Zeppo on the "fine letter." He tells Zeppo to make two copies of the letter and to throw away the original. When he finishes that task, Groucho wants him to throw away the copies and just send a stamp via air mail. And so, Groucho has dismissed the complete letter as worthless, as well as the entire process of writing business letters.

Letters are only the tip of the iceberg of confusion surrounding business practices. Contracts and their baffling legal language present a fear of the lay public that they were the target of unscrupulous businesses or deceitful lawyers. This fear concerns the small type in contracts, densely printed and hard to read with a glut of obfuscatory phrases, and if signed, would be binding. The famous contract scene in *A Night at the Opera* is not about opera. Opera is just a framework. The scene is really about deceitful business practices. Chico and Groucho could be talking about exporting corn from Kansas to Sicily instead of negotiating for the rights to an opera singer. There is no mention of opera or an elucidation of artists' rights or other matters specific to opera in this contract. It's simply Chico and Groucho literally tearing apart generic legal contracts with their overuse of untrustworthy language. Once more we are about to witness the interplay between the "smart" Groucho and the "stupid" (but street smart) Chico and we look forward to it.

As they stand, each resting one foot on Lasparri's stomach (in bar room style), they are about to negotiate the contract for the "greatest tenor in the world." The contract is on a very long piece of paper, longer than a standard size, infinitely longer. There is some legal jousting at the beginning to define the rules of procedure. Chico (who always appears to be an illiterate; nonetheless with a bountiful helping of street smarts) demands that Groucho read the contract to him. Groucho agrees, and starts their verbal duel by asking him if he can hear. Chico is wary of the question. He tells Groucho that he hasn't heard anything yet, and asks him if he has said anything. Groucho tells him that he hasn't said anything worth hearing, and Chico explains that this is why he hasn't heard anything. He asks Groucho if he can read. Groucho says that he can't see it because the paper is too long. If his arms were a little longer he could read it. Finally he gets the "fine print" in focus when he holds the contract at arm's length.

Groucho cautions Chico to pay attention to the first clause because it is important ("The party of the first part shall be known in this contract as the party of the first part"). Immediately we hear the phrase that confuses people most, containing those "dreary parties": the party of the first part and the party of the second part.[7] Groucho thinks it's a neat turn of phrase, but Chico isn't sure and he asks Groucho to read it again. This time he thinks it sounds a little better. Chico may not have a formal education, but he understands the nuances of language, especially legal language. He wants this contract to be clear, and is dismayed by some of the language that appears to be lucid, but isn't.

He tells Groucho that he wants to hear the first part again. Groucho asks him if it's the party of the first part that he wants to hear. Chico tells him that he wants to hear "the first part of the party of the first part." Groucho says that they shouldn't quarrel about a little thing like this, and offers to take this sentence out of the contract. With that, Groucho tears off the section containing that sentence. Chico does the same with his copy, and asks Groucho how much is left. Groucho tells him that he has about a foot and a half remaining on this long sheet. Groucho continues with a recitation of the definition of the "party of the second part," and Chico asks a question ("Why can't the first part of the second party be the second part of the first party?"). Many people believe that the wrestling over words and phrases is a technique that lawyers use to make their thoughts obscure.[8] Their reason for this emphasis on words is that they are making an attempt at expressing thoughts with understandable precision.[9]

Neither Groucho nor Chico can agree on the phrases in the contract. They agree on the fact that the contract should not include these words. So they tear off the offending clauses until they each have only a small strip of paper. It is a severe condemnation of lawyers and legal contracts; they have ripped up and thrown away all but a tiny shred of the original contract, implying that contracts are mostly worthless. In more modern vernacular, the tearing of the contract suggests that contracts are a rip-off!

Left with just a small strip of paper in their hands, Chico wants to know what the remaining paragraph means. Not to worry, assures Groucho, it's a standard part of every contract; it stipulates that a contract will not be binding if any of the parties are not of sound mind.[10] Chico isn't sure. It's all right, Groucho promises; it's a customary part of every contract. It's called a sanity clause. Chico laughs. You can't fool me, he says; "There ain't no Sanity Claus." And so, the contract is destroyed, language is destroyed, and we laugh at the foolish attempt at lawyers trying to confuse Groucho and Chico. Their wordplay in this scene is reminiscent of the vy-a-duck scene in *The Cocoanuts*, the scientific investigation scene in *Animal Crackers*, and the tootsie-frootsie scene in *A Day at the Races*. These interludes not only comment on the subjects "discussed," but they show us the concern for the slippery meanings of language itself. In this contract scene Chico's comment at the end also tells us that the language of contracts can be childish. We are grownups, he tells us; we don't believe in Santa Claus any more; we want action, not only words.

Feibleman thinks that the Brothers are most at ease when they attack the pomposities of big business and the language and sanctity of contracts.[11] If we interpret their "ease" at their choice of target, it's true. Throughout their career they preferred to harass the establishment, whether or not others more talented than they were wrote their scripts. Even in their private lives, there is clear evidence of these attitudes, as we see in some of Groucho's letters. But the presentation of their attacks was far from calm. Frenzy, sometimes visible, other times just beneath the surface, dominates their windmill tilting. Deflating pomposity is their strong suit, and it is clearly evident when their scripts point at portentous lawyers and what appears to be an absurd legal process. We see this in Chico's trial in *Duck Soup*, and other references sprinkled throughout the films.

Lawyers are pompous when they enter a courtroom; it is a calculated stance to give them an air of importance, especially when arguing a case.[12] On shipboard in *Monkey Business*, Groucho goes into the stateroom of Alky Briggs and his wife, in an attempt to elude the crew. He hides in the closet while Alky and his wife, Lucille, have an argument. When Alky leaves, Lucille talks to Groucho and tells him that he can't hide, she knows he's in the closet. He comes out and assumes the manner of a legal prosecutor asking questions of a witness for the defense. He asks her if she has seen him enter the closet. She hasn't, so he asks her if he's in the closet now. She says no. Then, he concludes, how does she know he was in the closet? Turning to an imaginary judge he brings his questioning to a close, without letting Lucille answer his final question. He then says, in an assumptive, stentorian finality, "Your honor, I rest my case." Groucho has made his real point: His legal arrogance is enough to "rest his case," with a faulty corollary, created by badgering Lucille.

Nonetheless Lucille is impressed with Groucho's legal manner. She flirts with him, telling him that she didn't know that he was a lawyer. She tells him that he's awfully shy for a lawyer. And he answers with a self-condemning pun ("You bet I'm shy. I'm a shyster lawyer"). But maybe that's exactly what she's seeking. She admits that she's having marital difficulties with Alky, and asks for his legal help. Once more, Groucho's legal persona sounds self-important, as he offers counsel after Lucille presents a plea for women's rights with the freedom to enjoy herself as she wants. She tells him she wants life, laughter, gaiety and "hot-cha-cha." Groucho responds, his speech makes him sound like a divorce lawyer, and at the same time, the same old Groucho whose real quest is for sex and money ("You take the children, your husband burns down the house ... you take the insurance, and I take you").

Groucho's role as a lawyer is an enhanced development of his character as a salesman, an auctioneer, and a public speaker. There's good reason for a comment on speechmaking in the Brothers' films. Americans are addicted to the habit of making speeches; not only the after-dinner variety, but even speechmaking before dinner, at political gatherings, even speeches at home.[13] When we look at Captain Spaulding's entrance in *Animal Crackers* we see that Groucho's speechmaking is unlike it is in any of the other films. He is stiff, formal, and Victorian. It is like the mockery of old-fashioned letter writing occurring later in the film. Groucho says that he is happy about the magnificent display of effusion shown to him. The other guests at Mrs. Rittenhouse's home interrupt his starched rhetoric by singing a short verse from "Hooray for Captain Spaulding," the song that eventually was Groucho's theme song on his radio and television show *You Bet Your Life* twenty years later. Groucho starts his stiff speech again, and the assembled guests drown him out with the same song. They simply want to eliminate this speech, to scoff at flowery speeches (as do Kaufman and Ryskind). This interruption occurs several times until Groucho gets the idea and interrupts himself by starting to sing the song. "Well, somebody's got to do it," he says.

Of course, the ultimate speech is the after-dinner version. It is a challenge. The speaker must present material different than a general orator because people have just eaten and a speech that's too serious might bring on indigestion.[14] But it's not a challenge for Groucho; he's completely relaxed and feels comfortable making this kind of speech.

In *The Cocoanuts* Mrs. Potter (Dumont) asks him to make a speech after dinner at a banquet she hosts to announce the engagement of her daughter. His speech is to introduce Dumont to the guests so that she can make her announcement. He interweaves clichés from other speeches, out of context with what he should be talking about. He mixes up these clichés, too ("On behalf of the Rotary Club of Minneapolis, I want to take the occasion of welcoming you to Waukegan").[15] He lapses into a parody of a phrase often used in speeches honoring a retiree from a corporation ("...in recognition of my many years of service to the railroad, you are presenting me with these ties"). Finally, he shifts the tone of his remarks and moves into the absurd ("Off in the thin night, the tumbling of a leaf can be heard. Down through the trees and the babbling brook as it wends its way onward...") reminding us of his *Strange Interlude* speech in *Animal Crackers*. The camera focuses on Harpo, who interrupts Groucho's speech by leaving the table with an expression of bored disgust on his face. But that doesn't stop Groucho. He continues his disjointed phrases ("Western cattle opened at 15½, yearlings and spring veal showed firm tone and eggs were a little touchy on a falling market") until he finally introduces Dumont ("I now take great pleasure in presenting to you the well-preserved, and partly pickled, Mrs. Potter"). Dumont asks the villainous Harvey Yates, her future son-in-law, to make a speech. Apparently uncomfortable and embarrassed, he assumes the stance of an unprepared speaker, starting by saying that he's not much of a speech maker, but he thanks Groucho/Hammer for calling on him. Groucho won't let him get away with his shy excuses. Groucho invites Yates to call on him sometime. When Yates starts to reply, Groucho interrupts by inviting him to come see his flower beds. Yates starts to speak again and Groucho continues to interrupt. Each time Yates tries to speak, Groucho describes another facet of his flower garden in his usual punning fashion ("I've got short pansies and long pansies ... next spring I'm getting in some early bloomers"). Yates, defeated, uses a polite excuse to try to extricate himself from this hostility by thanking everyone and repeating that he hadn't intended to make a speech after all. Groucho tells him that he certainly succeeded, and doesn't let him lean on that hackneyed exit line of the unprepared speaker.

At the opening night of the New York Opera Company in *A Night at the Opera*, Mrs. Claypool (Dumont) is the primary patron of the opera company. She has to make a speech to the audience before the curtain rises. She is terrified at the prospect. Groucho volunteers to make appropriate remarks to announce the opening of the new season. He has sharpened his teeth for the task of making a biting commentary on the pomposity of such speeches. At the same time, he makes his usual belittling remark about Dumont, implying her financial instability. He tells the audience that the opera season is the result of Dumont's generous checks. He's sure the familiar strains of Verdi's music will "come back to you tonight — and Mrs. Claypool's checks will come back in the morning." As in *The Cocoanuts*, part of Groucho's speech is introductory, as he offers a brief verbal résumé for Lassparri, the arrogant Machiavellian opera singer ("His mother was a well-known bass singer, and his father was the first man to cross spaghetti and bicarbonate of soda, thus causing and curing indigestion at the same time").

Chico's "radio" speech in *Opera* is more formal, but it is absurd, part of the ballyhoo used by cities to promote themselves. Chico's speech makes him sound stupid once again, but his being logically illogical is his unique way of making a satiric comment. It is a technique borrowed from his vy-a-duck and scientific-theory-of-crime-solving scenes with Groucho. But now Chico is at center stage; he speaks alone. The mayor of New York at a reception in front of city hall asks him to tell the radio audience about the transatlantic flight that Harpo, Ricardo Baroni, and Chico have just completed. After telling the audience that the first time they started they ran out of gasoline and had to go back, then they took twice as much fuel. This second time, he says, they were just about to land, just three feet from the landing strip, and they ran out of gasoline again. On their third try they flew halfway across the ocean and they realized they forgot the airplane. They try to find a solution by sitting down and talking it over (in mid-air, without an airplane?). Then, he says, they thought of a great idea. They decided not to take any gasoline and not to take an airplane, either ("We take-a steamship"). Harpo, who makes the next speech, starts by drinking many glasses of water. He is stalling for time, just as Groucho does in *At the Circus* in the banquet scene at Margaret Dumont's mansion ("I'll have another cup of coffee"). As Harpo continues to drink, he dribbles water down his chin. It eventually washes away his fake beard and exposes the fraud. As well as engendering the usual chase for the stowaways/illegal immigrants, Harpo's stalling implies that the prolific use of water pitchers and the drinking of water by public speakers is a device to eat into their allotted speaking time.

The Brothers were no strangers to ballyhoo. Their early years in vaudeville (with their mother managing their careers) were nine parts ballyhoo and one part talent. For all their sophistication, sometimes big cities used the techniques of ballyhoo — the uproar of ticker-tape parades and public gatherings to attract tourists — to identify themselves with greatness. These parades and gatherings are the rituals of society and in the 1920s official welcomes became the rule, rather than the exception, when New York's official greeter, Grover Whelan, welcomed sports figures with the same accord offered to international political figures. It was simply fun for the citizens of New York to throw ticker tape and fragments of telephone books out of windows along lower Broadway as parades honoring these notables proceeded uptown to city hall. Practically anyone with enough moxie and the right kind of press agent could promote such a public event.[16]

Business contracts, law practices, letter writing, legal language, and speech making all come under the critical eye throughout the films. There is no one institution signified, no one person to blame. We can correct these problems; we're all guilty of them. But we need to find the main Hunger-dunger with whom we can lodge our complaints.

16. Grand Slam

Every afternoon George Kaufman played bridge. He loved the game, and liked to play it as well as poker, often with his friends from the Algonquin Round Table, or with his friends in the newspaper world. Chico Marx was a compulsive gambler and would bet on anything, often foolishly. But he loved card playing, In fact, all the Brothers played cards regularly from their earliest years onward. In Nacogdoches the police arrested them on the front porch of their hotel for playing Euchre, a card game involving gambling.[1] Their mother, Minnie, would invite booking agents to her home in an attempt to persuade them to schedule her brood on another road trip. She served a hearty meal, cooked by her husband, and followed by a poker game. Card games, previously considered a form of gambling, became fashionable in American society during the 1930s. So popular was card playing, it had become a social necessity.[2] Card games were another way to escape from the suffocating reality of the outside world. Contract bridge was not only widespread as a social outlet, but some people thought it was a good way to divert conversation from the possibility of "dangerous" political discussion; there was a noticeable wave of discontent with the government in those hard times.[3] So, it's not surprising that card games, particularly bridge, show up as a target in some of the Brothers' films.

In *Animal Crackers,* Harpo and Chico start to play bridge with Dumont and Mrs. Whitehead. It is a short scene, running a little more than four minutes, but it illustrates how important this game has become in the American social landscape, with its tediously complicated rules, jargon, and other trappings. Of course, Chico and Harpo destroy all semblances of order and balance that the game had become. Victor Heerman directed it in the style of a vaudeville blackout. Chico asks Dumont if she wants to play "honest" without defining the alternative. She says that she thinks so. As if to threaten her if she will not play honestly, Harpo puts a blackjack on the table. When Dumont tells him to put the blackjack away, Harpo tries to slap her hand with it, but instead uses one of his trademarked comic devices and hits his own hand. He makes his wrist go limp and blows on his hand to try to soothe the pain.

Dumont tells Chico to cut the cards so he can pick his partner. He tells her that there's no need for that, Harpo is his partner, but Dumont insists that he has to play by the rules. At this point, they haven't started to play, but all honesty disappears instantly, as does the formality of the game itself. Honest playing is never in the cards with these two Brothers. And they avoid propriety at any cost.

Chico has arranged the cards so that both he and Harpo pick an ace of spades, making them partners automatically. When Dumont questions how there could be two aces of spades in the deck, Chico says that Harpo has thousands of them, as if to say that they are up his sleeve like the cutlery that Harpo is famous for dropping. When Harpo jumps up and sits on Mrs. Whitehead's lap, the other three players, including Chico, tell him to settle down. Chico offers a punning excuse for Harpo's behavior ("He thought it was Contact Bridge").

Harpo starts to shuffle the cards, but actually does nothing to them. He divides the deck in two piles and riffles both piles, one in each hand, without overlapping the piles in order to mix them. He finishes and extends the deck to Chico for him to cut the cards. Instead, Chico raps the table twice with his knuckles to signify that he doesn't want to cut. Harpo begins to deal but Dumont stops him. She wants to cut the cards. When she does, by dividing the deck in two, Harpo puts the two piles back together just as they were before she cut.

The blatant cheating begins. Harpo starts to deal, only using one hand, holding the deck in his right hand and moving his thumb across the deck to dislodge the next card so that he can deal it. He licks his left thumb (not his right) each time he deals a card, to make it easier to slide each one off the deck. After a few seconds, he deals in the normal manner, with both hands, but shows Chico the face of the cards before dealing them so that Chico can approve or reject a card that Harpo is about to deal to him. As he deals to himself, he discards the cards he doesn't want in a pile, except when he's about to deal an ace, saving them for his own hand. When he deals a card to Chico he shows it to him before he deals it. If Chico doesn't want it, Harpo throws it away, completely off the table. He finishes dealing, and puts another card from his lap into his own hand. Harpo's dealing techniques will allow the two Brothers to win. The two women can do nothing to stop them. Harpo ignores convention: He changes his hand with Chico, and he exchanges his hand with Dumont's without her seeing him do it.

They begin bidding by confusing all the rules. Dumont is exasperated and says that she doesn't understand what they are doing. Mrs. Whitehead

Animal Crackers (1930). The exasperating bridge game: (from left) Margaret Irving, Chico, Margaret Dumont, Harpo (Paramount Pictures).

realizes that there is something wrong with the way the Brothers are playing, and she suggests that they begin bidding again. But she's tangling with the wrong guys when she tries to restore a semblance of logic as well as the discipline of the formal rituals surrounding bridge. Harpo raises his forefinger, and Chico interprets ("He bids one"). When Mrs. Whitehead wants to know *one what* (like Zeppo wanting Groucho to clarify the *where* he hopes his Hungerdunger letter will find the addressee), Chico is evasive about their bids ("'At's all right, you find out"). As well, Dumont insists on knowing what Harpo has bid. Chico tells her that they will tell her later, and he offers to bid two. Now, Mrs. Whitehead wants to know what Chico has bid ("Two what?"). Chico continues the confusion, referring to Harpo's previous bid, by saying that he will bid two of the same that Harpo bid, without saying whether it is clubs, diamonds, hearts, or spades.

Chico asks Harpo if he has a hundred aces, referring to the method of keeping score. Harpo shows two fingers, which Chico interprets as two hundred. We don't know if Harpo is referring to the method of scoring, or that he has two hundred aces stored up his sleeves, even though he has rolled the sleeves of his coat and shirt up to his elbows before sitting down to play, and is playing with his bare arms showing. Our Harpo is enough of a magician to be able to hide two hundred cards up his shortened-sleeve coat. Once the game begins, the boys are not only disreputable in their bidding, they make misplays the norm. Kaufman seems to be enjoying himself, satirizing bridge. (This isn't the first time he focused on bridge as a setting for his humor. His satirical one-act play, *If Men Played Cards as Women Do*, was on Broadway in 1926, two years before the stage version of *Animal Crackers* opened on the Great White Way.)

As they continue playing, Harpo does all the gauche, things that disrupt the acceptable standards of honest play: When Mrs. Whitehead says that she doesn't know what card to lead, he looks at her hand and plays a card for her and as a result he's able to take the trick; he tears up and throws away a card he's about to play because Chico counsels him against it; he continues taking tricks slamming an ace of spades on the table, more vehemently each time; he has four of them (just part of the 200?). Finally, Dumont is frustrated and quits the game, taking Mrs. Whitehead with her. As she gets up to leave, Whitehead discovers that her shoes are missing. As the two women leave, we see that Harpo has stolen them and is wearing them. Chico recognizes the theft and laughs. Harpo stands up and teeters on these high-heeled shoes as he tries to walk. Blackout.

The references to bridge-playing in other films, slight as they are, reinforce how popular the game was. When Groucho introduces Herman Gottlieb to Dumont in *A Night at the Opera*, he not only spoofs the ritual of introductions, as he merely mentions their names as a shortcut to formal introduction. ("Mr. Gottlieb, Mrs. Claypool, Mrs. Claypool, Mr. Gottlieb. Now if you four people want to play bridge, don't mind me, go right ahead").

Referring to the two methods of bidding in bridge, Groucho invites Dumont to his land auction at Cocoanut Manor in *The Cocoanuts*. It is an opportunity for Groucho to give language an ironic twist ("You must come over. There's going to be entertainment, sandwiches, and the auction. If you don't like auction, you can play contract"). No matter how popular the game of bridge, Groucho thinks that people spend too much time on the game. He asks Dumont to guard Freedonia's war plans in *Duck Soup*, telling her that they are as valuable as her life ("and that's putting them pretty cheap"). He tells her to watch over them like a cat watches over her kittens. He asks her if she has ever had kittens, and he answers his own question ("No, of course not. You're too busy running around playing bridge"). Bridge terminology makes up a greater part of the game, and is for its players, a sign of acceptance when they can have conversations about the game using its jargon. To anyone who doesn't know anything about the game, the jargon is a foreign language, as it is with any sport or patois in any closely knit society. In *Horse Feathers*, someone has locked Chico and Harpo in an apartment. To escape, they saw through the floor. However, they crash through to the floor below and slam onto the top of a table, around which are four housewives playing bridge. After the flying dust and plaster settles, Chico remarks on the card game to Harpo ("Well, partner, I guess we made a grand slam").

Just as bridge playing was popular during the Depression, there was an increase in a variety of gambling activities, partly because many people hoped for a big return on their wagers at a time when so many people didn't have steady jobs.[4] It is like the hopes and dreams that people have today when they buy state-sponsored lottery tickets. One of the most widespread gambling devices in the 1930s was slot machines, and worthy of a visual reference in *Horse Feathers*. Harpo, standing in a speakeasy, watches a man desperately and unsuccessfully trying to hit the jackpot in a slot machine. Frustrated, the man steps aside, and Harpo inserts a button from his raincoat into the slot and wins. Moving from fantasy to satiric irony, and still in the speakeasy, he sees a streetcar conductor wearing a change maker on his belt. He puts a nickel (that he had won from the slot machine) into the money changer, puts his hat under it, and pushes the coin release lever. All the money (i.e., the "jackpot") pours into Harpo's hat. Then Harpo puts a nickel into the speakeasy's pay phone. He holds his hat under the coin return slot, but nothing happens. He inserts a second nickel, the phone rings, and he picks up the receiver. The phone pays off as silver comes pouring from the phone into his hat.

As racetracks profited from the increase in attendance (people who were unemployed with little chance of finding new jobs, had plenty of free time), legal pari-mutuel betting grew, too. But there still remained at race tracks people who sold information about the race horses. Called by a variety of slang names — tipsters or touts were two of the more common — these men were acting illegally, and what's more, their information was of dubious quality. They often sold daily bulletins to bettors at prices that ranged anywhere from ten cents to $1,000 a copy.[5] Of course, with any form of gambling there's always a chance to win, but it's more probable that the bettor will lose. The illegal touts knew this, and tried several ways to pry money from their customers. In a sequence in *A Day at the Races*, Chico is an ice cream vendor at the race track ("tootsie-frootsie ice cream"). He really is a race track tout masquerading as an ice cream vendor to fool the police, and Groucho is the bettor, his prey and potential customer. Chico tries to get Groucho to spend as much money as he can in order to learn the identity of the "hot tip" in the next race.

Groucho approaches a bettor's window and wants to bet on a horse named Sun Up. Chico confronts him, offering him "something hot." Groucho declines, saying that he doesn't like hot ice cream. Chico confides in him that he sells tips on horses, and that he has a horse that afternoon that can't lose. Chico tells Groucho that it will cost only one dollar to find out who the winning horse will be. Groucho declines, but Chico coerces Groucho into spending the money for his tip, and he gives Groucho a slip of paper. Groucho reads it and it is a series of letters. Groucho likens it to an optometrist's eye chart. He asks Chico what it means and Chico tells him it's the name of the horse in code. He tells Groucho that he has to look in the code book to find out the horse's name. When Groucho tells him that he has no code book, Chico says that he has one, and that it's free. However, there's a one dollar printing charge. When Groucho cannot decipher the code book, Chico offers him a free "Master Code Book." Groucho is skeptical, and asks him if there is a printing charge. Chico tells him that there isn't, but there is a two dollar delivery charge. Groucho complains, and asks why there's a delivery charge because, after all, he's standing right next to Chico. Chico concedes and lowers the price to one dollar because it's such a short distance, but Groucho tries to lower the price to fifty cents by offering to stand closer, whereupon Chico threatens to move farther away to keep the price at one dollar. After selling Groucho more dubious material, at exorbitant prices, Groucho discovers that the name of the horse recommended in Chico's information manuals is Rosie. When he tries to bet on her, he learns that the race is over. The winner was Sun Up, Groucho's original selection, not chosen from Chico's hot tip. Of course, Chico has furtively bet on Sun Up with the money he bilks from Groucho. The scene ends with Groucho, his arms full of the books he has just bought. He throws them back into the ice cream pushcart and starts to sell ice cream, as Chico had, hoping to find someone as gullible as he has been in order to recoup his misspent money.

Groucho takes over Chico's job as an ice cream vendor–tout. He realizes that trying to play the game of life within the rules of mainstream society is crazy. He cannot possibly succeed. So he changes from what he had assumed heretofore was normal (his conformity to the rules of betting at the race track) to what he had assumed was insane (Chico's devious and somewhat illegal way of making a living). Chico's manipulation of the system wasn't so crazy after all, and now Groucho sees it. Eyles contends that the Marx Brothers are really sane and it is the rest of us who are out of step.[6] There is no question that Eyles's conclusion is valid, and it is an important one. But we need to not only think about what Eyles is saying, but to come to a greater realization.

As a whole, the Marx Brothers films suggest that we should peek at ourselves regularly and critically to question our own actions. When Harpo and

Chico sit down to play bridge, they destroy all semblance of order within the accepted beliefs about order and chaos, sanity and insanity. Even though Dumont reproaches them about their unorthodox play, they insist on continuing it. Dumont is frustrated because the boys have turned the highly structured game of bridge (and her world) upside down, so she is defeated; she quits the game leaving the room with Mrs. Whitehead in tow. At the beginning of the game, we cringed as we watched the boys flout the rules; we continued to laugh at their improper actions anyway. As we wince and giggle at Harpo and Chico's gauche card playing, we conclude that they really aren't crazy, after all. If we change our perspective and look at the world as they do, we come to the realization that they want us to laugh at and scold ourselves for trying to fit into a society that is crazier than we are.

17. A Very Strange Interlude

Parodies and lampoons are rampant in the Marx Brothers' films. They are usually subtle and sophisticated, but often they require an elevated awareness of the references they make. Sometimes these references are so clear that it is obvious that a wide audience will understand them. Some of the references in the films are primarily a passing mention of the titles of works. In two Marx Brothers films the scripts delve into the contents or the techniques used by the authors or playwrights of the referenced works. These references are fully realized parodies.

When Paramount released *Horse Feathers* in 1932, the film version of Theodore Dreiser's famous novel, *An American Tragedy*, was still fresh in people's minds. Dreiser's novel, published in 1925, quickly became, and remains, his best-known work. It became a Broadway play in 1926,[1] and a film version opened in 1931. This dramatic story had touched a collective nerve among theatre goers, and as a film, it reached a wider audience. It was an obvious target for S. J. Perelman and Will Johnstone when they wrote *Horse Feathers*. (So ubiquitous is this story of social struggle that it has engendered several other films, novels, and plays since then. One of the more recent, Woody Allen's 2006 film *Scoop*, parodies the brutal canoe scene.)

Dreiser's tale tells of Clyde Griffiths and his struggle for social success. Griffiths has made Roberta Alden pregnant, and subsequently murders her by taking her for a canoe ride and pushing her overboard in the middle of a lake, where she drowns. The scene is the highlight of the story — its essence — and is a vicious and ugly comment on an obsessive determination and drive for social acceptance and financial security within the trappings of class struggle. To call it a study of upward mobility would give it a cynical and naïve label.

In *Horse Feathers*, there is a reference to Dreiser's play, and particularly to the scene at the lake. Groucho, as Professor Wagstaff, the president of Huxley College, is lured into a canoe by Connie Bailey, the so-called "college widow." She is a ravishing platinum blonde, played by Thelma Todd. Connie is trying to get the football team's signals from him, in order to sell these valuable secrets to a rival team. Groucho is in a role reversal of the traditional romantic scenes that take place with the lovers in a canoe. He sits under an umbrella in the canoe, idly playing a cute love song on the guitar while Connie does the hard work of rowing. Groucho interrupts his playing to comment that "this is the first time I've been in a canoe since I saw *An American Tragedy*." There is no subtlety about the reference in this scene. Groucho's next remarks satirize the play and the scene, as well as provide a sly double entendre.

In Dreiser's story, there is some dramatic foreshadowing when Griffiths and Roberta rent their canoe. The man who rents the boats asks them if they want a boat with a rounded bottom or a flat bottom, further stating that although the rounded bottom boat is more likely to tip over, it is easier to row. They choose the round bottom, an ominous prophesy, rather than the safer, flat bottom. The reference in *Horse Feathers* starts when Connie tells Professor Wagstaff that he's "perfectly safe" in this canoe. Groucho isn't convinced, and in saying so he makes the ambiguous anatomical, and mildly sexual, reference when he talks about his request to the canoe renter ("I was going to get a flat bottom, but the girl at the boat house didn't have one"). The superficial joke is funny; the deeper, sexual reference is more meaningful and sophisticated. It might have been excised by the Hays Office if it had been less ambiguous, and thus, as with several other sexual references in the films, was acceptable to the censors.

Within a few minutes, after a physical struggle with Groucho, Connie falls overboard and she cries out for a lifesaver. Groucho takes a roll of Lifesavers from his pocket and tosses one toward her as the scene ends. In today's cynical world, critics might see this little joke as an early foray into product placement. Not really. The concept of product placement used as a persuasive, subliminal marketing technique was unknown in the 1930s. No matter how contemptuous Perelman was toward advertising, it's probably just a simple humorous reference, an adolescent play on words. It's more of an attempt to produce a quick laugh, probably the result of the work of a journeyman gag writer, and certainly not on a par with the sophisticated wit for which Perelman is famous.

The references to advertising or other products occur in several of the films. In *The Big Store* Groucho makes reference to the rhyming jingles used by Burma Shave in their advertising by drawing a parallel with Byron; in the stateroom scene in *A Night at the Opera* he calls sleeping Harpo a bag of Jell-O; in *Horse Feathers* Chico makes reference to the Camel cigarettes slogan ("I'd walk a mile for a Cal-o-mel"); in *A Day at the Races* there is the memorable reference to Dodge automobiles when Groucho introduces himself to the medical staff at the Standish sanitarium; and in *At the Circus* Groucho says that Chico's slicker makes him think of Scott's Emulsion, a cod liver oil, with a picture of a fisherman wearing a slicker on its label.

The allusion to *An American Tragedy* was not the first literary reference in the Marxian portfolio. In the Broadway production of *Animal Crackers* in 1928, Groucho proposes marriage to two dowagers at the same time, invoking the style and technique of Eugene O'Neill's famous and controversial (for the 1920s) play *Strange Interlude*, that opened at the John Golden Theater in New York in January of that year, just a little less than nine months earlier than the *Animal Crackers* opening. The play was part of a growing movement toward a change in theatre style. That it produced controversy and conversation is an understated way of describing its dramatic and cultural impact. It was perfect for parodying, and Kaufman and Ryskind pounced on it.

O'Neill's was one of the few modern plays to use the Shakespearean technique of soliloquy where the actors speak their inner thoughts directly to the audience while having a conversation with other characters. O'Neill's play, "a stream-of-consciousness novel despite its dramatic structure," is related to Strindberg's expressionist plays and James Joyce's novel *Ulysses*, that use similar techniques. Authors often use the stream of consciousness technique in the modern novel because it enables characters to present the myriad thoughts of their introspection to the reader.[2] This brooding and novelistic approach, applied to drama by O'Neill, allowed him to express certain subtleties of plot and character that previously only novels had been capable of suggesting.[3]

In the film version of *Animal Crackers*, Groucho proposes marriage to both Mrs. Rittenhouse (Margaret Dumont) and Mrs. Whitehead (Margaret Irving), saying that if he were Eugene O'Neill he could tell them what he really thinks of them. Lucky for them, he continues, that the Theatre Guild isn't producing this play. He informs them that he's about to have a strange interlude. Before he speaks, he says, "Whim Wham." It is another password, like swordfish; a technique, a "button" he pushes, that allows him to change his character from a raffish Dr. Jekyll to a sepulchral Mr. Hyde. He changes the timbre of his voice and his style of speaking to express his "inner thoughts." Groucho's digression is a pensive meditation presented in a deep, hollow tone of serious thought. Groucho moves toward us for a close-up (when they filmed *Animal Crackers*, the camera was immobile). We see that he has turned his body away from the two women. He moves toward us, enabling him to speak his inner thoughts in a soliloquy directly to the camera and, therefore, the audience in the movie theatre. He starts with an insulting thought by referring to them as baboons and then asks "what makes you think I'd marry either one of you?" Then, in a dramatic non sequitur, he intones to himself that it's strange how the wind blows that night. The wind has a thin, eerie voice, he says. It reminds him of poor old Marsden. Groucho then speaks to us again by exclaiming how happy he could be with either of these two if both of them just went away.

It is a complete parody. There is no doubt that it is a direct reference to O'Neill's play, even using the name Marsden, one of his characters. In *Strange Interlude* Nina speaks to three men simultaneously, and in the middle of that conversation, all four speak their inner thoughts, as if they were a jazz quartet "speaking" to each other in a call-and-response passage by trading four-bar improvisational solos. We can almost substitute Groucho's soliloquy with O'Neill's words, if we compare the Groucho and Marsden monologues.

Eyles suggests that the technique, the tone of "heavy, introspective melancholy" used by Groucho, "mocks the portentousness of this kind of theatre."[4] Groucho is not as solemn as he appears. He delivers this mock-serious comment with a little smile on his lips, as if he's just thought of, and is about to make an ad lib monstrous pun or other outrageous play on words. It is this expectant little smile that he often used thirty years later on his television show, *You Bet Your Life*, when he would pause for a moment with a slight smile on his face as a prelude to a humorous remark about something that one of the contestants says. His smile telegraphs the imminence of his punch line, and at the same time allowing us to believe that he's trying to think of just the right words to say to make a withering, humorous comment. He repeats the technique of speaking directly to us in *Horse Feathers* when Chico starts his usual piano solo. Groucho comes forward to the camera and says directly to us: "I've got to stay here but there's no reason why you folks shouldn't go out to the lobby until this thing blows over."

When the allusions in the films are fleeting and swift, they don't offer anything more than using titles as references, rather than using more detailed parodies or lampoons to make their point. In *A Day at the Races*, Groucho makes a reference to *Three Men on a Horse*, a comedy written by John Cecil Holm and George Abbott that opened on Broadway in 1935; it was a success, running until January 1937, and revived many times since. In the play, three gamblers who bet on horses find that they have discovered the perfect "system" of selecting the winning horses when they realize that one of the other characters in the play is able to pick the winners of horse races during his daily commuter ride to work in New York City.[5] The three gamblers figuratively swoop onto this other character, hoping to reap the rewards of his acumen.

In *A Day at the Races* Groucho is in his room at the Standish Sanitarium with Flo Marlowe the femme fatale character (played to the hilt by Esther Muir), a big, slinky blonde, much too tall and unassailable for Groucho and his brothers. They are, after all, physically short. Esther is not, and she commands the screen in her every scene with her sultry and larger-than-life manner, oozing sexuality. She is a comely and physically attractive woman, often referred to as a "filly" by the Broadway wise guys in Damon Runyan's short stories about horse players, gamblers, and newspapermen in the 1920s who congregated around Times Square, frequenting its restaurants and bars.

Chico and Harpo burst into Groucho's room to warn him that Flo is trying to lure him into a compromising situation, and thus cause the wealthy Mrs. Upjohn (Margaret Dumont) to withdraw her offer of financial support to the sanitarium, and her romantic association with Groucho. In the frenzy of trying to get Flo to leave, Chico and Harpo, failing with persuasive rea-

A Day at the Races (1937). Flo (Esther Muir): "Closer! Closer!" Dr. Hackenbush (Groucho): "If I hold you any closer, I'd be in back of you" (Metro-Goldwyn-Mayer).

soning, both pounce on her, jumping on her lap. Then Harpo pats his own knee in a symbolic gesture that suggests that Groucho should jump on, too. "Oh, no," says Groucho, "not me. Not three men on a horse." The reference is obvious. But the subtlety has additional layers of meaning. Both the play with that title and the Marx Brothers film have a theme of betting on horses. In the Thirties and Forties, horse racing was at the height of its popularity in America, producing excitement, a chance to gamble, and another escape from the sobering reality of the Great Depression.[6]

Both expounding on the content or technique of a play with parody, as with *Strange Interlude*, or the simple mention of a title, as does the observation about *Three Men on a Horse*, occur frequently in the films. In *At the Circus* there is a quick reference to another title, much in the same way as there is to *Three Men on a Horse*, but it is more obtuse, more subtle.

During a conversation that takes place in front of a gorilla cage, Groucho, about to leave and apparently searching for the right exit line, turns to the cage, puts his hand through the bars and shakes hands with the anthropoid, saying, "Goodbye, Mr. Chips." It's as if the writers were sure that they had to have an exit gag line, and didn't quite know what to do, because there is no allusion to Mr. Chips in the film. So they used the comic technique of creating an incongruity.

If we look beneath the surface of the incongruity of the reference to Mr. Chips, it becomes a different matter. When Groucho shakes hands with the gorilla, his remark is confusing and apparently shallow if we don't know the James Hilton novel *Goodbye, Mr. Chips*. But if you know the reference, it is a fiendishly sophisticated reference to that tale about a seemingly timid British public school teacher who eventually overcomes his original shyness in his personal life and goes on to have a distinguished career as a hard-driving, but well-loved (by the students), taskmaster and educator. Depending on one's point of view, Chips can be an overbearing and frightening gorilla (demanding excellence from his students), or a Mr. Milquetoast, trapped in a symbolic cage where he seems emotionally too distant to have a meaningful relationship with women. Groucho's sophisticated reference to the gorilla/Milquetoast of Chips is similar to his ad lib topical reference to Kip Rhinelander's miscegenation lawsuit in 1925.

In *A Night at the Opera* the Brothers use this same sort of quick literary reference. Henderson, a detective, searches Groucho's suite, looking for Harpo, Chico, and Ricardo Baroni (Allan Jones). Once again, two of the Marx Brothers are stowaways. In the midst of being questioned about the whereabouts of the stowaways, Groucho folds his arms, hides his head in his folded arms and mutters, "I vant to be alone." It is a clear and unabashed reference to Greta Garbo's reputed statement when photographers and newspaper reporters besieged her with requests for interviews. She used the words to intimidate the paparazzi and to escape from their questioning. The phrase, however, became the popular way to mimic the enigmatic and reclusive Swedish film star, in the same way a comic might use a well-known phrase or gesture in order to characterize a contemporary personality. This brief verbal reference continues to be the legendary joke by which most people knew Garbo.[7] Garbo supposedly disowned the phrase as her plea for solitude.[8] But that didn't stop the Marx Brothers. Nothing ever did.

In *A Night at the Opera* we see another topical reference perhaps lost, or about to be, on contemporary audiences. In the contract scene, Groucho hands Chico the written contract that they're about to negotiate, telling him that it is a duplicate of the original. He asks Chico if he knows what a duplicate is. Chico free-associates on the word duplicate and says, "Those five kids up in Canada," referring to the world-famous Dionne quintuplets, born in 1934, notable because they were the first quintuplets to survive infancy.

In *A Night in Casablanca* there is a quick reference to the Humphrey Bogart film *To Have and Have Not*, based on Ernest Hemingway's novel with the same title. In the Bogart film, there is a scene with Lauren Bacall standing in Bogart's hotel room and saying to him, in a sultry way with ambiguous sexual overtones, "If you want anything, all you have to do is whistle."[9] After the film's 1944 release, this seductive line became a catchphrase throughout the United States. Of course, two years later the writers of *A Night in Casablanca* used it and they turned it into an unmistakable sexual innuendo for the Brothers.

A Night in Casablanca has Groucho as a hotel manager (once again). He's confronted by the hotel's nightclub singer, Beatrice Rheiner, who is looking for a lost toupee (not hers, one of the other characters'). Groucho, as usual, makes a romantic advance, while alluding to the Bogart-Bacall scene. When Beatrice invites Groucho to join her at the supper club that evening, she tells him that she wants him to hear her sing. "You don't have to sing," croons Groucho with an upward flick of his eyebrows, "just whistle."

The Marx Brothers-Humphrey Bogart connection doesn't end there. There is an obvious similarity in the title of this film and another Bogart film, *Casablanca* (1941). Although the intent of *A Night in Casablanca* apparently was not to comment on Bogart's *Casablanca*, the legal department at Warner Brothers, the producers of the Bogart film, attempted to institute a lawsuit against the Marx Brothers for infringing upon their "title." Groucho, with his tongue fully lodged in his own cheek, and metaphorically drawing himself up to his full height (5'7½") wrote a sly letter filled with ironic righteous indignation to Warner's legal department, saying that he thought he would institute a countersuit for infringing on the word "brothers" by Warner Broth-

A Night in Casablanca (1946). Groucho told Warner Brothers that the Marx Brothers were Brothers long before Warner Brothers were Brothers: (from left) Chico, Groucho, Harpo (United Artists).

ers, because "professionally, we were brothers long before you [Warner Brothers] were."[10]

Perhaps this was calculated promotional publicity by Groucho to generate more ticket sales for *A Night in Casablanca* even though by the time *A Night in Casablanca* was shot, as he wrote to Sheekman, Groucho felt such animosity toward what the Marx Brothers films had become that at the end of a day of movie work, he would go home and play his guitar and try to forget the distasteful experience.

If *A Night in Casablanca* was not a parody of Bogart's *Casablanca*, detective story films were. The "Who-Dunnit?" is a staple of feature film genres, even though they are not necessarily the best films.[11] The "hardboiled detective" usually featured in *film noir* features and exemplified by Dashiell Hammett and Raymond Chandler characters was popular in the Thirties and Forties. Chandler, who created cynical private eye Philip Marlowe, explained that he wrote his stories in that manner merely as a method of projecting character.[12] *The Big Store* satirized certain features common to these pessimistic detectives.

Usually the protagonist, the detective, is in dire economic straits. His lack of income forces him to live virtually in his office. But the period of insolvency is usually only temporary, because a significant assignment — a murder or a jewel robbery — could mean a fee of several thousand dollars.

Sam Spade, Dashiell Hammett's famous character, sits in his San Francisco office at the beginning of the film version of *The Maltese Falcon*. In *The Big Store*, Groucho is a seedy-looking private detective named Wolf J. Flywheel. He lives in his office. Harpo is his bodyguard, chauffeur (as he is in *Duck Soup*), secretary, assistant, and valet, evidently living in the office with him. In the typical Chandler or Hammett films the impoverished detective eats his meals in his office, usually leaving behind the evidence of other surreptitious meals eaten there. His meals are frequently limited to coffee and a sandwich rather than a more elaborate and substantial meal. Not in *The Big Store* under Harpo's guidance.

Harpo prepares a complete breakfast for Groucho: bacon, eggs, coffee, and toast. He has additional resources to prepare many similar full meals. We see he has laying chickens hidden in a rear room, ready to give forth more fresh breakfasts. His domestic responsibilities extend to valet services when we see a clothesline with wash drying on it, as well as other evidences of household accoutrements. In *Love Happy*, Groucho is Sam Grunion, another hardboiled detective. He has traveled around the world to solve a crime. He uses the same breezy, underworld patois heard in the Chandler and Hammett films. With all of their references to crime-solving and detectives, *The Big Store* and *Love Happy* are not the attack on scientific crime detection as practiced by Chico in *Animal Crackers*, but instead they just focus on the hardboiled detective as a character.

Go West is a complete spoof of the western genre of film. Harpo offers a visual comment when he wears a ten-gallon hat with a crown so tall it looks as if it would actually hold ten gallons of liquid. There's also a parody of the classic western barroom gun duel. Harpo and Red Baxter, the owner of the saloon, are the antagonists. The scene takes place in Red's saloon, in front of the bar, with Harpo and Red approaching each other slowly and cautiously, step by step. Their slow, meticulous steps are an exaggeration of similar scenes in movie westerns. They stare at each other, waiting for the right psychological moment, each appearing to have the judgment of knowing when the other combatant is ready to draw his six-shooter, each exercising a visible amount of control. There is complete silence in the saloon. They have reached the decisive moment. They both draw their guns. But Harpo draws a whisk broom with a pistol's handle from his holster. He dusts off Red. He has deflated the tension comically. The tension built up in this scene is the expression of "control" between hero and villain in westerns.

In classic western films, we often see a rugged individual (the protagonist, representing "good") in duel scenes, where he gives the appearance of unshakable control. It is a point of honor for him not to shoot first, and for his gun to remain in its holster until the exact moment of combat.[13]

A variation of the cowboy gun duel is the portrayal of the "surprise" rescue, often shown in detective films, too. Groucho, Chico and Harpo steal into Red's office so that they can pry open the safe to recover a deed that he has stolen from them. Red and his assistant, Breecher, discover them and hold Groucho and Chico at gunpoint. Almost immediately, Red drops his gun because Harpo enters behind him and sticks a toy cannon in his back. In swift succession there are a series of "surprise" entrances: Harpo drops his cannon because Breecher sticks a gun in his back, instantly followed by the female lead, Eve Wilson, who sticks a gun in his back, followed by an Indian accomplice of Red's who sticks a gun in her back, instantly followed by the male lead, Terry Turner, who sticks a gun into the Indian's back. The rapid entrance of the characters in a long line, "good" after "bad," each carrying a gun and each asking the one in front to drop his gun makes the point with a minimum of words, based on the type of scene in western films where usually the heroes are surprised by the villains, or vice versa, at the climax of the film, and held at gunpoint. It is a melodramatic exposition, like in Gothic romances or old-fashioned crime dramas.

Allied to the satire of the romantic ideal is a brief visual punch at the aspects of romantic adventure films — the swashbuckler genre — typified by Errol Flynn, Douglas Fairbanks, and more recently, Johnny Depp. Even though *Go West* is a parody of western films, the reference to swashbucklers creeps in. During the climactic chase scene, the Brothers attempt to steal a railroad train as Chico and Harpo have a "swordfight" with the train's engineer and fireman. They fight with oil cans, using the long spouts as swords. Harpo and Chico win the fight by squirting the faces of the trainmen with oil.

A common and trite show business practice is the custom of hiring unknown actors to play major dramatic roles, or to thrust an unknown actor into the spotlight when the star is not able to perform. The popular concept among many people is that an unknown actor will become a star overnight if he or she can get "one big break" on Broadway. Films, especially the 1933 musical *42nd Street*, have perpetrated this idea for years, mythical as it is. Overnight success is usually the result of years of hard work. Nonetheless, producers will occasionally cast unknowns. In *Room Service* Groucho is a disreputable theatrical producer who has unknown actresses pay him for the privilege of appearing in his play. Part of the plot of *Love Happy* revolves around a struggling theatrical group. Chico is looking for a job and says that he has heard that they want to cast unknowns in the show. That's the compelling reason that he should be in the cast ("I'm the most unknown and unheard-of actors [*sic*] who's never been on Broadway").

There are several references to radio in their films. Radio broadcasting emerged in 1920 not only as a social, cultural, and technological force, but also as an economic influence. The first broadcasting station opened in Pittsburgh in that year;[14] by 1930 there were nearly 13 million radios in American homes.[15] Radio station WJZ, eventually acquired by NBC, broadcast its first program in 1921 from Newark, New Jersey.[16] Radio grew so rapidly that it became a major part of American mass culture. Chico makes a passing reference to it in *The Cocoanuts* with an outrageous pun. Groucho shows Chico a map of the area that he's going to auction and describes it as having a radius of approximately three-quarters of a mile. He asks Chico if he knows what radius means and Chico says he does ("It's-a WJZ").

By 1940 there were nearly 900 broadcasting stations and 52 million radios in homes, offices, and automobiles. Radio coverage made sporting events even more popular, especially baseball, football, and boxing. Announcers like Graham McNamee and Clem McCarthy were well-known favorites. McNamee projected the atmosphere and the excitement of a sports event rather than accurate reporting.[17] Boxing announcers were often criticized by listeners because of their inaccuracy of reporting.[18] During the fight scene between Zeppo and Alky Briggs in an old barn at the climax of *Monkey Business*, Groucho "announces" the fight as if it was a professional boxing match and he was trying to capture its excitement as a radio announcer. He creates the flavor of being present at ringside with words ("Oh, baby, what a great fight! Zowie! Zowie! Zowie!"). But he turns his own words into a new role for himself. After he counts the zowies (silently) he turns himself into a baseball commentator ("Three zowies and a man gets a base on balls"). Eyles thinks that his abrupt change from boxing to baseball is an illustration of how the brothers attack inexact language.[19]

Harpo makes a satirical comment on this barn fight, too. It's also a reference to fight managers and army generals wielding unquestionable control. The camera cuts to Harpo during the fight scene. He sits on a horse backwards, facing the horse's tail as he watches the fight. He wears a large hat with a prominent brim and has a serious look on his face. Harpo has turned up the front edge of the brim so his hat looks like a colonial tricorn. He has his right hand inserted in his shirt, with just his wrist showing. He holds an empty wine bottle in his left hand and looks through the neck and into the bottle as if he were viewing the fight through a small telescope. He's not Napoleon, but instead, looks like George Washington directing his troops in battle, as he takes his right hand out of his shirt and waggles it back and forth, silently directing the fight; he is a boxer's manager and master puppeteer at the same time, thoroughly engrossed in his work.

In another fast turnaround from playing one role to another, Groucho continues his narration of the fight to change his presentation to that of a radio commercial spokesman. He mocks the dependence on advertising in network radio ("This program is being brought to you through the courtesy of the Golden Gate Furniture Company with three stores: 125th Street, 125th Street, *and* 125th Street"). No doubt, we see Perelman's malevolence toward advertising influencing the script.

In *Horse Feathers*, the radio announcer of the college football games asks Groucho to describe on air the game between Huxley College and its arch rival Darwin College on Thanksgiving, the final game of the year's schedule. Groucho uses the same technique of incongruity that he uses later in *At the Circus* with the *Mr. Chips* reference. When he announces the college football game he digresses to include an incongruous "human interest" announcement about a "Mrs. Moskowitz" giving birth to twins, ending with him screaming, "Okay, Mr. Moskowitz!" Mr. and Mrs. Moskowitz? We don't know who they are, they aren't characters in the film, nor do their names have any connection with the film or any other characters. But the incongruity and the harsh sound of their surname is a basic comic technique, probably created for the sole purpose of provoking laughter. The sound and the comic non sequitur of this slight digression is so confusing that even if we don't know what it means, it's still funny.

■　■　■

When Kaufman and Ryskind include the parody of *Strange Interlude* as a humorous digression in *Animal Crackers*, they add another, more serious, satirical dimension to the usual Marx Brothers fare. Perhaps with just as calculated a reason, Perelman and Johnstone's insertion of the send-up of *An American Tragedy* in *Horse Feathers* does the same; it launches another cultural observation balloon to burst, with the Brothers as their alter egos. In two of their films they make extended references as fully realized, but shortened, parodies of both *An American Tragedy* and *Strange Interlude*. They make glancing reference to other literary vehicles (films, novels, and plays) but they mostly concentrate these references to works produced as popular culture rather than the more literary and certainly more serious focus of the O'Neill and Dreiser dramas. Topical, superficial references are plentiful throughout the Brothers' films. With their boundaries set at immediate comedic gratification accompanied by joyous laughter with no deeper meaning, they are easy soap bubbles for the Marx Brothers to puncture. But the serious, literary, almost pompous balloons are a larger target. And they are even easier, and more meaningful, for them to deflate.

18. A Brace of Woodpeckers

Maybe because the music they played and the songs they sang in vaudeville were lowbrow, the Brothers and their writers thought that denigrating opera and classical music was appealing to their audiences. By the 1920s opera was beginning to be part of mass culture in America. Within ten years, opera and classical music was so pervasive that Auturo Toscaninni appeared on radio conducting a specially recruited orchestra initially performing one concert a week for ten weeks.[1] Before radio made opera and classical music popular, most people were not willing to listen to such music. By the end of the Thirties, more than 10 million families each week listened to opera and classical music on radio.[2]

In *The Cocoanuts, Animal Crackers, A Night at the Opera,* and *At the Circus,* the Brothers parodied opera, or commented on classical music, either visually, verbally, or aurally. In each of *Cocoanuts, Crackers,* and *Opera,* there are short sequences of aural reference to the rhythmic repetition of the "Anvil Chorus" from Act II of Giuseppe Verdi's *Il Trovatore.* The Brothers bang and clang various objects such as silverware, tin plates, and even a cash register drawer to reproduce the rhythmic effect of this familiar passage. In *A Night at the Opera,* the "Anvil Chorus" is a musical interlude in the opera in which on-stage gypsies, working at forges at their camp, swing their hammers and clank down onto anvils with the emphasis on the second and fourth beat of each bar, synchronized to the notations for the timpani in the orchestral score.

The most hilarious Marxian reference to this operatic passage takes place at the registration desk in the Hotel de Cocoanut. Groucho has to leave the front desk and his parting words to Chico and Harpo are, "Don't forget to register." Harpo goes behind the registration desk and opens the cash drawer to the register to steal whatever money is in it. He's infatuated with the sound from the register as the drawer opens and as he closes it. He opens the drawer again, closes it again, and then starts to whistle the "Anvil Chorus," opening the drawer of the register by punching its keys, and closing it with his stomach, mimicking the same rhythm of the orchestral kettledrums. Chico joins him, making rhythmic sounds, both vocally and with the desk bell, to complete the reference to this dissonant operatic interlude. They are a two-man symphonic orchestra.

Later in the same film, at Mrs. Potter's party to celebrate the engagement of her daughter, the Brothers perform a parody of the drinking song from Georges Bizet's *Carmen*— the "Couplets du Toreador"— with Hennessy, the humorless detective at the hotel, playing Escamillo, the toreador.

In *A Night at the Opera* the Brothers insert the sheet music for "Take Me Out to the Ball Game" onto the music stands of each member of the orchestra before they begin the overture to *Il Trovatore* so that the orchestra will mistakenly play the baseball song and disrupt the opening night performance of the New York Opera Company. After adding the new "music," Harpo and Chico, dressed in white tie and tails, enter the orchestra pit. We've never seen Harpo dressed in any semblance of conformity to the norms of male formal wear (he wears formal attire briefly in *At the Circus*, but as usual, it is disheveled). It was customary at premiere performances, and perhaps on opening night, for the orchestra and the audience to dress formally. La Scala even stipulates this as their dress code and it is printed on the tickets to performances.[3]

Harpo carries a trombone, Chico a violin as they take their places in the orchestra, ready to play with them. The conductor raps on his music stand with his baton, a signal to the musicians to get ready for the overture. As a mimicking answer to the conductor's aural call to attention, Chico raps on his stand with his violin bow. Harpo joins his brother, and raps on his stand. While all three (including the conductor) rap, Groucho offers the observation that there must be "a brace of woodpeckers" in the orchestra. After order is restored and the orchestra is once more about to begin the overture, Harpo picks up his trombone and puts a violin bow across its slide. He is prepared to play. The conductor waves "no" with his baton. Harpo, always a mimic, waves "no" in return, with his bow. The waving continues until Harpo advances on the conductor and starts a "swordfight" with him, using his bow versus the conductor's baton. With decorum restored, once again the orchestra begins the overture. After a few pages of the musical score, they mistakenly play the baseball song previously inserted into their sheet music. Harpo takes a baseball out of his pocket. He and Chico have a catch in the orchestra pit, with Groucho appearing in the audience dressed as a ballpark vendor as he yells "Peanuts! Peanuts!" Their energetic disruption of the orchestra and operatic music feeds into the American preference for lowbrow cultural entertainment, and at the same time upsets the social stuffiness of an upright and overdressed audience. The incongruity of Groucho's peanut vendor among the assembled upper crust implies a call for a relaxation of the stifling and uncomfortable formal rules of conduct. Many Americans considered opera a species of alien highbrow entertainment[4] and, as a result, they had no patience to try to understand it. Categorically, they wanted simply to have no part of it.

Marxist criticism of opera aims at more than just its music. Earlier in *A Night at the Opera*, after a performance of Leoncavallo's *Pagliacci* at the Milan Opera House, Groucho approaches Lassparri who has just finished singing the traditional role of Canio. Lassparri wears the traditional white satin or silk clown suit for that role: jumper top, trousers, and tall hat, all adorned with large black cloth-covered buttons. A photograph of opera singer Manuel Salazar as Canio, in June 1924, shows him in this same costume.[5] A self-caricature of Enrico Caruso shows him wearing it for the same role.[6] Groucho makes an anti-intellectual comment on Lassparri's costume when he asks him if it hurts his stomach when he sleeps on those big black buttons.

Music and costumes aren't the only things about opera that come under fire. The business of opera — patronage by the affluent — is a major theme that runs just below the surface of the love story of *A Night at the Opera*, although we can argue that the business of opera is the main story and everything else is secondary. Traditionally, financial subsidy came from "old money," but those of recent wealth often offered financial support as a means of strengthening and forwarding their entrance to high society, or just enhancing their position in the social order.[7] Groucho explains to the *nouveau riche* Dumont how her support of opera will allow her to enter society. He tells her that she should invest $200,000 in the New York Opera Company, and he has arranged it. She doesn't quite follow his thinking. He clarifies the concept for her ("Don't you see? You'll get into society. Then you can marry me and they'll kick you out of society").

A secondary theme is the adoration of foreign opera stars (in this film, from Italy) by American opera companies. Before the Twenties and Thirties, American companies featured only prominent foreign stars. Opera goers in America lionized these foreign stars believing that they were better than any American performer could be.[8] And, it was common to use these highly paid foreign stars, even during the Thirties, when opera was available free on radio. There was still a demand for live, popular-priced opera.[9] *Opera* makes this point without rancor or irony, but with ridicule. Herman Gottlieb, the manager of the New York Opera Company, wants to "import" a foreign opera star, Rudolfo Lassparri, to New York. Groucho brings us down to reality. Gottlieb tells Dumont about his plan to hire "the greatest tenor in the world." She asks how much Gottlieb would have to pay Lassparri. He replies that it doesn't matter how much. He's worth $1,000 a night. Groucho perks up when he hears this and thinks that it's outrageous to pay someone that much money just for singing ("Why, you can get a phonograph record of Minnie the Moocher for seventy-five cents. For a buck and a quarter you can get Minnie").[10] With his joke, he equates a sophisticated art form with lowbrow pop music. But Groucho, always calculating, decides to sign Lassparri himself so that he can realize some income out of the exorbitant nightly fee that the tenor will command.

He confronts Chico backstage at the opera house in Milan, and they begin to negotiate a deal for Lassparri as a preamble to the Sanity Claus scene. It is a backroom business deal between two unscrupulous businessmen whose only concern is the deal and with crass indifference to the cultural importance of opera itself. Groucho tells Chico that he's looking for the greatest tenor in the world. Chico claims that he is his manager. Groucho tells him that he wants to sign him with the New York Opera Company because America is waiting to hear him sing. But Chico isn't sure ("He can sing loud, but he can't sing that loud"). This leads them to continue to conclude their deal with the contract scene and its sanity clause.

On opening night, after the Brothers destroy the performance of the orchestra's playing of the overture; they turn their fiendish attention to the production itself. Harpo and Chico invade the stage in appropriate costume and they blend in with the cast, looking for opportunities to upend Lassparri's performance by creating havoc via a series of visual gags. At one point, Harpo emerges from the chorus and approaches a shirtless male dancer and his female partner. He holds his partner aloft, and Harpo strikes a match across the man's taut, bare abs. Harpo lights a cigarette with the match. As Lassparri rips the dress off one of the women in the cast, in keeping the requirements of his role, Harpo takes this as a cue to resume his usual role of chasing blondes through the scenery, except that what he does this time is more fun, and more tactile. Mimicking Lassparri, he maniacally attacks several women in the cast and rips off their dresses. Eventually someone calls the police to try to stop the Brothers, and the chase begins. The Brothers scramble about backstage, swinging through the flies of the theatre, from rope to rope just out of reach of the cops. Their weight on these ropes for changing scenery raises or lowers backdrops, incongruous to the scene that the actors are performing, while the opera is in progress. This creates further frustration for Lassparri as he sings his role. The confusion escalates: One moment Lassparri stands in the scene as it should be, and a new backdrop is lowered, inconsistent in its visual, showing trains at a railroad station. Immediately after, the Brothers lower a new backdrop inadvertently, showing an Italian vendor's pushcart with a sign next to it advertising a taxicab company. As the Brothers swing, Tarzan-like, on the ropes, their continuous swinging makes various backdrops fall and rise rapidly. One even falls in front of Lassparri, blocking him from the sight of the audience, but he continues, struggling to sing. Eventually they upend the entire performance.

Although their disruption of the orchestra, destruction of music, and annihilation of the opera performance is in keeping with the usual physical destruction associated with Marx Brothers films, their actions lack the maniacal glee of their unstructured, ad lib mayhem in their previous films, and before that, their stage musicals. In *Opera* it is obvious that the Brothers rehearsed their manic chaos. Thalberg controlled this film with a firm hand, and the scenes of confusion really look practiced. All those weeks in tryouts on the road did it! But, it looks like the writer or team of writers constructed each step of these scenes under Thalberg's strict orders to make the turmoil more orderly and more pleasant for the audience. Most likely Paramount planned the devastation of their surroundings just as carefully. But they give the appearance of occurring to the Brothers on the spur of the moment, just as when Groucho speaks dialogue in his relaxed manner it appears improvised. The opera destruction sequences were more about interference than total physical destruction, designed to appeal to audiences who may or may not have had any reference to their earlier films or previous theatrical history, and therefore could not compare them critically with the Brothers' earlier efforts. These composed scenes of destruction are in keeping with Thalberg's viewpoint for success: the presentation of the Brothers in a more gentle way. These scenes don't call for reform under the strict definition of satire; they call for chuckles and laughter.

Thalberg replaced the harsh anarchy of *Duck Soup* with a pleasing form of comic disruption, allowing audiences to enjoy this tearing-down of that highbrow icon called grand opera, without the appearance of any antipathy lurking behind it. Unlike *Duck Soup* where audiences were angered by the apparent belittling of government at a time when the newly elected president Franklin D. Roosevelt was building confidence among the American population, *A Night at the Opera* did not disturb opera lovers to complain about the Brothers' symbolic act of the destruction of opening night at the New York Opera Company. The differences between the two are clear. Americans wanted Roosevelt to succeed (and by inference, to jump-start their own survival). They were inflamed about *Duck Soup* because it went beyond their tolerance for criticism of a federal government that was trying to help them during the Depression. Criticism of opera, in comparison, was relatively neutral and not politically or socially inflammatory. *Opera* allows us to laugh at high society and ourselves. However, in 1933, criticism of the economically struggling America was no laughing matter.

If opera is the target in *A Night at the Opera*, *At the Circus* exorcizes symphonic performance of classical music. Harpo and Chico take a symphony orchestra to a specially built floating platform, their stage for the evening. Dumont has hired them as entertainment for her highbrow and formally dressed guests. The orchestra begins to play the prelude to Act III of Wagner's *Lohengrin*. Immediately, Harpo cuts them loose from their mooring, and they drift out to sea oblivious to their changing surroundings as they continue to play. Harpo clinically severs them from our consciousness, implying an anti-intellectual attitude toward classical music. None of Dumont's guests are present; they have been delayed by Groucho's procrastinating after-dinner speech ("I'll have another cup of coffee") to allow enough time for the circus to be set up on the front lawn of Dumont's mansion so that the guests can see the circus rather than hear the concert. The jettisoning of the orchestra combined with the offering of the circus in its place are comments on the plebeian stance that suggests that lowbrow entertainment should triumph over highbrow culture, enhancing the popular notion that even Dumont's socially prominent guests would prefer lowbrow entertainment, given the choice.

In *Monkey Business* Harpo takes on classical music single-handedly during the party scene at Joe Helton's lavish home. The camera shows us that part of the entertainment for the evening is a performance by a female harpist accompanying a female singer, singing a piece of classical music. As the camera moves in for a closeup, we see that it is Harpo's right hand and arm (with his sleeve rolled up) playing the harp, substituting for the woman's own hand (Harpo hides upstage of the harpist so that we don't see his body). Harpo steps away so that we see him fully. He frightens the harpist by making one of his angry faces through the harp's strings. He takes over and begins to play. But he continues to build on the surreal. In place of his right hand and arm, he has substituted a dress mannequin's hand and wrist, using it to pluck the harp strings for a few moments before revealing his ruse to the camera. He makes this revelation in Harpo-like fashion: He scratches his neck with the mannequin's hand while playing the harp with his left hand. He uses other mood-destroying comic business to lighten the seriousness of the classical music he's playing. He hits his nose with his hands while plucking the strings, scratches the soles of his feet (with his shoes on) while playing, thumbs his nose at the female singer during one of the glissando motions of his right hand, and pulls a harp string as if it is a bowstring, aiming it at the singer as she holds a note with a tremolo. Then he drapes his raincoat over his head while playing. He doesn't want to see or hear the singer. When she finishes, he stands next to his harp with his hands clasped over his head, moving them back and forth like a professional boxer indicating that he has won the match. His actions suggest that we shouldn't take his playing, or the music itself, seriously. It's no wonder that Dalí admired Harpo.

Chico presents visual comment on music and pianists each time he plays the piano. His technique of playing, "shooting" the keys with an outstretched forefinger and elevated thumb as if his hand were a pistol, or "wiping" the keys with his forefinger as if it was a paintbrush, ridicules accepted piano-playing techniques. The epitome of his insouciance comes in *Go West* when he plays piano in a saloon and rolls an apple across the keys to produce an achromatic musical scale.

Frequently Harpo "discovers" his harp in bizarre places, and sometimes creates a harp from other objects that suggests the potential for conversion into his beloved instrument. In *Go West* he makes an Indian loom into a harp. In some of the films, he, acting alone or with Chico, physically destroys a piano, whereupon Harpo "finds" his harp in the innards. His single-minded vision is exquisitely creative. He uses the piano strings attached to their frame that immediately, when turned upright, resembles a harp. The destruction of pianos, like the physical destruction of the opera performance, is a symbol of the destruction of the accepted conventions of music, just as traditional New Orleans jazz at the beginning of the twentieth century was a logical progression from European chamber music, and subsequently replaced it as the embodiment of popular music of its time.

The music that Harpo and Chico play is a mixture of pseudo-classical, semi-classical and popular music, including jazz, appealing to the mass common denominator of movie audiences. Sometimes they play all three forms within the same musical score. The juxtaposition of the physical destruction of instruments with the subsequent instrumental improvisation on the resulting flotsam (whether or not it's intended to be highbrow or lowbrow) represents a pointed attack on traditionally accepted standards of music appreciation. All of the abbreviated tripartite Marx Brothers played musical instruments throughout their lives. Aside from Chico and Harpo whose playing we see most frequently in the films, Groucho actually played guitar (see the canoe–*An American Tragedy* scene in *Horse Feathers*) usually for his own amusement. Plucking or shooting or strumming their instruments, the three Brothers evolved into a virtual Descent of Woodpeckers, vilifying a society that was much too formal for their Everyman tastes, and perhaps for ours.

19. Upside Down

Other than aspects of the satire and social criticism in these films, a general observation of Marx Brothers films flavored with some of the noteworthy remarks by film critics is apt. These critics wrote about the Brothers, often placing them in the history of comedy, and describing their contribution to it. They analyzed the characters that the Brothers developed, or wrote about satire and how it applied to them. For the greater part of the Marxes' career, critics and reviewers wrote about them, dissected their Broadway musicals and, finally, their films. In general, these critics and reviewers contributed some intelligent insights into the Brothers' films with an enlightened overview of their work. Their comments help us to understand the films better.

We see and hear how language plays such an important part of the comedy in the films. Groucho or Chico point their harangues at language itself, however illogical they may seem. Siegfried Kracauer thinks that Groucho's diatribes are a specific comment on our use of language as communication. However illogical they seem to be, Groucho's "word cascades wreak havoc on language."[1] Their function is to destroy the heretofore accepted uses of language. He thinks that Groucho's "impossible delivery ... tends to obstruct the sanctioned functions of speech.... Silly and shrewd, scatterbrained and subversive, his repartees are bubbling self-assertions rather than answers or injunctions.... Whatever Groucho is saying disintegrates speech all around him."[2] More than just destroying speech, we observe how Groucho snipes at social, cultural, political, and economic conventions with a sharpshooter's eye, as does Chico (aside from shooting the piano keys) as he destroys conventional logic in cahoots with Groucho.

Allied to Hayakawa's concepts of pre-symbolic language, Eyles contends that phrases like the misplacement of the words in the phrase "property values have increased 1929 since 1,000 percent" are so familiar to us that we don't really hear this inversion.[3] These inversions occur throughout the films as the Brothers upset language and logic, the normal rhythm of living at the opera,

171

at the races, in the big store, or in Freedonia. Even our routine acts are upset.[4] Symbolically, the Marx Brothers turn the world upside down.

Feibleman suggests that Groucho's destructive attacks on language are composed of platitudes, because comedy often centers on their use in language, and with repetition they infer their demolition. Epigrammatically he contends, "Great tragedy consists of the invention of platitudes; comedy in their destruction."[5]

Raymond Durgnat offers that the ridicule of language in the films with puns is suggestive that the Brothers are really "immigrants" who do not fully understand the English language, "inventing plausible logical and verbal patterns ... which lead straight into utter absurdity."[6] It is common for "immigrants" to use puns, sometimes inadvertently, as a relief to ease the difficulties of grasping an idiomatic, informal language, as American English is. How can someone, for whom English is a second language, understand the idiom "he sat in his shirtsleeves?" Or how do you explain Groucho's introduction of the cultural differences between eee-ther and eye-ther when he corrects Margaret Dumont's pronunciation in *Duck Soup*?

We see that the satire in the films is stronger verbally than it is visually because the Brothers are verbal comedians, even though they may have physically destroyed scenery, costumes, and musical instruments, and occasionally used visual routines to communicate language, as they do in the nightshirt and mirror routine in *Duck Soup* when Harpo tries to fool Groucho into thinking that he's looking at himself in a mirror. The physical destruction is not satire on the same scale as their script writers conceived. The visual aspects, expressed violently or humorously, are secondary in significance to the verbal impact of the films. But traditional film criticism stressed the importance of the visual over the verbal, at least before the introduction of sound.[7]

Nonetheless, the more important target of the satire in these films is not just language but our social habits. The films do indeed "mimic the whole world of solemnity and conventions."[8] Grierson contends that it is the function of the Marx Brothers films to "destroy all evidence of social equilibrium."[9]

These critics imply that this questioning of American society implies contempt for American culture. Robert Warshow suggests that this contempt is "popular among middle-class intellectuals because [the Brothers] express a blind and destructive disgust with society that the responsible man is compelled to suppress in himself."[10] Schickel finds this same characteristic in Groucho's treatment of Margaret Dumont, maintaining that "the abuse to which she was subjected must have satisfied the deep yearnings of many people."[11] Dumont was a symbol of the establishment, and most people don't have the ability to stand up to it and effect change. Seeing her bewilderment in the hands of the Brothers provides that relief.

But contempt suggests destruction of a problem rather than offering an alternative. The Marx Brothers offer alternatives; however, they rarely verbalize them. They imply them, as Freud suggests, in their devastating invective. The films appeal for a more relaxed life devoid of formality and assumptions about what we should expect from everyday living.

Because the Marx Brothers are outside the confines of the restrictive society, they are able to criticize it. When Durgnat refers to the Brothers as immigrants, he sees them as "third class citizens," questioning society's values until they finally "learn to conform"[12] to the majority. Warshow agrees. He says that the Marx Brothers' nihilism ("Whatever It Is, I'm Against It") is characteristic of men who are dispossessed from society.[13]

Henri Bergson's study of laughter offers insight as well, with an apt description of humor that we can apply to the Brothers' films. Bergson speculates that the inelasticity of human beings, that is, any rigid attitudes people might have, is the basis for humorous criticism. He suggests that human beings should adapt to circumstances around them rather than live by rote and ignore change. An entire society can be viewed as a single human being in this same manner; a society which is stereotyped, inert, rigid, or fixed, is ready for criticism in a comic way.[14]

But there's more to the incisive comedy that criticizes American behavior in these thirteen films. Edgar Anstey suggests that the films had a greater scope than functioning as a mere attack on American society. He believes that in going from vaudeville to film, the Marx Brothers challenged "the solemnities of the wider world which lay within the range of the camera."[15] Feibleman concurs. He interprets the films as more than superficial criticism of American foibles; they are criticism of modern life in general.[16]

These critics seem to have understood Kaufman's concept of how to structure the Marx Brothers plays and films. Nonetheless the primary criticism of the films persisted for many years after they retired, even after Chico and Harpo died. Vincent Canby compared their films with George Feydeau's *A Flea in Her Ear*. Canby thinks that the Marx Brothers films "are collections of brilliant individual routines, while each farce by Feydeau is a single breathless routine in itself."[17]

Widening our lens, we see more than a collection of brilliant individual routines. After seeing their films — good and bad — the focused observer understands that the Brothers may seem to be outsiders, but beneath their criticism of the world around them, they ask probing questions in their own way, trying to understand others, infused with the need to have their peers and cultural authority figures shed the skin of social, and uncompromising, rigidity. In turning their world upside down, the Marx Brothers want us to be more relaxed and open to change, and to accept all of its social manifestations.

20. Whim Wham

It takes just two little words.

It's the middle of the brilliant *Strange Interlude* scene. Captain Spaulding turns his attention from Dumont and Mrs. Whitehead and speaks directly to the camera and, by extension, directly to us sitting in the movie theatre or in front of our television set. He demolishes the invisible fourth wall of the theatre separating the stage from the audience, states his thoughts aloud, and turns back to the two women to continue to speak with them. At one point, he's about to talk to us again, and he lets us know with a simple, two-word self-prompt. Spaulding says, "Whim Wham," followed by that dead-on parody of a character in Eugene O'Neill's play expressing his thoughts to us out loud.

That is the essence of this chapter's title: expressing a summary of some ideas we have concluded about satirical social criticism in the Marx Brothers films, as well as some other analytical thoughts, the fundamental significance of their work, their place in film history, and the traditions in theatre history that their characters represent. And so:

Whim wham.

The primary significance of the Marx Brothers films is that they are the result of a conscious effort by their writers to create social satire, more notably in the first six films, from *The Cocoanuts* to *A Night at the Opera*. Their first two, *The Cocoanuts* and *Animal Crackers*, are mostly filmed presentations of their last two Broadway shows. (They filmed *The Cocoanuts* at Paramount's Astoria, Queens, studio at the same time they were performing *Animal Crackers* at the 44th Street Theatre in New York, probably causing Margaret Dumont to make a mistake. In *The Cocoanuts*, she tries to fend off Groucho's non-stop sales pitch by saying "I must be going." It is a line from the lyric of "Hooray for Captain Spaulding" in *Animal Crackers*.) Although the writers infused the films with many of their old vaudeville routines, as their musical comedies on Broadway had been, they steered them away from being simple comedies. They refined the stories and added the tartness of satire to flavor them with their own social condemnation.

The Brothers' unique presentation adds a significant facet to this satire, especially when Groucho and Chico speak. If Groucho's written dialogue is, "Let's go to the movies," it's a simple invitation. As Doherty concludes, both Groucho and Mae West's delivery of a line of dialogue could turn it from innocent to suggestive. Groucho's visual presentation could produce the same double entendre. If he says the same line — "Let's go to the movies" — even with no difference in intonation, but he simply wiggles his eyebrows at the end of the sentence, it becomes a steamy sexual innuendo. With just that little raising of his eyebrows, we laugh at what Groucho implies and the sheer irony of it. If you read Groucho's or Chico's lines aloud without their distinctive vocal inflections or physical mannerisms, a great deal of the humor doesn't come through; it is less interesting.

Some of the Brothers' films are important in the history of cinema, because they were made around the same time as sound began to be dominant. Loud, direct, and brash, the Brothers just burst onto the screen. Their writers created rushed, caustic dialogue, synchronized to the rapid social and political changes taking place outside the theatre in real life. It was a more pronounced social attack than the dialogue written into their scripts before the stock market crash of 1929. There was no subtlety in their goal of tearing down big business, manners, and social rituals. Subtlety came from the ambiguous language and the cultural references sprinkled generously throughout their work.

Nothing appeared to be sacrosanct to their writers, just as everything had been fair game for the Marx Brothers on the Broadway stage and in vaudeville. No matter how many of the old vaudeville routines appeared in these films, Perelman, Ryskind, and Kaufman were recognized satirists whose work before (and after) their association with the Brothers fell resoundingly into this genre. The dialogue in their scripts encompassed a greater world of focus and reference and knew no bounds. Kaufman was one of the main proponents of dramatic satire in America during his career,[1] even though he denied it with a sarcastic quip. Frequently, in public, he disassociated himself from satirists because "satire is what closes Saturday night."[2] This is a classic Kaufman wisecrack, a way to respond to a serious question without an answer that might make him sound pompous and self-important.

Groucho answered the question about satire for him, leaving no doubt about its part in their films. He affirmed that the scripts were a conscious attempt at creating satire. As well, he modified his assessment by putting the films into perspective, both analytically and historically, adding his own conclusions about film history. Without expressing any trace of irony, he offered the thought that there was no more satire in Hollywood, and subsequently no more Marx Brothers films:

> There are no more Marx Brothers movies ... because we did satire, and satire is *verboten* today. The restrictions — political, religious, and every other kind — have killed satire. If Will Rogers[3] were to come back today, he couldn't make a living. They'd throw him in the clink for being subversive.[4]

Looking at the entire body of the thirteen Marx Brothers films, we see that their satirical intent falls into broad categories. These targets are historical events, political practices, economic conditions, manners and customs, literary subjects, and popular entertainment reflecting the socio-cultural background of that time. Although many subjects within these categories come under fire in the films, the writers learned not to focus on sensitive issues when they broadened the subjects to satirize and to encompass larger themes, such as Roosevelt's efforts to help the country recover from the financial crisis in the Thirties. The box office disaster of *Duck Soup* was an important lesson. The larger themes of the stock market crash and the Depression were mentioned in a few fleeting references in *Animal Crackers, Monkey Business,* and *Opera,* and they are an acceptable exception. Thalberg had the maturity to temper or reject ideas that he thought would be objectionable to audiences. George Oppenheimer, one of the *A Day at the Races* writers, remembered that he presented a scene about European psychoanalysts to Thalberg. It was a comment on the visible influx of both Austrian and German psychoanalysts to the United States during the 1930s. Thalberg laughed uproariously at the dialogue, but rejected it because it was "too satirical."[5]

The Brothers' comeback and the renewal of their success after the poor box office returns of *Duck Soup* were because of Thalberg's contributions. His concept of softening their characters in *A Night at the Opera,* of integrating comedy into plot, and the idea of market-testing the comedy scenes as vaudeville blackouts during out-of-town tryouts, were innovative, creative, and helpful toward producing their most successful box office returns. This market testing made the comedy stronger, but as a whole the concept didn't work. The "Sanity Clause" scene, the overstuffed stateroom scene, the heroes of the air scene, the farcical hotel room scene, and the destruction of the opening night performance are splendid, and they fit well in the plot. If an editor excises them, they can stand alone and the plot does not suffer. Of course, *Opera* wouldn't be a Marx Brothers movie without them.

What Thalberg really achieved was the goal that he envisioned for them before they signed a contract with him. Thalberg softened the Brothers' characters and made them more likable. The significance of this softening is that *A Night at the Opera* became the watershed for the Brothers for the remainder of their career. Although other critics may differ, we can see the turning point in one scene: the steerage scene. Before that scene it is the Marx Brothers as usual, albeit somewhat reserved: comedy scenes, the usual haphazard romantic advances to Dumont by Groucho, the sarcastic comments to women ("Do you Rumba?" "Why, yes." "Well, take a rumba from one to ten"), and the penurious Groucho, always thinking about money even when it is inappropriate ("Will you marry me? Did he [Mrs. Rittenhouse's deceased husband] leave you any money? Answer the second question first").

But here we have Chico and Harpo doing their usual musical interludes that heretofore were jammed into the films in the vaudeville tradition as disassociated musical performances, more of a relief from the general sarcasm than a necessity to further the story. Although entertaining, these earlier musical asides had no relation to the story and no connection with the other characters in the films. This time, the boys play their songs with an audience that is visibly entertained (rather than an invisible audience or one that doesn't seem to care). The children in steerage gather around the piano as Chico plays for them with his natural charm resonating with them. When he's finished, Harpo sits at the piano and starts to play furiously for them, and the kids love his comic energy. He rapidly changes to his lyrical harp solo. We see the two Brothers perform and we sense the pleasure they're offering to the audi-

A Night at the Opera (1935). The turning point of their career: Harpo and the children (Metro-Goldwyn-Mayer).

ence within the film. It is similar to Harpo's Punch and Judy scene in *Monkey Business*, where we see how much the kids enjoy Harpo as a clown. When the boys play their musical solos, we sense their pleasure at performing, too. We are part of the steerage group, ready to upset Dumont *et al.* and their WASP snobbery. We can relax as the scene unfolds. Harpo and Chico are no longer strangers to us, they belong to our family; we would like to have them for brothers! It is the pivotal moment in this film, and in the Marx Brothers' career. Everything changed forever after this scene.

Behind the irreverent characters that the Brothers created for themselves, we see some deep-rooted theatre traditions. They were born in the United States, as were the men who wrote Broadway musicals and films for them, but their humor reveals a subliminal immigrant mockery. Their writers understood the plight of the immigrant even though they hadn't experienced it directly themselves (nor had the Brothers). They wanted to keep this immigrant mockery exhibited by them in their earlier vaudeville years to reinforce the idea that the Marx Brothers were a metaphor for social outsiders (their noses pressed against a window pane, looking in on an established world of WASP sovereignty in America and trying enter and gain membership and acceptance to the general population). Beyond Durgnat's characterization of the Brothers themselves as immigrants "struggling along in a strange land ... while contemplating, irreverently, its strange customs and institutions,"[6] they demeaned other immigrant groups quite pointedly. The intent of mocking newly arrived immigrants was not intolerance or a belittling, but rather to identify with their plight.

And so, the layer of immigrant characterization often bubbled to the surface in their vaudeville years. The Brothers played stock immigrant characters frequently, as did other vaudeville acts featuring such characters. These immigrant portrayals were common in American vaudeville. The obvious evidence of this is Chico's character. His Italian accent and portrayal of ersatz stupidity allowed immigrants in their audiences to laugh at themselves, and the more established citizens in the audience to feel superior. Groucho's role of a school teacher in their early attempts at humor is that of a German schoolmaster.

It's not surprising that some of this apparent intolerance of immigrants is in the films, even though the Brothers represent liberal thinking and the quest for freedom from repugnance toward any factions of society that is at odds with the predominant WASP Establishment. We cringe at such unconcealed bigotry now, but making jokes at the expense of ethnic groups was acceptable during the years when vaudeville was prominent in popular culture. After vaudeville receded from widespread appeal with the emergence of movies as the preferred mass entertainment medium, ethnic bigotry continued to be visible. Throughout the heyday years of vaudeville during and after the greatest waves of immigrants from Europe came to the United States, these crudely drawn immigrant characters were easily identifiable to recent émigrés sitting in theatre audiences in cities everywhere. They could cackle out loud and perhaps feel a little superior to the more recent group of arrivals sitting near them in the audience. It was the way to lessen the uneasiness felt by newly landed immigrants, as one ethnic group arrived and eventually became comfortably settled. It was also how the Brothers, and other vaudeville acts, could get audiences laughing, so that theatre managers would not cancel them because of audience indifference to their singing, dancing, comedy, juggling, rat-and-cat acts, and other variety show performances. Making jokes at the expense of immigrants may not seem funny to us now, and is even embarrassing, but this dynamic is a theatrical tradition starting with the Greek theatre in the fifth century B.C.

Nearly fifteen hundred years later, in a more recent version of this tradition, Groucho's character is like that of the Yankee, or Jonathon, character seen in colonial American drama; he is an American who by his perception of other humans and their gullibility is able to overcome them by his sharper, "slicker," more clever dealings.[7] The Yankee character has traveled from theatre in colonial times through minstrel shows, vaudeville, and burlesque. The blackout comics at Minsky's Burlesque may not have been drawing-room sophisticated, but they were following in the same tradition. Such disrespectful criticism of ethnic groups is one way of "slipping the unacceptable past the censors,"[8] just as Archie Bunker did in the *All in the Family* television series and stand-up comedians still do. To demean a group of people is a convoluted way of criticizing a society that humiliates other social groups, alien or not. It is harsh and cruel. Nonetheless, it is a way for societal outsiders to take their noses off the symbolic window panes and to enter the warmth and comfort of the Establishment's living room with complete acceptance.

Verbal humor is the humor of the Marx Brothers, both by natural inclination and the coincidence of the development of sound in films. With sound, "the humor in films shifted abruptly from visual to verbal, and a new crowd of comics were imported from the New York stage and from vaudeville" to satisfy the needs of the most up-to-date technology.[9] Even silent Harpo's pantomime comes from verbal references rather than the pure visual comedy of Chaplin, Buster Keaton, or Marcel Marceau. Harpo's humor is a graphic way of expressing a traditional verbal pun. He sometimes uses a form of charade to pantomime a word, a thought, or a sentence to Chico, therefore creating a visual way of expressing verbal communication rather than a visual device to express a thought or emotion that is usually associated with a film or a staged play. Not just with humor, he communicates verbally in visual form. In *Horse Feathers*, when he has to say the password, he shows a large fish with a sword stuck into its mouth.

In general, the films attacked relatively provincial and minor social irritations of their time (except for war, which is never a minor social irritation). They continue to be relevant to contemporary life. In the 1960s, thirty years after they made their most anarchic films, the Marx Brothers re-emerged as anti-establishment heroes of their time. They didn't give a damn about convention, and they were willing to ridicule any institution.[10] Anti-establishment irreverence continues to be a popular attitude in contemporary culture, especially comedy. The Marx Brothers, W.C. Fields, and Mae West, all remembered as slayers of their contemporary societal dragons in their time, remain as cultural heroes with widespread audience appeal.

When actors become superstars, they are often associated with the characters they play, and at the same time, audiences remember the names of the roles for which they are famous, but can't remember the actors' names. At a higher level of identification, we may not remember the names of the characters they play, but we do remember their real names. The actors have become icons. The Marx Brothers fall into this category, and so does Margaret Dumont. It is a way of star identification, as true today as it was in the 1930s. For the Brothers, this star identification leads many people to a wrong conclusion: that the jokes in the films were ad lib, and the Brothers wrote them.

Of course, it's not true. In their formative years they used whatever material they could from other vaudeville acts, just as many other acts did who were on the lower rungs of vaudeville. When Kaufman and Ryskind wrote the Broadway show *The Cocoanuts*, they would not allow any alteration of the script; they conceived all the wisecracks. Just as with Mae West, a lot of the humor came from Groucho's natural and relaxed delivery. The words on paper don't have the comedic effect that Groucho and his brothers gave to them. It was Groucho's skill in delivering memorized material as if he had just thought of it that made the difference, and led to the audience's belief that he was creating the humor as he spoke.[11] Herman Mankiewicz settled the issue of authorship with a sharply ironic essay in *The New Yorker* suggesting that Groucho did, indeed, write his scripts, just as other contemporary performers whose delivery was natural and easy, wrote their own material.[12]

The Brothers made a contribution — their real contribution — to the writers and directors of their films. It was just being the Marx Brothers. The characters they had established during their long career allowed the writers and directors to create their roles in their films.

Satirical lambasting is in all of the films to some degree, and is in various forms: parody, irony, spoof, lampoon, burlesque, or basic send-up. It's clear that satire is more noticeable and more dominant in the Paramount films. Subsequently, in *Opera* and *Races* there is less of it and it is milder, by Thalberg's design. And the intensity of the satire continued to diminish after *A Day at the Races*. Andrew Sarris thinks that the Brothers "burned themselves out somewhere between *A Night at the Opera* and *A Day at the Races*."[13] But the reason isn't the Brothers' own creative decline, or the lack of concern by producers and the director of *Races* upon Thalberg's death. There is no single reason. There are several, and the Marxes had no control over them. Obviously, the restrictions imposed by the Code had a sobering effect on everything produced by the Hollywood studios, but we can see other explanations.

The production of films changed significantly by 1935 when Thalberg produced *Opera*. The fear of failure during the Depression was so omnipresent in Hollywood that studios were exceedingly cautious about every film they undertook. Undoubtedly this was a factor in creating scripts for the Brothers; the studios didn't want to take the chance of repeating the box office failure of *Duck Soup* at the height of the downturn in 1933. Of course, Hollywood had functioned in a different, more cheerful environment ten years earlier. It cost less to produce silent films than films with sound. Investment money flowed easily. Film production was more haphazard, more of an art than a science. So, the studios seemed to be almost casual about moviemaking.

The Marx Brothers were undoubtedly getting too old to play the roles they had been playing for a quarter-century. They were no longer the juvenile, irreverent, anti-establishment cut-ups who had ploughed a wide swath through rural America and then Broadway. In 1935 Chico was 48, Harpo 47, and Groucho, 45. So Groucho's intimation in his correspondence with Sheekman that they were "tired" was a reasonable appraisal.

Movies had become big business by the mid–Thirties and the production staff at the Hollywood studios reflected the seriousness associated with any large corporate venture. With the use of sound and its added cost, the film industry had to approach filmmaking as a big business might. The artistic and marketing decisions were becoming less hasty and more calculated. There was a noticeable loss of creative improvisation. Detailed scripts with the dialogue precisely timed deprived directors and actors of the freedom to extemporize as was common during the era of silent films. Consequently, there ensued a loss of spontaneity and individuality by directors and actors who had been associated with the independent productions before they became large corporations. Simply, spontaneity disappeared. Film production became more expensive in the 1930s and required heavy financing, often predicated by a dependence on the movie-star system to try to ensure reasonable box office returns. It was rare that filmmakers departed from tried-and-true formulas.[14]

A more conservative and profit-conscious Hollywood stifled the Brothers' inclination toward making highly critical satires. Hollywood producers wanted to make family-friendly comedies and not create harsh, satirical attacks on government and large corporations. Groucho's comments in various letters imply that there was a great deal of emphasis placed on production meetings where various executives would make administrative decisions influencing the outcome of the films. Hollywood negated individuality in the big business of filmmaking by the time the Brothers made *Circus* and *Go West*. MGM skewed administrative changes more toward corporate interests than creative satisfaction. Graham Greene thought that *At the Circus* represented the Marx Brothers caught up in the stifling atmosphere of the big business of filmmaking, and that they were finally "imprisoned in the Hollywood world."[15]

MGM wanted to repeat the pattern of success established in *Opera* and *Races*, without the pre-production care of those earlier films. No longer were the comedy scenes tried out, tested, and revised. There was only one writer assigned to each; gone was the considerable advantage of nurturing a creative team effort to produce the best possible films. The Brothers were "just another comedy team shifted into the obvious changing backgrounds."[16]

The writers of the films did not intend every joke in their early, socially critical films as a satirical condemnation or a call for profound cultural repair. Some things are simply gentle jibes that make us laugh at ourselves or at the characters on the screen. These jokes are funny even out of the context of the plots. By design, in the first five films made for Paramount, the plots were secondary to the comedy. We can easily identify the comic routines that were rehashed from their Broadway successes and their vaudevillian roots. The one exception is *Duck Soup*; there are only a few of the old vaudeville routines included. Even though the plot is superficial and skimpy, and continues to be secondary to the film's main purpose — the satirical elements are interspersed with the story. Contrary to the criticism of the film at its original release, a careful observation reveals the real impact of the entire film, and its real significance: *Duck Soup* is a scathing critique of politics, paranoid international diplomacy, and needless war. Within its script structure, for example, Gehring concludes that the lemonade sequence in *Duck Soup* reflects the result of misunderstandings in diplomatic relations.[17] Gehring's analysis is finely honed and perceptive. In real life, little misunderstandings between diplomats, blended with an elevated display of paranoia, actually can result in a devastating war between nations. There is always room for discussion, but as we see *Duck Soup* today, it is the most knowing of political statements, the most satirical of all their work for Paramount, and, in fact, the entire body of the thirteen Marx Brothers films.

Whether or not the Brothers or their writers realized the long-lasting implications of their work when they created it, the films are a lucid expression of the thinking of the writers who wrote them in an attempt to have an irreverent impact on the cultural landscape of their generation. When they identified subjects that were on people's minds (i.e., *their* minds), they wrote about them sarcastically, humorously, and satirically. It was how these writers usually worked, and how they gained their reputations. The only way they could hope to effect a change was to write humorously about the problems they saw.

But they knew that they weren't omnipotent. Once they identified a facet of life that was ripe for change, they did not think that they could egocentrically rub their palms together in a gloating gesture, symbolic as it may have been, and believe that they could bring about a tangible "correction of man's foibles and follies" just by writing a pointed comedy. That would have been too naïve, too cynical, and just as arrogant as the characters and themes that were the subjects of their scripted derision.

■ ■ ■

The characters that the Marx Brothers created in the vaudeville years are clearly defined. Each one is an individual with a different interpretation of the surrounding world. As a group, they are upstarts. They delight in making a mockery of life's details with wisecracks. Part of their appeal to movie audiences (but not so attractive to Kaufman in the 1920s) is that they appear to be so unpredictable. On stage, in their rambunctious youth, they tore apart scenery, or harassed other actors, at whim. They sometimes made a physical shambles of their onstage surroundings, and mocked their own performances as they were presenting them.[18] The wisecracking attitude they created extended throughout their film career, learned on the streets of New York and Chicago, at first exhibited and nurtured in vaudeville, and finally brought to maturity by the most sarcastic writers for Broadway and Hollywood, with a wider scope than merely laughing at the roaches in Nacogdoches. Their brickbats struck a chord in the burgeoning dissatisfaction with American society and politics beginning after World War I and building to a crescendo in the 1930s when they began making films for Paramount.

The fact remains that the subjects of the satire in the films are classic and broad enough to transcend their own generation, and to remain applicable to audiences in the twenty-first century. Their importance remains: These films offer a varied menu of cultural realizations to contemporary audiences, and their internal sagacity keeps them fresh. We realize that many of those same issues are true today. Even the most innocent jokes that they sprinkle throughout their work add to an overall montage of social criticism. Beneath all this disarming barrage of jokes, puns, pratfalls, and demonic energy, the significance of the films is that they are a demonstrative plea for change, for reform. It is a plea that's just as applicable now as it was then. We get the point: Maybe we should do something tangible to effect a change, or at least have a better understanding of the problem. We nod knowingly in collusion with the Brothers; we snicker in agreement. When we leave the theatre, or turn off our television sets, we try to recall and repeat some of the puns and jokes and songs word for word. Later, we start to realize that there's something more going on, something more significant, than the temporary gratification we feel when we see three or four brothers flailing about, bombarding us with a salvo of jokes. We realize what the Marx Brothers really mean, beneath the laughter.

Appendix: Credits of the Films Discussed

Included here are the 13 films with the basic information for each: production studio, release date, cast, director(s) and writer(s). You can find more production information about the films on the Internet Movie Database (www.imdb.com) and on various websites created by Marx Brothers fans.

The Cocoanuts   Paramount. Released August 3, 1929.

Cast: Zeppo (Jamison), Groucho (Mr. Hammer), Harpo (Harpo), Chico (Chico), Margaret Dumont (Mrs. Potter), Oscar Shaw (Bob Adams), Mary Eaton (Polly Potter), Cyril Ring (Harvey Yates), Kay Francis (Penelope), Basil Ruysdael (Detective Hennessy), Gamby-Hale Ballet Girls (Themselves), Allan K. Foster Girls (Themselves)

   Directors: Robert Florey, Joseph Santley; *Writers:* George S. Kaufman (play), Morrie Ryskind (adaptation).

Animal Crackers   Paramount. Released August 28, 1930.

Cast: Groucho (Captain Jeffrey T. Spaulding), Harpo (The Professor), Chico (Signor Emanuel Ravelli), Zeppo (Horatio Jamison), Margaret Dumont (Mrs. Rittenhouse), Lillian Roth (Arabella Rittenhouse), Louis Sorin (Roscoe W. Chandler), Hal Thompson (John Parker), Margaret Irving (Mrs. Whitehead), Robert Greig (Hives, the butler), Edward Metcalf (Inspector Hennessey)

   Director: Victor Heerman; *Writers:* George S. Kaufman (play), Morrie Ryskind (play and screenplay), Bert Kalmar and Harry Ruby (music and lyrics: "Hooray for Captain Spaulding," "Why Am I So Romantic?").

Monkey Business   Paramount. Released September 19, 1931.

Cast: Groucho (Groucho), Harpo (Harpo), Chico (Chico), Zeppo (Zeppo), Thelma Todd (Lucille Briggs), Rockcliffe Fellowes (J.J. "Big Joe" Helton), Harry Woods (Alky Briggs), Ruth Hall (Mary Helton), Tom Kennedy (First Mate Gibson)

   Director: Norman Z. McLeod; *Writers:* S.J. Perelman and Will B. Johnstone (original screenplay), Arthur Sheekman (additional dialogue).

Horse Feathers   Paramount. Released August 19, 1932.

Cast: Groucho (Professor Quincy Adams Wagstaff), Harpo (Pinky), Chico (Baravelli), Zeppo (Frank Wagstaff), Thelma Todd (Connie Bailey), David Landau (Jennings)
   Director: Norman Z. McLeod; *Writers:* S.J. Perelman, Will B. Johnstone, Bert Kalmar, Harry Ruby, Arthur Sheekman.

Duck Soup   Paramount. Released November 17, 1933.

Cast: Groucho (Rufus T. Firefly), Harpo (Pinky), Chico (Chicolini), Zeppo (Lt. Bob Roland), Margaret Dumont (Mrs. Gloria Teasdale), Raquel Torres (Vera Marcal), Louis Calhern (Ambassador Trentino), Edgar Kennedy (Lemonade Vendor), Leonid Kinsky (Agitator)
   Director: Leo McCarey; *Writers:* Bert Kalmar, Harry Ruby, Arthur Sheekman (additional dialogue), Nat Perrin (additional dialogue).

A Night at the Opera   Metro-Goldwyn-Mayer. Released November 15, 1935.

Cast: Groucho (Otis B. Driftwood), Harpo (Tomasso), Chico (Fiorello), Margaret Dumont (Mrs. Claypool), Kitty Carlisle (Rosa Castaldi), Allan Jones (Ricardo Baroni), Walter King (Rodolfo Lassparri), Sigfried Rumann (Herman Gottlieb), Robert Emmett O'Connor (Henderson)
   Director: Sam Wood; *Writers:* James Kevin McGuinness (story), George S. Kaufman and Morrie Ryskind (screenplay), Al Boasberg (dialogue and additional material), Robert Pirosh and George Seaton (drafts).

A Day at the Races   Metro-Goldwyn-Mayer. Released June 11, 1937.

Cast: Groucho (Dr. Hugo Z. Hackenbush), Harpo (Stuffy), Chico (Tony), Margaret Dumont (Emily Upjohn), Allan Jones (Gil Stewart), Maureen O'Sullivan (Judy Standish), Sig Rumann (Dr. Leopold X. Steinberg), Esther Muir (Flo Marlowe), Douglass Dumbrille (J.D. Morgan), Leonard Ceeley (Whitmore)
   Director: Sam Wood; *Writers:* Robert Pirosh and George Seaton (story and screenplay), George Oppenheimer (screenplay).

Room Service   RKO-Radio. Released September 30, 1938.

Cast: Groucho (Gordon Miller), Harpo (Faker Englund), Chico (Harry Binelli), Lucille Ball (Christine Marlowe), Ann Miller (Hilda Manny), Frank Albertson (Leo Davis), Cliff Dunstan (Joseph Gribble), Donald MacBride (Gregory Wagner), Philip Loeb (Timothy Hogarth), Philip Wood (Simon Jenkins), Alexander Asro (Sasha Smirnoff), Charles Halton (Dr. Glass)
   Director: William A. Seiter; *Writers:* Allen Boretz and John Murray (play), Morrie Ryskind (screenplay).

At the Circus   Metro-Goldwyn-Mayer. Released October 20, 1939.

Cast: Groucho (J. Cheever Loophole), Harpo (Punchy), Chico (Antonio Pirelli), Margaret Dumont (Mrs. Dukesbury), Kenny Baker (Jeff Wilson), Florence Rice (Julie Randall), Eve Arden (Peerless Pauline), Nat Pendleton (Goliath), Fritz Feld (Jardinet),

James Burke (John Carter), Jerry Marenghi (Little Professor Atom), Barnett Parker (Whitcomb)
    Director: Edward Buzzell; *Writer:* Irving Brecher.

Go West   Metro-Goldwyn-Mayer. Released December 6, 1940.

Cast: Groucho (S. Quentin Quale), Harpo (Rusty Panello), Chico (Joseph Panello), John Carroll (Terry Turner), Diana Lewis (Eve Wilson), Walter Woolf King (Beecher), Robert Barrat (Red Baxter), June McCloy (Lulubelle), George Lessey (Railroad President)
    Director: Edward Buzzell; *Writers:* Irving Brecher, Buster Keaton (uncredited).

The Big Store   Metro-Goldwyn-Mayer. Released June 20, 1941.

Cast: Groucho (Wolf J. Flywheel), Harpo (Wacky), Chico (Ravelli), Margaret Dumont (Martha Phelps), Tony Martin (Tommy Rogers), Virginia Grey (Joan Sutton), Douglass Dumbrille (Mr. Grover), William Tannen (Fred Sutton), Marion Martin (Peggy Arden), Virginia O'Brien (Kitty), Henry Armetta (Guiseppi), Anna Demetrio (Maria), Paul Stanton (Arthur Hastings), Russell Hicks (George Hastings), Bradley Page (Duke)
    Director: Charles Reisner; *Writers:* Nat Perrin (story), Sid Kuller, Hal Fimberg, Ray Golden (screenplay).

A Night in Casablanca   United Artists. Released May 10, 1946.

Cast: Groucho (Ronald Kornblow), Harpo (Rusty), Chico (Corbaccio), Charles Drake (Lt. Pierre Delmar), Lois Collier (Annette), Sig Rumann (Count Pfefferman/Heinrich Stubel), Lisette Verea (Beatrice Rheiner), Lewis Russell (Governor Galoux), Dan Seymour (Capt. Brizzard), Frederick Gierman (Kurt), Harro Mellor (Emile), David Hoffman (Spy), Paul Harvey (Mr. Smythe)
    Director: Archie Mayo; *Writers:* Joseph Fields and Roland Kibbee (original screenplay), Frank Tashlin (additional material).

Love Happy   United Artists. Released March 3, 1950.

Cast: Harpo (Harpo), Chico (Faustino), Groucho (Sam Grunion), Ilona Massey (Madame Egelichi), Vera-Ellen (Maggie Philips), Marion Hutton (Bunny Dolan), Raymond Burr (Alphonse Zoto), Melville Cooper (Throckmorton), Paul Valentine (Mike Johnson), Leon Belasco (Mr. Lyons), Eric Blore (Mackinaw), Bruce Gordon (Hannibal Zoto), Marilyn Monroe (Grunion's client)
    Director: David Miller; *Writers:* Harpo Marx (story), Frank Tashlin and Mac Benoff (screenplay).

Chapter Notes

Chapter 1

1. Stefan Kanfer, *Groucho: The Life and Times of Julius Henry Marx* (New York: Alfred A. Knopf, 2000), 370.

2. *Ibid.*

3. Vincent Canby, "Captain Spaulding Is Now a Lion," *New York Times*, April 13, 1967, 45.

4. Kanfer, *Ibid.*

5. George S. Kaufman, who wrote the Marx Brothers' Broadway show *The Cocoanuts*, reputedly was standing in the wings at one performance with a colleague. His associate, seeing that Kaufman was paying no attention to him, asked him why. Kaufman held up his hand, saying, "I may be wrong but I thought I just heard one of the original lines."

6. Edgar Johnson, "The Nature and Value of Satire," in *A Treasury of Satire*, ed. Edgar Johnson (New York: Simon and Schuster, 1945), 36.

7. Johnson, *passim.*

8. Letter, Leonard Lyons to Groucho Marx, October 26, 1960, Library of Congress, Marx Papers, Box 2.

9. Letter, Groucho Marx to Leonard Lyons, November 4, 1960, Library of Congress, Marx Papers, Box 2.

10. Roberta Smith, "Reflections Though a Surrealistic Eye: Dalí and the Camera," in *Weekend Arts: Fine Arts Leisure, The New York Times*, June 27, 2008, E28.

11. Earl Wilson, "It Happened Last Night: Dali Confides in Me: He's Not Mad — Just Crazy," *New York Post*, November 20, 1944, 32, cited in Michael R. Taylor, "*Giraffes on Horseback Salad* 1937," in *Dalí & Film*, ed. Matthew Gale (New York: The Museum of Modern Art, 2008), 150.

12. Salvador Dalí, *The Secret Life of Salvador Dalí*, trans. Haakon M. Chevalier, New York, 1942, London, 1948, 345, cited in Michael R. Taylor, "*Giraffes on Horseback Salad* 1937," 8.

13. Randy Kennedy, "Mr. Surrealist Goes to Tinseltown," in *Arts & Leisure, New York Times*, June 29, 2008, 21.

14. Maria Seton, "Salvador Dali + 3 Marxes =," *Theatre Arts*, October 1939, 734–40, *passim.*

15. John Willett, *The Theatre of Bertolt Brecht* (New York: New Directions, 1959), 124.

16. Martin Esslin, *The Theatre of the Absurd*, Anchor Books (Garden City, New York: Doubleday & Co., 1961), 237.

17. George Plimpton, "Philip Roth's Exact Intent," *New York Times Book Review*, February 23, 1969, 25.

18. Douglas Martin, "Robert Volpe, Art-Theft Expert, Dies at 63," *New York Times*, December 5, 2006, B7.

19. Groucho Marx, *The Groucho Letters: Letters from and to Groucho Marx* (New York: Simon and Schuster, 1967), 8.

20. *Room Service* was an adaptation of the Broadway comedy of the same name, and was the only adaptation of another work included in this group of defined films. Morrie Ryskind, one of the key writers for the Marx Brothers, wrote the screenplay.

21. Frank M. Whiting, *An Introduction to the Theatre* (rev. ed.; New York: Harper & Brothers, 1961), 20.

22. Gilbert Highet, *The Anatomy of Satire* (Princeton: Princeton University Press, 1962), 233.

23. *Ibid.*, 241.

24. *Ibid.*

25. James K. Feibleman, *Aesthetics* (New York: Duell, Sloan and Pearce, 1949), 92.

26. *Ibid.*, 82.

27. *Ibid.*

28. *Ibid.*

29. Jean-B.P. Molière, "Preface" to *Tartuffe*, trans. and ed. by Haskell M. Block (New York: Appleton-Century-Crofts, 1958), 3.

30. Robert C. Elliott, *The Power of Satire* (Princeton: Princeton University Press, 1960), 271.

31. Sigmund Freud, *Wit and Its Relation to the Unconscious* (London: Kegan Paul, Trench, Trubner & Co., Ltd., n.d.), 150.

32. *Ibid.*

33. L.J. Potts, *Comedy* (New York: Capricorn Books, 1966), 153.

34. Albert Cook, *The Dark Voyage and the Golden Mean* (New York: W.W. Norton & Co., 1966), 48.

35. Raymond Durgnat, "Mechanism of the Gag," *Films and Filming*, August 1965, 15.

36. Highet, 5.

37. Kyle Crichton, *The Marx Brothers* (New York: Doubleday & Co., 1950), 287.

38. Kip Rhinelander was a New York socialite who sued his wife for divorce a few years earlier because he believed that she had hidden the fact that one of her ancestors was black. In the 1920s this was scandalous, considering Rhinelander's social status in society. The case was a media sensation but most people had forgotten about it by the time *Animal Crackers* opened on Broadway. Apparently Groucho's impromptu remark reopened a nearly healed wound.

39. Cook, *Ibid.*

40. An apocryphal quote attributed to Groucho, and often appearing on contemporary tee shirts, is: "Outside of a dog, a book is man's best friend. Inside a dog it's too dark to read."

41. Richard Schickel, *Movies: The History of an Art and an Institution* (New York: Basic Books, 1964), 197.

42. Conversation with Maxine Marx, Chico's daughter, April 18, 1967.

Chapter 2

1. Bosley Crowther, *The Great Films: Fifty Golden Years of Motion Pictures* (New York: G.P. Putnam's Sons, 1967), 108.

2. Jean Roy, "Groucho Marx ou le mot qui tue," *Cahiers du Cinéma*, October 1977, 52.

3. Crichton, 117.

4. Schickel, *Movies: The History of an Art and an Institution*, 126.

5. James F. Clarity and Eric Pace, "Marcel Marceau, Renowned Mimic, Dies at 84," *New York Times*, September 24, 2007, B8.

6. Abel Green and Joe Laurie, Jr., *Show Biz from Vaude to Video* (New York: Henry Holt and Co., 1951), 7.

7. Groucho Marx and Richard J. Anobile, *The Marx Bros. Scrapbook* (New York: Darien House, 1973), 17.

8. Crichton, 108.

9. Date shown on a photo of a commemorative plaque at the old Opera House, Nacogdoches. Photo by Annie Jones, October 8, 2008.

10. Nacogdoches, Texas, Wikipedia, http://en.wikipedia.org/wiki/Nacogdoches, Texas (accessed June 16, 2008).

11. Mechelle Ball, "Downtown Art Studio Was Known as 'Old Opera House' 70 Years Ago," *The Sunday Sentinel,* June 22, 1986, 12 A.

12. Crichton, 113.

13. *Ibid.*, 114. Also cited in http://en.wikipedia.org/wiki/Nacogdoches, Texas.

14. Nacogdoches, Texas, "History," Wikipedia, *http://en.wikipedia.org/wiki/Nacogdoches, Texas.*

15. Stephen F. Austin State University, "A Tour of Nacogdoches — Downtown Area," *http://www.cets.sfasu.edu/nachis.html.*

16. Wes D. Gehring, *The Marx Brothers: A Bio-biography* (Westport: Greenwood Press, 1987), 66.

17. "It's 3 Marx Brothers Now, Zeppo Quits Stooge Role," *New York Herald Tribune*, March 31, 1934, 8.

18. Crichton, 292.

19. Thomas Doherty, *Pre-Code Hollywood* (New York: Columbia University Press, 1999), 195.

20. Tim Dirks, *"Duck Soup," http://www. filmsite.org/duck.html.*

21. Arthur Marx, *Life with Groucho* (New York: Simon and Schuster, 1954), 188.

22. "MGM (Metro-Goldwyn-Mayer) Ruling 1930s Hollywood: Depression-Era Dominance," *www.filmreference.com* (accessed June 15, 2008).

23. Arthur Marx, *Ibid.*

24. Marx and Anobile, 209.

25. *Ibid.*, 203.

26. Arthur Marx, *Ibid.*

27. *Ibid.*, 193.

28. "MGM Ruling 1930s Hollywood...," *Ibid.*

29. Arthur Marx, 194.

30. Arthur Marx, 191.

31. Teichmann, 207.

32. "Marx Bros. Use 11 Different Acts in 11 Shows in Windup Vaude Wk.," *Variety*, August 26, 1936, 89.

33. Douglas W. Churchill, "News and Gossip from Hollywood," *New York Times*, October 20, 1935, sec. 10, 5.

34. Marx and Anobile, 209.

35. Doherty, 179–80, *passim*.

36. *Ibid.*

37. Bob Thomas, *Thalberg* (Garden City, New York: Doubleday & Co., 1969), 286.

38. Howard Teichmann, *George S. Kaufman: An Intimate Portrait* (New York: Atheneum, 1972), 209.

39. Arthur Marx, 200.

40. "Flashes from Studios," *New York Times*, October 10, 1937, sec. 11, 5.

41. "Imagine Three Marx Brothers Playing 'Straight,' Yet They Do," *New York Herald Tribune*, September 18, 1938, sec. 6, 3.

42. Eileen Creelman, "Picture Plays and Players," *New York Sun*, November 14, 1939, 16.

43. Arthur Marx, 209.

44. Letter, Groucho Marx to Arthur Sheekman, June 24, 1939, Marx Papers, Box 2. Cited hereinafter as Marx to Sheekman.

45. Marx to Sheekman, October 27, 1939, Marx Papers, Box 2.

46. *Ibid.*

47. Marx to Sheekman, March 4, 1940, Marx Papers, Box 2.

48. Marx to Sheekman, July 20, 1940, Marx Papers, Box 2.

49. Marx to Sheekman, May 29, 1940, Marx Papers, Box 2.

50. Marx to Sheekman, June 12, 1940, Marx Papers, Box 2.

51. Marx to Sheekman, July 1, 1940, Marx Papers, Box 2.

52. Marx to Sheekman, October 10, 1940, Marx Papers, Box 2.

53. "Hollywood News," *New York Herald Tribune*, April 12, 1941, 6.

54. Marx to Sheekman, March 11, 1941, Marx Papers, Box 2.

55. *Ibid.*

56. *Ibid.*

57. Laurence Greene, "We're Through, Groucho Marx Confesses," *New York Post*, April 10, 1941, 5.

58. Malcolm Goldstein, *George S. Kaufman: His Life, His Theater* (New York: Oxford University Press), 1979, 109.

59. Arthur Marx, 204.

60. Arthur Whitelaw, theatrical producer of *Minnie's Boys*, interview, New York, August 16, 1968.

61. "Marxes Not Through Yet," *Morning Telegraph* (New York), February 2, 1942, 2.

62. Letter, Groucho Marx to Sam Zolotow, December 5, 1945, Marx Papers, Box 2.

63. Letter, Groucho Marx to Sam Zolotow, January 23, 1946, Marx Papers, Box 2.

Chapter 3

1. Goldstein, 52.

2. Howard Teichmann, *George S. Kaufman: An Intimate Portrait* (New York: Atheneum, 1972), 101.

3. *Ibid.*, 94.

4. Moss Hart, *Act One* (New York: Random House, 1959), 274.

5. Goldstein, 130.

6. *Ibid.*, 51.

7. *Ibid.*, 109.

8. Goldstein (citing conversation with Ryskind), 129.

9. Simon Louvish, *Monkey Business: The Lives and Legends of the Marx Brothers* (New York: St. Martin's Press, 1999), 175.

10. Goldstein, 18.

11. Internet Broadway Database, *The Cocoanuts, http://www.ibdb.com* (accessed July 18, 2008).

12. Goldstein, 126.

13. Goldstein, 194.

14. Dorothy Herrmann, *S.J. Perelman: A Life* (New York, G.P. Putnam's Sons, 1986), 40–41.

15. *Ibid.*, p. 42, citing the *Brown Jug*, October 1924, 17.

16. S.J. Perelman, *Dawn Ginsbergh's Revenge* (New York: Horace Liveright, 1929), 51.

17. The date attributed to this event cannot be correct. Although Perelman reports that he was at a performance of *Animal Crackers* in October 1931, the Broadway show actually closed in April of 1929. By October 1931 the film version of the show had already been released. And so had *Monkey Business*. Written by Perelman and Johnstone, *Monkey Business* was released in September 1931, one month before Perelman talks about this evening at the theatre where he had a first meeting with Groucho in his dressing room. It was supposedly at this meeting that Groucho in-

troduced his idea of Perelman writing for the Brothers.

18. S.J. Perelman, "The Winsome Foursome," *Show*, November 1961, 35.

19. *Ibid.*

20. *Ibid.*, 36.

21. *Ibid.*

22. See first page of Chapter 4: You Can Get Stucco.

23. Perelman, "The Winsome Foursome," 38.

24. *Ibid.*, 37.

25. Marx and Anobile, 46.

26. Goldstein, 246.

27. Marx and Anobile, *Ibid.*

28. Arthur Marx, 193.

29. *Ibid.*

30. Marx and Anobile, 154.

31. Crichton, 299.

32. Crichton, 288.

33. Goldstein, 51.

34. Crichton, 299.

35. Doherty, 5–9, *passim.*

36. *Ibid.*, 181.

Chapter 4

1. Lewis Jacobs, *The Rise of the American Film* (New York: Teachers College Press, 1968), 547.

2. Marx and Anobile, 116.

3. Internet Movie Database, *The Broadway Melody* and *The Cocoanuts, http://www.imdb.com.*

4. Louvish, p. 206.

5. Johnny Roventini had been a bellhop at the Hotel New Yorker. Executives from Philip Morris were in the hotel one day in 1934 when one of them, thinking that this small 24-year-old bellhop (Johnny was only 3'11") might be used as part of their promotion, gave Johnny a dollar and asked him to page "Philip Morris" throughout the lobby. Johnny, unaware that Philip Morris was the name of a cigarette and not a person, walked about the lobby shouting out "Call for Philip Morris!" His clear, high-pitched voice and pronunciation of Morris ("Mor-rey-ee-ss") were memorable, and the executive hired him to repeat the "call" for Philip Morris on a radio show that they were sponsoring. Both radio listeners and studio audiences reacted favorably to Johnny's distinctive voice. The company offered him a contract and he re-

mained with Philip Morris well into his eighties.

6. Marx and Anobile, *Ibid.*

7. Harvey Wish, *Contemporary America* (rev.; New York: Harper & Bros., 1955), 334.

8. Jack Kofoed, *The Florida Story* (Garden City, New York: Doubleday & Co., 1960), 258.

9. Singer-comedienne Sophie Tucker was one of the most popular entertainers during the first third of the twentieth century. She was billed as "The Last of the Red Hot Mamas" because of her outsized personality and corpulence.

10. Florida Marketing Bureau, *Annual Fruit and Vegetable Report, 1928–1929* (Jacksonville, Florida: Florida State Marketing Bureau, n.d.), 5.

11. Michael Gannon, *Florida: A Short History* (Tallahassee, Florida: University Press of Florida, 1993), 77.

12. Carita D. Corse, *Florida, Empire of the Sun* (Tallahassee, Florida: Florida State Hotel Commission, 1930), 9.

13. Frank P. Stockbridge and John H. Perry, *Florida in the Making* (New York and Jacksonville, Florida: The deBower Publishing Co., 1926), 99.

14. Frederick Lewis Allen, *Only Yesterday*, Perennial Library (New York: Harper & Row, 1959), 231.

15. *Ibid.*, 227.

16. W.T. Cash, *The Story of Florida* (New York: The American Historical Society, 1938), 586.

17. Charlton Tebeau and Ruby Leach Carson, et al. *Florida from Indian Trail to Space Age,* Vol. 2 (Delray Beach: The Southern Publishing Co., 1965), 59.

18. Allen, *Only Yesterday*, 231.

19. Gannon, 77.

20. Allen, *Only Yesterday*, 230.

21. Allen, *Only Yesterday*, 228.

22. Peter Applebome, "Perhaps a Boor (or a Bore), But Imus Makes It Work," *The New York Times*, November 4, 2007, 42.

23. Mary Louise "Texas" Guinan was a former vaudeville and stage actress who opened a speakeasy in 1929 on West 54th Street in New York, where she would greet her customers with "Hello, suckers!" The wealthy elite flocked to her club.

24. Gannon, *Ibid.*

25. Tebeau and Ruby Leach Carson, et al., 57.

26. Gannon, 82.

27. Burton Rascoe, introduction to *Boom*

in Paradise, by Theyre Weigall (New York: Alfred H. King, 1932), xiii.

28. In the argot of theatre professionals, when an actor commands the stage with an uncommon presence, he is described, admirably, in a number of ways. "He tears up the scenery" is one of them. The Marx Brothers literally would sometimes tear up the scenery — turn it into a shambles — when they were crisscrossing the country, highballing through countless vaudeville theatres. Even when they eventually made it to Broadway, there was no stopping them.

29. Goldstein, 127.

Chapter 5

1. Allen, *Only Yesterday*, 92.
2. Irving L. Allen, *The City in Slang: New York Life and Popular Speech* (U.S.: Oxford University Press, 1993), 72.
3. Allen, *Only Yesterday*, 210.
4. Eyles, 66.
5. Frederick Lewis Allen, *Since Yesterday*, Bantam Matrix Editions (New York: Bantam Books, 1940), 13.
6. Allen, *Only Yesterday*, 91.
7. *Ibid.*
8. *Ibid.*, 82.
9. Paul Sann, *The Lawless Decade* (New York: Crown Publishers, 1957), 111.
10. *Ibid.*, 211.
11. *Ibid.*
12. *Ibid.*, 186.
13. Eyles, 55.

Chapter 6

1. Thomas Doherty, *Pre-Code Hollywood* (New York: Columbia University Press, 1999), 44.
2. Jacobs, 508.
3. A Hooverville was a common name for shanties built by homeless men between 1931 and 1933, usually constructed on unused land in metropolitan areas. One of the more notable was in Central Park in New York City.
4. Doherty, *Ibid.*
5. Film Reference, "MGM (Metro-Goldwyn-Mayer) Ruling 1930s Hollywood: Depression-Era Dominance" in *http://www.filmreference.com/encyclopedia/*.
6. Jacobs, 422.

7. Turner Classic Movies, "Forbidden Hollywood Introduction," *http://www.tcm.com*.
8. "The Changing Value of the Dollar," *Banking*, September, 1958, 58.
9. U.S. Department of Commerce, Bureau of the Census, *Statistical Abstract of the United States: 1968* (Washington, D.C.: Government Printing Office, 1968), 347.
10. *Ibid.*, 266.
11. *Ibid.*, 279.
12. *Ibid.*, 280.
13. Dixon Wecter, *The Age of the Great Depression* (New York: The Macmillan Co., 1948), 229.
14. Wish, *Contemporary America*, 506.
15. Irving Settel, *A Pictorial History of Radio* (New York: Bonanza Books, 1960), 73.
16. *Ibid.*
17. Settel, 92.
18. *Ibid.*, 73.
19. Morrison and Commager, II, 553.
20. Wish, 302.
21. Wecter, 230.
22. Morrison and Commager, II, *Ibid.*
23. Wish, 302.

Chapter 7

1. Samuel Eliot Morison and Henry Steele Commager, *The Growth of the American Republic* (2 vols., 3d ed. rev.; New York: Oxford University Press, 1942), II, 642.
2. Eyles, 76.
3. E. David Cronon, ed., *The Cabinet Diaries of Josephus Daniels* (Lincoln, Nebraska: University of Nebraska Press, 1963), 125.
4. *Ibid.*, 25.
5. *Ibid.*
6. *Ibid.*, 517–18, *passim*.
7. John Dewey, ed., *New York and the Seabury Investigation* (New York: The City Affairs Committee of New York, 1933), 38.
8. Morison and Commager, II, 519.
9. Doherty, 194.
10. Frank H. Simonds, "Economic Expansion," in *The Shaping of American Diplomacy*, ed. by William A. Williams (Chicago: Rand McNally & Co., 1956), 664.
11. *Ibid.*, 667.
12. *Ibid.*
13. Morison and Commager, II, 502.
14. *Ibid.*, 504.
15. Doherty, 193.

Chapter 8

1. Richard Hofstader, *The Paranoid Style in American Politics* (New York: Alfred A. Knopf, 1965), 3.

2. Sidney Fay, *The Origins of the World War* (2d ed. rev.; New York: The Macmillan Co., 1930), 38–39.

3. *Ibid.*

4. Rushton Coulborn, "The Causes of War and the Study of History," *Journal of Social Philosophy*, IV (October, 1938), 57.

5. Morison and Commager, II, 461.

6. Fay, *Ibid.*

7. Hofstader, 24.

8. Hofstader, 25.

9. Woolworth, or more formally, F.W. Woolworth, is now a sporting goods company, Foot Locker. But in the 1930s it was one of the largest retail chains in the world, with its discounted merchandise sold at fixed prices, usually five or ten cents an item.

10. Morison and Commager, II, 642.

11. Mumford, *The Culture of Cities*, 273.

12. Morison and Commager, II, 644.

13. Hans J. Morgenthau, *In Defense of the National Interest* (New York: Alfred A. Knopf, 1951), 30–31.

14. Fay, 548.

15. Hofstader, 31.

16. *Ibid.*, 25.

17. Morgenthau, 54.

18. *Ibid.*

19. *Ibid.*, 55.

20. H.C. Engelbrecht, *Revolt Against War* (New York: Dodd, Mead & Co., 1937), 24.

21. *Ibid.*, 64.

22. Joseph Blotner, "Speaking of Books: Faulkner's *A Fable*," *New York Times Book Review*, May 25, 1969, 39.

23. Margaret Thorp, *America at the Movies* (New Haven: Yale University Press, 1939), 190.

Chapter 9

1. H.W. Whicker, "Doctors of Dullness," *North American Review*, July, 1929, 116.

2. James T. Hamilton, "Inaugural Conference at Reed College," *School and Society*, September 14, 1935, 382.

3. Whicker, 115–16, *passim.*

4. John Tunis, "College President," *Harper's Magazine*, February, 1937, 259–67.

5. Harold J. Laski, "Self-Determination for Faculties," *New Republic*, June 21, 1933, 149–50.

6. "The Qualifications of a University President," *Christian Century*, November 11, 1936, 1846.

7. Tunis, *passim.*

8. Eyles, 64.

9. Settel, 49.

10. Harvey Wish, *Society and Thought in America*, Vol. II: *Society and Thought in Modern America* (2d. ed.; New York: David McKay Co., 1962), 452.

11. Wish, Contemporary America, 322.

12. "Circuses or Colleges," *Collier's*, March 1, 1930, 66.

13. "Pennsy's Bitter Dose and Reducing Diet for Stadium Fever," *Literary Digest*, February 21, 1931, 34.

14. Dexter Keezer, "Putting College Athletics in Their Place," *School and Society*, February 20, 1937, 261.

15. *Ibid.*, 262.

16. Max Lerner, *America as a Civilization* (New York: Simon and Schuster, 1957), 734.

17. Wecter, 220.

18. John R. Tunis, "Who Cares About Amateur Sport?" *American Mercury*, January 1937, 94.

19. Ann Carter, "Poor Professors," *Forum and Century*, February, 1935, 90.

20. *Ibid.*

21. Merle Curti, *et al.*, *An American History*, II, 467.

22. John H. McNeely, "Salaries of College Teachers: Comparisons," *School Life*, February 1932, 111.

23. Wish, *Society and Thought in America*, II, *Ibid.*

24. Wish, *Contemporary America*, 313.

25. *Ibid.*

26. Howard W. Odum, *American Social Problems* (New York: Henry Holt & Co., 1939), 334.

27. Wish, *Contemporary America*, 503.

28. "The College Is No Cloister," *Catholic World*, September, 1935, 641.

29. Allen, *Since Yesterday*, 51.

30. Clarence Enzler, *Some Social Aspects of the Depression (1930–1935)* (Washington, D.C.: The Catholic University of America Press, 1939), 115.

31. Lerner, *Ibid.*

32. Lee Sieg, "Who Are the Good Teachers?" *School and Society*, October 15, 1932, 483.

33. Whicker, 116.

34. Edgar J. Goodspeed, "The Twilight of the Professors," *Atlantic Monthly*, August 1935, 211.

35. Harold Arlen and E.Y. Harburg, "Lydia the Tattooed Lady" (New York: Leo Feist, 1939).

Chapter 10

1. Sheila John Daly, *Blondes Prefer Gentlemen* (New York: Dodd, Mead & Co., 1949), 206.

2. *Ibid.*, 202.

3. "Must I Pet to Be Popular?" *Ladies Home Journal*, January, 1932, 7.

4. Ben Lindsey, *An Answer to the Critics of Companionate Marriage* (New York: New York Public Library, 1929), vii.

5. Kathleen Norris, *Companionate Marriage* (New York: The Paulist Press, n.d.), 2–3, *passim*.

6. Fuller brushes were sold door-to-door starting in 1906, and the salespeople were so ubiquitous that the company became well-known nationally. Their dominance in their field was powerful enough that they became part of popular American culture. In fact, a feature-length comedy with Red Skelton, *The Fuller Brush Man*, was released in 1948. The company is still in business.

7. Ernest W. Burgess, "The Wise Choice of a Mate," in *Successful Marriage*, ed. by Morris Fishbein and Ernest W. Burgess (Garden City, New York: Doubleday & Co., 1947), 20.

8. Lindsay Brooke, "Mr. Ford's T: Mobility With Versatility," *New York Times*, July 20, 2008, Automobiles section, 1.

9. Allen, *Only Yesterday*, 83.

10. Denis de Rougemont, *Love in the Western World*, trans. by Montgomery Belgion (New York: Harcourt, Brace and Co., 1940), 111.

11. *Ibid.*, 13.

12. *Ibid.*, 72.

13. Lerner, 582–83, *passim*.

14. Wish, 312.

15. Doherty, 182.

Chapter 11

1. de Rougemont, 31.

2. Burma-Vita Co., *Jingle Book*, vol. 1

(Minneapolis, Minnesota: The Burma-Vita Co., 1938), unpaginated.

3. de Rougemont, 201.

4. *Ibid.*, 268

5. *Ibid.*, 262.

6. Frances Parkinson Keyes, "Love and Marriage," *Good Housekeeping*, March 1929, 292.

7. Lerner, 589.

8. Lester W. Dearborn, "Extramarital Relations," in *Successful Marriage*, ed. by Marris Fishbein and Ernest W. Burgess (Garden City, New York: Doubleday & Co., 1947), 163–72, *passim*.

9. Kingsley Davis, "Divorce," *Ibid.*, 461.

10. de Rougemont, 269

11. Gladys D. Shultz, *Widows Wise and Otherwise* (Philadelphia: J.B. Lippincott Co., 1949), 136.

12. *Ibid.*, 137.

13. Edward Westermarck, *The History of Human Marriage*, vol. 1 (3 vols., 5th ed. rev.; New York: The Allerton Book Co., 1942), 462.

14. Chicago Stamps, "Our Stamp Collecting President," *http://www.chicagostamps.com*.

15. Edward Sheldon, *Romance*, in *Best Plays of 1909–1919*, ed. Burns Mantle (New York: Dodd, Mead and Co., 1945), 147.

16. Eyles, *The Marx Brothers*, 20.

Chapter 12

1. Amy Vanderbilt, *Amy Vanderbilt's Complete Book of Etiquette* (Garden City, New York: Doubleday & Co., 1952), 186.

2. *Ibid.*, 218.

3. S.I. Hayakawa, *Language in Thought and Action* (New York: Harcourt, Brace and Co., 1939), 66–79, *passim*.

4. "Bull Market in Ballroom Stepping," *Literary Digest*, January 2, 1937, 21.

5. Jerome Beatty, "Can You Dance with Your Wife?" *American Magazine*, December 1933, 100.

6. "Bull Market in Ballroom Stepping," *Ibid.*

7. Encyclopedia of Chicago, Lewis A. Erenberg, "Dance Halls," from Lewis A. Erenberg, *Swingin' the Dream: Big Band Jazz and the Rebirth of American Culture*. 1999, *http://www.encyclopedia.chicagohistory.org*.

8. Beatty, 24.

Chapter 13

1. Allen, *Since Yesterday, passim.*
2. Ocean Liner, *http://en.wikipedia.org/wiki/Ocean_liner.*
3. Jacobs, *The Rise of the American Film*, 240.
4. Basil Woon, *The Frantic Atlantic* (New York: Alfred A. Knopf, 1927), 177.
5. Timothy S. Green, "High-Seas Society," *Horizon*, Summer 1968, 112.
6. Green, 107.
7. John Grierson, *Grierson on Documentary*, ed. Forsyth Hardy (rev. ed.; Berkeley and Los Angeles: University of California Press, 1960), 56.
8. "Tips on Tipping," *Delineator*, July, 1936, 15.
9. Vanderbilt, 319.
10. Al Cerrachio, "Ship Travel in Third Class," *http://www.cruisemates.com/articles/onboard/steerage.cfm.*
11. Allegheny-Kiski Valley Historical Society, Chronicle Page, "Their Journey to America," *http://www.akvhs.org.*

Chapter 14

1. Donald E. Lundberg, *Inside Innkeeping* (Dubuque, Iowa: Wm. C. Brown Co., 1956), 121.
2. Surprisingly, this ethnic reference, with its slur word, has remained in the film. Many other scenes that were subsequently thought to be distasteful or socially rude, were cut from the original releases of the films.
3. Norman S. Hayner, *Hotel Life* (Chapel Hill, North Carolina: The University of North Carolina Press, 1936), 172.
4. Dev Collans with Stewart Sterling [Prentice Winchell], *I Was a House Detective* (New York: E.P. Dutton & Co., 1954), p. 80. Cited hereinafter as Collans (pseud.).
5. Collans (pseud.), *passim.*
6. Lundberg, 120.
7. James Feibleman, *In Praise of Comedy* (London: George Allen & Unwin, Ltd., 1939), 224.
8. Collans (pseud.), 16.
9. *Ibid.*, 40.
10. *Ibid.*, 16.
11. Duncan Matheson, "The Technique of the American Detective," *Annals of the American Academy of Political and Social Science*, CXLI (November 1929), 216.
12. *Ibid.*

Chapter 15

1. Allen, *Only Yesterday*, 140.
2. Merle Curti, *The Growth of American Thought* (2d. ed.; New York: Harper & Brothers Publishers, 1951), 708.
3. Allen, *Only Yesterday*, 147.
4. John B. Opdycke, *Take a Letter, Please* (New York and London: Funk & Wagnalls Co., 1937), 192.
5. Maurice Weseen, "Better Business Letters," *Outlook*, August 24, 1927, 544.
6. Alfred B. Chambers, *The New Century Standard Letter-Writer* (Chicago: Laird & Lee Publishers, 1900), *passim.*
7. John Mason Brown, "Seeing Things: Language, Legal and Literary: Part I," *Saturday Review*, June 21, 1952, 32.
8. *Ibid.*, p. 31.
9. David Mellinkoff, *The Language of the Law* (Boston and Toronto: Little, Brown and Co., 1963), 22.
10. Henry Black, *Black's Law Dictionary* (4th ed.; St. Paul, Minnesota: West Publishing Co., 1951), 1507.
11. Feibleman, 224.
12. Mellinkoff, 27.
13. A.C. Edgeton, *A Speech for Every Occasion* (New York: Noble and Noble, 1949), xi.
14. Alexander Burton, *After Dinner Speeches* (New York: Edward J. Clode, 1921), 8.
15. This is a classic technique of satirical writing, reminiscent of the introduction that Victor Borge, the humorist and concert pianist, would use ("Before we start, the Steinway piano company has asked me to say that this is a Baldwin Piano").
16. Allen, *Only Yesterday*, 184–87, *passim.*

Chapter 16

1. "Old Nacogdoches Opera House" commemorative plaque.
2. Morison and Commager, *The Growth of the American Republic*, II, 556.
3. Wish, *Contemporary America*, p. 509.

4. Allen, *Since Yesterday*, p. 122.

5. Henry N. Pringle, *Crimes and Tragedies of the Race Tracks* (Washington, D.C.: International Reform Federation, 1931), p. 6.

6. Eyles, p. 48.

Chapter 17

1. Internet Broadway Database, *An American Tragedy*, *http://www.ibdb.com*.

2. John Gassner, *Masters of the Drama* (3d ed. rev. and enlarged; New York: Dover Publications, 1954), 656.

3. Joseph Wood Krutch, introduction to *Nine Plays by Eugene O'Neill*, The Modern Library (New York: Random House, 1954), xix.

4. Eyles, 38.

5. John Cecil Holm and George Abbott, *Three Men on a Horse*, in *Twenty Best Plays of the Modern American Theatre*, ed. with an introduction by John Gassner (New York: Crown Publishers, 1939).

6. Wecter, 243.

7. Michael Conway, *The Films of Greta Garbo* (New York: The Citadel Press, 1963), 17.

8. Raymond Durgnat and John Kobal, *Greta Garbo* (New York: E.P. Dutton and Co., 1965), 43.

9. Paul Michael, *Humphrey Bogart: The Man and His Films* (New York: The Bobbs-Merrill Co., 1965), 21.

10. Groucho Marx, *The Groucho Letters: Letters from and to Groucho Marx* (New York: Simon and Schuster, 1967), 14.

11. Ordean A. Hagen, *Who Done It?* (New York: R.R. Bowker Co., 1969), 439.

12. Dorothy Gardiner and Kathrine S. Walker, eds., *Raymond Chandler Speaking* (London: Hamish Hamilton, Ltd., 1962), 27.

13. Robert Warshow, *The Immediate Experience* (Garden City, New York: Doubleday & Co., 1962), 93.

14. Wish, *Contemporary America*, 301.

15. Morison and Commager, *The Growth of the American Republic*, II, 554.

16. Settel, 39.

17. Wish, 49.

18. "World at Ringside by Proxy," *Literary Digest*, October 5, 1935, 32.

19. Eyles, 58.

Chapter 18

1. Allen, *Since Yesterday*, 216.

2. Dickson Skinner, "Music Goes into Mass Production," *Harper's Magazine*, April 1939, 487.

3. "Dress Code at La Scala: The Final Episode, Part ROFL" *http://operachic.typepad.com/opera_chic/2007/01/dress_code_la_s.html*.

4. Howard Taubman, *The Making of the American Theatre* (New York: Coward McCann, 1965), 219.

5. New York Public Library, Lincoln Center Theatre Collection, Photograph of Manuel Salazar as Canio, June 15, 1924.

6. New York Public Library, Lincoln Center Theatre collection, self-caricature of Enrico Caruso appearing as Canio, n.d., in *The Robinson Locke Collection of Dramatic Scrapbooks,* Vol. CV, No. 1, unpaginated.

7. Irving Kolodin, *The Metropolitan Opera: 1883–1966* (rev. 4th ed.; New York: Alfred A. Knopf, 1966), 3–45, *passim*.

8. George A. Small, "American Dramatic Comedy: 1900–1950; A Study of Reflected Climate of Opinion in Changing Historical Perspective," unpublished Ph.D. dissertation, University of Pennsylvania, 1956, 44.

9. Philip L. Miller, "Opera, The Story of an Immigrant," in *One Hundred Years of Music in America*, ed. by Paul Henry Lang (New York: G. Schirmer, 1961), 76.

10. "Minnie the Moocher" is a jazz song recorded by Cab Calloway and his orchestra in 1931. It is most famous for its scat lyrics that include a call-and-response with audience participation.

Chapter 19

1. Siegfried Kracauer, *Theory of Film* (New York: Oxford University Press, 1965), 109.

2. *Ibid.*, 108.

3. Eyles, 40.

4. Raymond Durgnat, "The World Turned Upside Down," *Films and Filming*, September 1965, p. 12.

5. Feibleman, *In Praise of Comedy*, 225.

6. Raymond Durgnat, "Hoop de Doo for Mr. L. and Mr. H.," *Films and Filming*, November 1965, 18.

7. See: Mortimer J. Adler, *Art and Pru-*

dence (New York: Longmans, Green and Co., 1937); Béla Balázs, *Theory of the Film: Character and Growth of a New Art*, trans. Edith Bone (New York: Roy Publishers, 1953); Ernest Lindgren, *The Art of the Film* (London: G. Allen and Unwin, 1948).

8. "Marx Brothers," *New Statesman and Nation*, October 3, 1931, 405.

9. Grierson, Grierson on Documentary, 55.

10. Robert Warshow, *The Immediate Experience* (Garden City, New York: Doubleday & Co., 1962), 18.

11. Schickel, *Movies: The History of an Art and an Institution*, 126.

12. Durgnat, "Hoop de Doo for Mr. L. and Mr. H.," 17.

13. Warshow, *Ibid.*

14. Henri Bergson, *Laughter*, trans. Cloudesley Brereton and Fred Rothwell (New York: The Macmillan Co., 1912), *passim*.

15. Edgar Anstey, "*The Big Store*," *Spectator*, October 3, 1941, 331.

16. Feibleman, *In Praise of Comedy*, 224.

17. Vincent Canby, "Screen: *Flea in Her Ear*," *New York Times*, November 28, 1968, 66.

Chapter 20

1. Robert C. Hailey, "George S. Kaufman, Playwright and Satirist," unpublished Master's thesis, Miami University, 1949, *passim*.

2. Scott Meredith, *George S. Kaufman and His Friends* (New York: Doubleday, 1974), 89.

3. Will Rogers (1879–1935) was a Cherokee-American actor and humorist who would base his social and political criticism on current events reported in each day's newspapers ("All I know is what I read in the papers"). The format of his monologues continues to be used by stand-up comics and on broadcast comedy shows.

4. Groucho's use of the word "subversive" is a reference to the Entertainment blacklist, often called the Hollywood blacklist, during the 1940s and 1950s. "The Marx Brothers Now," *Newsweek*, March 17, 1958, 104.

5. George Oppenheimer, *The View from the Sixties* (New York: David McKay Co., 1966), 126.

6. Durgnat, "Hoop do Doo for Mr. L. and Mr. H.," 17.

7. Francis Hodge, *Yankee Theatre: The Image of America on the Stage, 1825–1850* (Austin, Texas: University of Texas Press, 1964), 4–6, *passim*.

8. Edward Rothstein, "How Jokes Guaranteed to Offend Teach Propriety Its Place," *New York Times*, July 8, 2000, B8.

9. Arthur Knight, *The Liveliest Art* (New York: The New American Library, 1957), 162.

10. George Seaton, "Books," review of *The Marx Brothers at the Movies*, by Paul D. Zimmerman and Burt Goldblatt, *Action*, January–February 1969, 39.

11. Goldstein, 128.

12. *Ibid.*

13. Andrew Sarris, *The American Cinema*, (New York: E.P. Dutton & Co., 1968), 247.

14. Oscar Handlin, *America* (New York: Holt, Rinehart and Winston, 1968), 1054.

15. Graham Greene, "The Marx Brothers at the Circus," *Spectator*, December 15, 1939, 864.

16. Eyles, 106.

17. Gehring, 68.

18. "Old Nacogdoches Opera House," photograph of commemorative historical marker, Nacogdoches, Texas, *Ibid.*

Bibliography

Works Cited

BOOKS

Allen, Frederick Lewis. *Only Yesterday*. Perennial Library. New York: Harper & Row, 1959.
_____. *Since Yesterday*. Bantam Matrix Editions. New York: Bantam Books, 1940.
Allen, Irving L. *The City in Slang: New York Life and Popular Speech*. U.S.: Oxford University Press, 1993.
Bergson, Henri. *Laughter*. Translated by Cloudesley Brereton and Fred Rothwell. New York: Macmillan, 1912.
Black, Henry. *Black's Law Dictionary*. 4th ed. St. Paul, MN: West Publishing, 1951.
Burgess, Ernest W. "The Wise Choice of a Mate." *Successful Marriage*. Edited by Morris Fishbein and Ernest W. Burgess. Garden City, NY: Doubleday, 1947.
Burma-Vita Co. *Jingle Book*. Vol. I. Minneapolis, MN: Burma-Vita, 1938.
Burton, Alexander. *After Dinner Speeches*. New York: Edward J. Clode, 1921.
Cash, W. T. *The Story of Florida*. New York: The American Historical Society, 1938.
Chambers, Alfred B. *The New Century Standard Letter-Writer*. Chicago: Laird & Lee Publishers, 1900.
Collans, Dev, with Stewart Sterling [Prentice Winchell]. *I Was a House Detective*. New York: E.P. Dutton, 1954.
Conway, Michael. *The Films of Greta Garbo*. New York: The Citadel Press, 1963.
Cook, Albert. *The Dark Voyage and the Golden Mean*. New York: W.W. Norton, 1966.
Corse, Carita D. *Florida, Empire of the Sun*. Tallahassee, FL: Florida State Hotel Commission, 1930.
Crichton, Kyle. *The Marx Brothers*. New York: Doubleday, 1950.
Cronon, E. David, ed. *The Cabinet Diaries of Josephus Daniels*. Lincoln: University of Nebraska Press, 1963.
Crowther, Bosley. *The Great Films: Fifty Golden Years of Motion Pictures*. New York: G.P. Putnam's Sons, 1967.
Curti, Merle. *The Growth of American Thought*. 2d. ed. New York: Harper & Brothers, 1951.
_____, Richard H. Shryock, Thomas C. Cochran, and Fred Harvey Harrington. *An American History*. 2 vols. New York: Harper & Brothers, 1951.
Dalí, Salvador. *The Secret Life of Salvador Dalí*. Translated by Haakon M. Chevalier. New York, 1942, London 1948. In Taylor, Michael R. "Giraffes on Horseback Salad 1937." *Dalí & Film*, edited by Matthew Gale, 140–53. New York: The Museum of Modern Art, 2008.

Daly, Sheila John. *Blondes Prefer Gentlemen*. New York: Dodd, Mead, 1949.

Davis, Kingsley. "Divorce." *Successful Marriage*. Edited by Marris Fishbein and Ernest W. Burgess. Garden City, NY: Doubleday, 1947.

de Rougemont, Denis. *Love in the Western World*. Translated by Montgomery Belgion. New York: Harcourt, Brace, 1940.

Dearborn, Lester W. "Extramarital Relations." *Successful Marriage*. Edited by Marris Fishbein and Ernest W. Burgess. Garden City, NY: Doubleday, 1947.

Dewey, John, ed. *New York and the Seabury Investigation*. New York: The City Affairs Committee of New York, 1933.

Doherty, Thomas. *Pre-Code Hollywood: Sex, Immorality, and Insurrection in American Cinema 1930–1934*. New York: Columbia University Press, 1999.

Durgnat, Raymond, and John Kobal. *Greta Garbo*. New York: E.P. Dutton, 1965.

Edgerton, A. C. *A Speech for Every Occasion*. New York: Noble and Noble, 1949.

Elliott, Robert C. *The Power of Satire*. Princeton: Princeton University Press, 1960.

Engelbrecht, H. C. *Revolt Against War*. New York: Dodd, Mead, 1937.

Enzler, Clarence. *Some Social Aspects of the Depression (1930–1935)*. Washington, D.C.: The Catholic University of America Press, 1939.

Esslin, Martin. *The Theatre of the Absurd*. Anchor Books. Garden City, NY: Doubleday, 1961.

Eyles, Allen. *The Marx Brothers: Their World of Comedy*. London: A. Zwemmer, 1966.

Fay, Sidney. *The Origins of the World War*. 2d ed. revised. New York: Macmillan, 1930.

Feibleman, James K. *Aesthetics*. New York: Duell, Sloan and Pearce, 1949.

_____. *In Praise of Comedy*. London: George Allen & Unwin, 1939.

Florida Marketing Bureau. *Annual Fruit and Vegetable Report, 1928–1929*. Jacksonville, FL: Florida State Marketing Bureau, n.d.

Freud, Sigmund. *Wit and Its Relation to the Unconscious*. London: Kegan Paul, Trench, Trubner, n.d.

Gannon, Michael. *Florida: A Short History*. Tallahassee: University Press of Florida, 1993.

Gardiner, Dorothy, and Kathrine S. Walker, eds. *Raymond Chandler Speaking*. London: Hamish Hamilton, 1962.

Gassner, John. *Masters of the Drama*. 3d ed. revised and enlarged. New York: Dover Publications, 1954.

Gehring, Wes D. *The Marx Brothers: A Bio-biography*. Westport: Greenwood Press, 1987.

Goldstein, Malcom. *George S. Kaufman*. New York: Oxford University Press, 1979.

Green, Abel, and Joe Laurie, Jr. *Show Biz from Vaude to Video*. New York: Henry Holt, 1951.

Grierson, John. *Grierson on Documentary*. Edited by Forsyth Hardy. Revised ed. Berkeley and Los Angeles: University of California Press, 1960.

Hagen, Ordean A. *Who Done It?* New York: R. R. Bowker, 1969.

Handlin, Oscar. *America*. New York: Holt, Rinehart and Winston, 1968.

Hart, Moss. *Act One*. New York: Random House, 1959.

Hayakawa, S. I. *Language in Thought and Action*. New York: Harcourt, Brace, 1939.

Hayner, Norman S. *Hotel Life*. Chapel Hill: The University of North Carolina Press, 1936.

Herrmann, Dorothy. *S. J. Perelman: A Life*. New York: G.P. Putnam's Sons, 1986.

Highet, Gilbert. *The Anatomy of Satire*. Princeton: Princeton University Press, 1962.

Hodge, Francis. *Yankee Theatre: The Image of America on the Stage, 1825–1850*. Austin: University of Texas Press, 1964.

Hofstader, Richard. *The Paranoid Style in American Politics*. New York: Alfred A. Knopf, 1965.

Holm, John Cecil, and George Abbott. *Three Men on a Horse*. In *Twenty Best Plays of the*

Modern American Theatre. Edited with an introduction by John Gassner. New York: Crown, 1939.

Jacobs, Lewis. *The Rise of the American Film*. New York: Teachers College Press, 1968.

Johnson, Edgar. "The Nature and Value of Satire." *A Treasury of Satire*. Edited by Edgar Johnson. New York: Simon and Schuster, 1945.

Kanfer, Stefan. *Groucho: The Life and Times of Julius Henry Marx*. New York: Alfred A. Knopf, 2000.

Knight, Arthur. *The Liveliest Art*. New York: The New American Library, 1957.

Kofoed, Jack. *The Florida Story*. Garden City, NY: Doubleday, 1960.

Kolodin, Irving. *The Metropolitan Opera: 1883–1966*. Revised 4th ed. New York: Alfred A. Knopf, 1966.

Kracauer, Siegfried. *Theory of Film*. New York: Oxford University Press, 1965.

Krutch, Joseph Wood. Introduction to *Nine Plays by Eugene O'Neill*. The Modern Library. New York: Random House, 1954.

Lerner, Max. *America as a Civilization*. New York: Simon and Schuster, 1957.

Lindsey, Ben. *An Answer to the Critics of Companionate Marriage*. New York: New York Public Library, 1929.

Louvish, Simon. *Monkey Business: The Lives and Legends of The Marx Brothers*. New York: St. Martin's Press, 1999.

Lundberg, Donald E. *Inside Innkeeping*. Dubuque, IA: Wm. C. Brown, 1956.

Marx, Arthur. *Life with Groucho*. New York: Simon and Schuster, 1954.

Marx, Groucho. *The Groucho Letters: Letters from and to Groucho Marx*. New York: Simon and Schuster, 1967.

_____, and Richard J. Anobile. *The Marx Bros. Scrapbook*. New York: Darien House, 1973.

Mellinkoff, David. *The Language of the Law*. Boston and Toronto: Little, Brown, 1963.

Meredith, Scott. *George S. Kaufman and His Friends*. New York: Doubleday, 1974.

Michael, Paul. *Humphrey Bogart: The Man and His Films*. New York: Bobbs-Merrill, 1965.

Miller, Philip L. "Opera, The Story of an Immigrant." In *One Hundred Years of Music in America*. Edited by Paul Henry Lang. New York: G. Schirmer, 1961.

Molière, Jean-B. P. Preface to *Tartuffe*. Translated and ed. by Haskell M. Block. New York: Appleton-Century-Crofts, 1958.

Morgenthau, Hans J. *In Defense of the National Interest*. New York: Alfred A. Knopf, 1951.

Morison, Samuel Eliot, and Henry Steele Commager. *The Growth of the American Republic*. 2 vols. 3d ed. revised. New York: Oxford University Press, 1942.

Norris, Kathleen. *Companionate Marriage*. New York: The Paulist Press, n.d.

Odum, Howard W. *American Social Problems*. New York: Henry Holt, 1939.

Opdycke, John B. *Take a Letter, Please*. New York and London: Funk & Wagnalls, 1937.

Oppenheimer, George. *The View from the Sixties*. New York: David McKay, 1966.

Perelman, S. J. *Dawn Ginsbergh's Revenge*. New York: Horace Liveright, 1929.

Potts, L.J. *Comedy*. New York: Capricorn Books, 1966.

Pringle, Henry N. *Crimes and Tragedies of the Race Tracks*. Washington, D.C.: International Reform Federation, 1931.

Rascoe, Burton. Introduction to *Boom in Paradise* by Theyre Weigall. New York: Alfred H. King, 1932.

Sann, Paul. *The Lawless Decade*. New York: Crown, 1957.

Sarris, Andrew. *The American Cinema*. New York: E.P. Dutton, 1968.

Schickel, Richard. *Movies: The History of an Art and an Institution*. New York: Basic Books, 1964.

Settel, Irving. *A Pictorial History of Radio*. New York: Bonanza Books, 1960.

Sheldon, Edward. *Romance. Best Plays of 1909–1919.* Edited by Burns Mantle. New York: Dodd, Mead, 1945.

Shultz, Gladys D. *Widows Wise and Otherwise.* Philadelphia: J. B. Lipincott, 1949.

Simonds, Frank H. "Economic Expansion." *The Shaping of American Diplomacy.* Edited by William A. Williams. Chicago: Rand McNally, 1956.

Stockbridge, Frank P., and John H. Perry. *Florida in the Making.* New York and Jacksonville, FL: deBower Publishing, 1926.

Taubman, Howard. *The Making of the American Theatre.* New York: Coward McCann, 1965.

Tebeau, Charlton, Ruby Leach Carson, et al. *Florida from Indian Trail to Space Age.* Vol. 2. Delray Beach: Southern Publishing, 1965.

Teichmann, Howard. *George S. Kaufman: An Intimate Portrait.* New York: Atheneum, 1972.

Thomas, Bob. *Thalberg.* Garden City, NY: Doubleday, 1969.

Thorp, Margaret. *America at the Movies.* New Haven: Yale University Press, 1939.

U.S. Department of Commerce. Bureau of the Census. *Statistical Abstract of the United States: 1968.* Washington, D.C.: Government Printing Office, 1968.

Vanderbilt, Amy. *Amy Vanderbilt's Complete Book of Etiquette.* Garden City, NY: Doubleday, 1952.

Warshow, Robert. *The Immediate Experience.* Garden City, NY: Doubleday, 1962.

Wecter, Dixon. *The Age of the Great Depression.* New York: Macmillan, 1948.

Westermarck, Edward. *The History of Human Marriage.* Vol. 1. 3 vols., 5th ed. revised. New York: Allerton, 1942.

Whiting, Frank M. *An Introduction to the Theatre.* Revised ed. New York: Harper & Brothers, 1961.

Willett, John. *The Theatre of Bertolt Brecht.* New York: New Directions, 1959.

Wish, Harvey. *Contemporary America.* Revised ed. New York: Harper & Bros., 1955.

_____. *Society and Thought in America.* Vol. II: *Society and Thought in Modern America.* 2d. ed. New York: David McKay, 1962.

Woon, Basil. *The Frantic Atlantic.* New York: Alfred A. Knopf, 1927.

PERIODICALS

Anstey, Edgar. "*The Big Store.*" *Spectator*, October 3, 1941.

Applebome, Peter. "Perhaps a Boor (or a Bore), But Imus Makes It Work." *New York Times*, November 4, 2007, New York City edition.

Beatty, Jerome. "Can You Dance with Your Wife?" *American Magazine*, December 1933, 24–25, 98–100.

Blotner, Joseph. "Speaking of Books: Faulkner's *A Fable.*" *New York Times Book Review*, May 25, 1969, 2, 34, 36, 38, 39.

Brooke, Lindsay. "Mr. Ford's T: Mobility with Versatility." *New York Times*, July 20, 2008, Automobiles section, New York City edition.

Brown, John Mason. "Seeing Things: Language, Legal and Literary: Part I." *Saturday Review*, June 21, 1952, 30–32.

"Bull Market in Ballroom Stepping." *Literary Digest*, January 2, 1937, 21–22.

Canby, Vincent. "Captain Spaulding Is Now a Lion," *New York Times*, April 13, 1967, New York City edition.

_____. "Screen: *Flea in Her Ear.*" *New York Times*, November 28, 1968, New York City edition.

Carter, Ann. "Poor Professors." *Forum and Century*, February 1935, 88–90.

"The Changing Value of the Dollar." *Banking*, September, 1958.

Churchill, Douglas W. "News and Gossip from Hollywood." *New York Times*, October 20, 1935.

"Circuses or Colleges." *Collier's*, March 1, 1930, 66.

Clarity, James F., and Eric Pace. "Marcel Marceau, Renowned Mimic, Dies at 84." *New York Times*, September 24, 2007, Section B, New York City edition.

"The College Is No Cloister." *Catholic World,* September 1935, 641–48.

Coulborn, Rushton. "The Causes of War and the Study of History." *Journal of Social Philosophy*, IV (October 1938), 57–68.

Creelman, Eileen. "Picture Plays and Players." *New York Sun*, November 14, 1939.

Durgnat, Raymond. "Hoop de Doo for Mr. L. and Mr. H." *Films and Filming*, November 1965, 14–18.

_____. "Mechanism of the Gag." *Films and Filming*, August 1965, 10–15.

_____. "The World Turned Upside Down." *Films and Filming*, September 1965, 8–12.

Goodspeed, Edgar J. "The Twilight of the Professors." *Atlantic Monthly*, August 1935, 210–14.

Green, Timothy S. "High-Seas Society." *Horizon*, Summer 1968, 106–13.

Greene, Graham. "The Marx Brothers at the Circus." *Spectator*, December 15, 1939.

Greene, Laurence. "We're Through, Groucho Marx Confesses." *New York Post*, April 10, 1941.

Hamilton, James T. "Inaugural Conference at Reed College." *School and Society*, September 14, 1935, 382–83.

"Hollywood News," *New York Herald Tribune*, April 12, 1941.

"Imagine Three Marx Brothers Playing 'Straight,' Yet They Do." *New York Herald Tribune*, September 18, 1938.

"It's 3 Marx Brothers Now, Zeppo Quits Stooge Role." *New York Herald Tribune*, March 31, 1934.

Keezer, Dexter. "Putting College Athletics in their Place." *School and Society*, February 20, 1937, 261–66.

Kennedy, Randy. "Mr. Surrealist Goes to Tinseltown." *New York Times*, June 29, 2008, Arts & Leisure, New York City edition.

Keyes, Frances Parkinson. "Love and Marriage." *Good Housekeeping*, March 1929, 22–23, 292, 295–96, 299.

Laski, Harold J. "Self-Determination for Faculties." *New Republic*, June 21, 1933, 149–50.

Martin, Douglas. "Robert Volpe, Art-Theft Expert, Dies at 63." *New York Times*, December 5, 2006, Section B, New York City edition.

"Marx Bros. Use 11 Different Acts in 11 Shows in Windup Vaude Wk." *Variety*, August 26, 1936.

"Marx Brothers." *New Statesman and Nation*, October 3, 1931.

"The Marx Brothers Now." *Newsweek*, March 17, 1958, 104–05.

"Marxes Not Through Yet." *Morning Telegraph*, February 2, 1942.

Matheson, Duncan. "The Technique of the American Detective." *Annals of the American Academy of Political and Social Science*, CXLI (November 1929), 214–18.

McNeely, John H. "Salaries of College Teachers: Comparisons." *School Life,* February 1932, 111, 117.

"Must I Pet to Be Popular?" *Ladies Home Journal*, January 1932, 7, 84, 86.

"Pennsy's Bitter Dose and Reducing Diet for Stadium Fever." *Literary Digest*, February 21, 1931, 34–36.

Perelman, S. J. "The Winsome Foursome." *Show*, November 1961, 35–38.

Plimpton, George. "Philip Roth's Exact Intent," *New York Times Book Review*, February 23, 1969, 2, 23–25.

"The Qualifications of a University President." *Christian Century*, November 11, 1936, 1846.

Rothstein, Edward. "How Jokes Guaranteed to Offend Teach Propriety Its Place." *New York Times*, July 8, 2000, Section B, New York City edition.

Roy, Jean. "Groucho Marx ou le mot qui tue." *Cahiers du Cinéma,* October 1977, 52–3.

Seaton, George. "Books." *Review of the Marx Brothers at the Movies*, by Paul D. Zimmerman and Burt Goldblatt. *Action*, January-February 1969, 38–39.

Seton, Marie. "Salvador Dalí + 3 Marxes=." *Theatre Arts*, October 1939, 734–40.

Sieg, Lee. "Who Are the Good Teachers?" *School and Society*, October 15, 1932, 481–85.

Skinner, Dickson. "Music Goes into Mass Production." *Harper's Magazine*, April 1939, 484–90.

Smith, Roberta. "Reflections Through a Surrealistic Eye: Dalí and the Camera." *New York Times*, June 27, 2008, Section E, New York City edition.

"Tips on Tipping." *Delineator*, July 1936, 15.

Tunis, John R. "Who Cares About Amateur Sport?" *American Mercury*, January 1937, 91–95.

Weseen, Maurice. "Better Business Letters." *Outlook*, August 24, 1927, 543–46.

Whicker, H. W. "Doctors of Dullness." *North American Review*, July 1929, 115–19.

Wilson, Earl. "It Happened Last Night: Dali Confides in Me: He's Not Mad — Just Crazy," *New York Post*, November 20, 1944, 32. In *Dalí & Film*, edited by Matthew Gale. New York: The Museum of Modern Art, 2008.

"World at Ringside by Proxy." *Literary Diges*t, October 5, 1935, 32–33.

WEBSITES

Allegheny-Kiski Valley Historical Society. Chronicle Page. "Their Journey to America." *http://www.akvhs.org* (accessed September 3, 2008).

Cerrachio, Al. "Ship Travel in Third Class." *http://www.cruisemates.com/articles/onboard/steerage.cfm* (accessed September 1, 2008).

Chicago Stamps. "Our Stamp Collecting President." *http://www.chicagostamps.com* (accessed April 12, 2008).

Dirks, Tim. "Duck Soup." *http://www.filmsite.org/duck.html* (accessed July 5, 2008).

"Dress Code at La Scala: The Final Episode, Part ROFL." *http://operachic.typepad.com/opera_chic/2007/01/dress_code_la_s.html* (accessed September 30, 2008).

Encyclopedia of Chicago. Lewis A. Erenberg, "Dance Halls." Lewis A. Erenberg, *Swingin' the Dream: Big Band Jazz and the Rebirth of American Culture.* 1999. *http://www.encyclopedia.chicagohistory.org* (accessed June 25, 2008).

Film Reference. "MGM (Metro-Goldwyn-Mayer) Ruling 1930s Hollywood: Depression-Era Dominance." *www.filmreference.com* (accessed June 15, 2008).

Internet Broadway Database. *An American Tragedy. http://www.ibdb.com* (accessed December 18, 2007).

Internet Broadway Database. *The Cocoanuts. http://www.ibdb.com* (accessed July 18, 2008).

Internet Movie Database. *The Broadway Melody* and *The Cocoanuts. http://www.imdb.com* (accessed August 17, 2008).

Nacogdoches, Texas. "History." Wikipedia. *http://en.wikipedia.org/wiki/Nacogdoches, Texas* (accessed June 18, 2008).

Nacogdoches, Texas. Wikipedia. *http://en.wikipedia.org/wiki/Nacogdoches, Texas* (accessed June 16, 2008).

Ocean Liner. *http://en.wikipedia.org/wiki/Ocean_liner* (accessed September 2, 2008).

Stephen F. Austin State University. "A Tour of Nacodoches — Downtown Area." *http://www.cets.sfasu.edu/nachis.html* (accessed June 18, 2008).

Turner Classic Movies. "Forbidden Hollywood Introduction." *http://www.tcm.com* (accessed August 14, 2008)

CATALOG

Gale, Matthew, ed. *Dalí & Film.* New York: The Museum of Modern Art, 2008.

UNPUBLISHED MATERIAL

·Hailey, Robert C. "George S. Kaufman, Playwright and Satirist." Unpublished Master's thesis, Miami University, 1949.
Jones, Annie. Photograph, Nacogdoches, Texas, October 8, 2008.
Joseph, Barbara A. "Patterns for Modern American Comedy Since 1923." Unpublished Ph. D. dissertation, Western Reserve University, 1953.
Marx, Maxine. Chico Marx's daughter. Conversation, April 18, 1967.
New York Public Library. Lincoln Center Theatre Collection. Photograph of Manuel Salazar appearing as Canio, June 15, 1924.
_____. Lincoln Center Theatre Collection. Self-caricature of Enrico Caruso appearing as Canio, n.d. In *The Robinson Locke Collection of Dramatic Scrapbooks*, Vol. CV, No. 1, unpaginated.
Small, George A. "American Dramatic Comedy: 1900–1950; A Study of Reflected Climate of Opinion in Changing Historical Perspective." Unpublished Ph.D. dissertation, University of Pennsylvania, 1956.
Whitelaw, Arthur. Theatrical producer of *Minnie's Boys*. Interview, August 16, 1968.

MUSIC

Arlen, Harold, and E. Y. Harburg. "Lydia the Tattooed Lady." New York: Leo Feist, 1939.

MANUSCRIPT COLLECTION

Library of Congress. Manuscript Division. The Groucho Marx Papers.

Works Consulted

BOOKS

Adler, Mortimer J. *Art and Prudence.* New York: Longmans, Green, 1937.
Agee, James. *Agee on Film: Reviews and Comments.* Boston: Beacon Press, 1958.
Allen, Frederick Lewis. *The Big Change.* New York: Harper & Brothers, 1952.
Balázs, Béla. *Theory of the Film: Character and Growth of a New Art.* Translated by Edith Bone. New York: Roy Publishers, 1953.
Barnouw, Erik. *A Tower in Babel: A History of Broadcasting in the United States.* 2 vols. New York: Oxford University Press, 1966–69.
Cooke, Alistair, ed. *Garbo and the Nightwatchmen.* London: Jonathan Cape, 1937.
Cornford, Francis M. *The Origin of Attic Comedy.* Anchor Books. Garden City, NY: Doubleday, 1961.
Corrigan, Robert W., ed. *Comedy: Meaning and Form.* San Francisco: Chandler Publishing, 1965.

Crowther, Bosley. *The Lion's Share*. New York: E.P. Dutton, 1957.

Daniels, Jonathan. *The Time Between the Wars*. Garden City, NY: Doubleday, 1966.

Dell, Floyd. *Love in the Machine Age*. New York: Farrar & Rinehart, 1930.

Dolph, Edward A. *Sound Off*. New York: Cosmopolitan Book, 1929.

Durgnat, Raymond. *The Marx Brothers*. Vienna: Österreichisches Filmmuseum, 1966.

Eastman, Max. *Enjoyment of Laughter*. New York: Halcyon House, 1936.

_____. *The Sense of Humor*. New York: Charles Scribner's Sons, 1921.

Feinberg, Leonard. *Introduction to Satire*. Ames: Iowa State University Press, 1967.

_____. *The Satirist: His Temperament, Motivation, and Influence*. Ames: Iowa State University Press, 1963.

Frye, Northrop. *Anatomy of Criticism*. Princeton: Princeton University Press, 1957.

Gallaway, Marian. *The Director in the Theatre*. New York: Macmillan, 1963.

Gassner, John, and Philip Barber. *Producing the Play, with the New Scene Technician's Handbook*. Revised ed. New York: Holt, Rinehart and Winston, 1953.

Greene, Laurence. *The Era of Wonderful Nonsense*. Indianapolis and New York: Bobbs-Merrill, 1939.

Gurko, Leo. *The Angry Decade*. New York: Dodd, Mead, 1947.

Kyrou, Ado. *Le Surréalisme au Cinéma*. Paris: Éditions Arcanes, 1953.

Lambert, Constant. *Music Ho!* London: Faber and Faber, 1934.

Lauter, Paul, ed. *Theories of Comedy*. Garden City, NY: Doubleday, 1964.

Levant, Oscar. *A Smattering of Ignorance*. New York: Doubleday, Doran, 1940.

Lindgren, Ernest. *The Art of the Film*. London: G. Allen and Unwin, 1948.

Lundberg, Donald E. *Inside Innkeeping*. Dubuque, IA: Wm. C. Brown, 1956.

Mars, François. *Le Gag*. Paris: Editions du Cerf, 1964.

Marx, Groucho. *Groucho and Me*. New York: Bernard Geis Associates, 1959.

Marx, Harpo, with Rowland Barber. *Harpo Speaks!* New York: Bernard Geis Associates, 1961.

Mead, Margaret. *And Keep Your Powder Dry*. New York: William Morrow, 1947.

Mumford, Lewis. *The Culture of Cities*. New York: Harcourt, Brace, 1938.

Nesbit, Wilbur D. *After-Dinner Speeches*. Chicago and New York: Reilly & Lee, 1927.

Nicoll, Allardyce. *Masks, Mimes and Miracles*. New York: Cooper Square Publishers, 1963.

Philbrick, Frederick A. *Language and the Law*. New York: Macmillan, 1949.

Rotha, Paul. *Documentary Film*. London: Faber & Faber, 1939.

Sadoul, Georges. *Histoire du Cinéma Mondial*. Paris: Flammarion, 1949.

Sandburg, Carl. *The American Songbag*. New York: Harcourt, Brace, 1927.

Slosson, Preston W. *The Great Crusade and After, 1924–1928*. New York: Macmillan, 1930.

Thompson, Alan R. *The Dry Mock*. Berkeley and Los Angeles: University of California Press, 1948.

U.S. Department of Labor. Bureau of Labor Statistics. *Monthly Labor Review*. October, 1931. Washington, D.C.: Government Printing Office, 1931.

Van Doren, Mark. *The Private Reader*. New York: Henry Holt, 1942.

Vos, Melvin. *The Drama of Comedy: Victim and Victor*. Richmond, Virginia: John Knox Press, 1966.

Winnington, Richard. *Drawn and Quartered*. London: The Saturn Press, 1948.

Wood, William A. *After-Dinner Speeches*. Chicago: T. H. Flood, 1914.

PERIODICALS

Allombert, Guy. "Les Marx Brothers un univers de démence consciente." *Image et Son*, April 1964, 56–59.

Artaud, Antonin. "Scenarios and Arguments." *Tulane Drama Review*, XI, No. 1, 1966.

"As Others See Us." *Living Age*, December 1932, 371–72.

Barnes, Howard. "The Playbill: Hart-Sherwood-Marx." *New York Herald Tribune*, January 14, 1934, Section 5, New York City edition.

_____. "The Playbill: Ridges Cast in *Jig Saw*." *New York Herald Tribune*, April 1, 1934, Section 5, New York City edition.

Bashky, Alexander. "Madness from Hollywood." *Nation*, August 31, 1932, 198–99.

Birrell, Francis. "The Marx Brothers." *New Statesman and Nation*, October 1, 1932, 374–75.

Bost, Pierrre. "Le Cinéma." *Annales Politiques et Littéraires*, June 10, 1936, 605–07.

Chafee, Zechariah, Jr. "The Disorderly Conduct of Words." *Columbia Law Review*, XLI (March 1941), 381–404.

Chavance, Louis. "The Four Marx Brothers as Seen by a Frenchman." *Canadian Forum*, February 1933, 175–76.

Churchill, Douglas W. "Extra Trouble in the Hollywood Paradise." *New York Times*, August 30, 1936, Section 9.

_____. "Hollywood Goes Back to Nature." *New York Times*, September 13, 1936, Section 10.

_____. "A Script Survives the Marxes." *New York Times*, July 24, 1938, Section 9.

Crowther, Bosley. "Comedies of Error." *New York Times*, February 23, 1941, Section 9.

_____. "Or Is It Corn?" *New York Times,* April 23, 1950, Section 2.

_____. "The Screen." *New York Times*, February 21, 1941.

_____. "The Screen in Review." *New York Times*, June 27, 1941.

_____. "Those Marx Men." *New York Times*, August 18, 1946, Section 2.

Dixon, Campbell. "Film Notes: The Marx Brothers." *Daily Telegraph* (London), March 2, 1936.

Dubreuilli, Simone. "Le Genie des Frères Marx?" *Paris-Soir Dimanche*, November 5, 1938.

Evans, Harry. "Movies." *Life*, September 26, 1930, 20.

Forrest, Mark. "Films." *Saturday Review* (London), October 3, 1931, 427.

_____. "The Films." *Saturday Review* (London), December 6, 1930, 738.

"4 Marx Brothers Now Are 3." *New York Herald Tribune*, July 22, 1933.

Hall, Mordaunt. "Changes in Gotham Dwelling." *New York Times*, December 10, 1933, Section 10.

_____. "Havens of Laughter." *New York Times*, October 18, 1931, Section 8.

_____. "Those Boisterous Marx Brothers." *New York Times*, August 21, 1932, Section 9.

Halle, Rita S. "Is My Daughter Safe at College?" *Good Housekeeping*, September 1929, 40–41, 227–34.

Hamilton, Sara. "The Nuttiest Quartette in the World." *Photoplay*, July 1932, 90–91.

Hardy, Forsyth. "*Horse Feathers*." *Cinema Quarterly* (Edinburgh), Winter 1932, 117.

"Harpo Marx Talks." *New York Times*. November 12, 1933, section 9.

Johnston, Alva. "The Marx Brothers: The Scientific Side of Lunacy." *Woman's Home Companion*, September 1936, 12–13, 73–74.

Kurnitz, Harry. "Return of the Marx Brothers." *Holiday*, January 1957, 95, 98.

Laura, Ernesto G. "Il Contributo dei Marx Brothers alla Nascita del Film Comico Sonoro." *Bianco e Nero*, November-December 1964.

Lee, Mabel B. "Censoring the Conduct of College Women." *Atlantic Monthly*, April 1930, 444–50.

Martin, André. "Harpo Marx à n'en plus finir." *Cinéma 64*, December 1964, 43–47.

_____. "Les Marx Brothers ont-ils une ame?" *Cahiers du Cinéma*, February 1955, 2–16.

_____. "Les Marx Brothers ont-ils une ame?" Part 2. *Cahiers du Cinéma*, March 1955, 24–38.

_____. "Les Marx Brothers ont-ils une ame?" Part 3. *Cahiers du Cinéma*, May 1955, 27–27, 58–60.
_____. "Les Marx Brothers ont-ils une ame?" Part 4. *Cahiers du Cinéma*, June 1955, 23–35.
"Marx Break Reported." *New York Times*, March 10, 1933.
"The Marx Brothers." *The Times* (London), September 19, 1932.
"Marx Brothers in Films." *New York Times*, May 19, 1929, Section 9.
"Marx Brothers Incorporate." *New York Herald Tribune*. April 4, 1933.
"A Marxian Experiment." *New York Times*, July 26, 1936, Section 9, New York City edition.
"Marxes m with Sam Harris on 6 Other Pix; Seek a Broadway Show." Variety, April 18, 1933.
"Marxmen Shoot to Kill." *New York Times*, November 19, 1939, Section 10.
McNeely, John H. "Salaries of College Teachers: Comparisons." *School Life*, February 1932, 111, 117.
"Music Features Marxes." *New York Times*, November 30, 1939.
Panofsky, Erwin. "Style and Medium in the Motion Pictures." *Critique*, January-February 1947, 5–18, 27–28.
"Personality: Groucho Marx, Trademark: Effrontery." *Time*, December 31, 1951, 29.
"Plucking A Few Notes from Harpo." *New York Times*, November 17, 1935, Section 9.
Rosten, Leo. "The Lunar World of Groucho Marx." *Harper's Magazine*, June 1958, 31–35.
Sarris, Andrew. "I Am a Whore." *Arts*, December 1966, 24–26.
"Those Marx Brothers." *New York Times*, May 4, 1930, Section 11.
"Three Mad Marxes Test Gags for Movie." *New York Times*, July 19, 1936, Section 2.
Troy, William. "*The Invisible Man*." *Nation*, December 13, 1933, 688.
Tunis, John. "College President." *Harper's Magazine*, February 1937, 259–67.
Winokur, Mark. "The Marx Brothers." *Film Quarterly*, vol. 13, no. 3, 1985, 161–71.
Woollcott, Alexander. "A Strong Silent Man." *Cosmopolitan*, January 1934, 55–57, 108.

Unpublished Material

Carlisle, Kitty. Letter to Bruno Zirato, Jr., describing her experiences in filming *A Night at the Opera*. February 15, 1969.
Joseph, Barbara A. "Patterns for Modern American Comedy Since 1923." Unpublished Ph.D. dissertation, Western Reserve University, 1953.
Rohauer, Raymond. "A Tribute to the Marx Brothers." Brochure commemorating a festival of Marx Brothers films. New York: The Gallery of Modern Art, 1967, unpaginated.
Ruby, Harry. Letter to Tino Balio, Director of the Wisconsin Center for Theatre Research. February 15, 1969.

Manuscript Collection

State Historical Society of Wisconsin. Wisconsin Center for Theatre Research. Manuscript Division. The Harry Ruby Collection.

Index

Numbers in **bold italics** indicate pages with photographs.

Abbott, George 1, 155
Adams, Franklin P. 30
advertising 12, 14, 42, 44, 102–103, 153, 163, 167
Algonquin Round Table 36, 145
Allen, Woody 8, 152
Animal Crackers 5–6, 18, 30–31, 35–36, 53, 61, 65, 69, 72, 75, 92–93, 97–100, 103–104, 106, 110, 115–16, 126, 134, 136–39, 141–43, 145, *147*, 148, 154, 160, 163–64, 174, 176, 185, 190*cln38*, 191*c3n17*
animals 46, 110, 136
anti-establishment 6, 12, 16, 30, 33, 57, 75, 82, 141, 172, 178, 180–81
Aristophanes 9–10
Astor, Caroline, and the Social Four Hundred 12
At the Circus 23–24, 37–38, 95, 106, 110, *111*, 117, 124, 134, 144, 154, 157, 163–65, 168, 182, 186
auctions and auctioneers 44–45, 49–51, 89, 104, 142

Bacall, Lauren 1, 158
The Beatles 57
bellhops 41–45, 52, 130–31
Benchley, Robert 35
Benny, Jack 33–35
Berle, Milton 16
Berlin, Irving 28
big business 1, 12, 25, 44, 59–61, 74, 91, 105, 107, 115, 120, 129–30, 136–39, 141, 144, 161, 166–67, 175; attacked by writers 27, 29, 31
The Big Store 23, 25, 102, 107, *108*, 136, 153, 159–60, 172, 187
Boasberg, Al 14, 34–35, 122
bodyguards 60–61
Bogart, Humphrey 1, 158

boxing 14–15, 162
Brecht, Bertolt 8
Breen, Joseph and the Breen Office 38–39
bridge 45, 145–49, 151
Butler, Nicholas Murray 30

Canby, Vincent 6
capitalism 43–44
Carmen 165
Casablanca 158–59
Chaplin, Charlie 4, 10, 36, 53, 59, 63, 75, 122–23, 131, 179
Chevalier, Maurice 8, 123
classical music 29, 164, 168–70
The Cocoanuts 6, 18, 28–30, 36, 38, 40–41, 43, 46, 48, 50–53, 55, 60–61, 72–73, 78, 89, 92, 101, 104, 107–10, 116, 126–27, *128*, 129, 134, 136, 141–43, 148, 162, 164, 174, 180, 185, 189*cln5*
companionate marriage 98–99
costumes 16, 42, 73–74, 86–87, 166, 172
courtroom trials 82

Dada 35–36
Dalí, Salvador 7–8, 35, 169
dancing, ballroom 23, 117–18, 177; the Lindy 125
A Day at the Races 2–3, 15, 21–24, 37, 39, 73, 100, 110, 114, 116, 118, 125–26, 133, 141, 149, 153, 155, *156*, 176, 181–82, 186
deflating pomposity 12, 15, 27, 29, 116–17, 141, 163, 175
department store merchandising 1, 136–37
depression 18, 21, 30, 35, 37, 54, 61, 63–65, 67–68, 70–72, 91–94, 118, 149, 157, 168, 176; and Hollywood 181–82
destruction of language 6, 31–32, 45, 56, 75–76, 95, 99, 101, 103, 109–10, 139–41, 162, 171–72; *see also* language

detectives and crime investigation 133–34,
    159–60
disguises 82
Doherty, Thomas 4, 18, 22, 77, 79, 101, 175
domestic tranquility 108–109
Dreiser, Theodore 1, 152–53, 163; *An
    American Tragedy* 1, 3, 152–54, 163, 170
Duck Soup 4, 6, 14, 17–18, 23, 35–37, 39,
    53, 72–73, 77, 79–80, 83, **86**, 87–88,
    103, 106, 108, 111, 116, 118, 126, 141, 148,
    160, 168, 172, 176, 181–82, 186
Dumont, Margaret 3, 38, 43–44, 47, 67,
    72, 75, 78, 80, 98–99, 102, **108**, **109**, **111**,
    115–17, 134, 144, **147**, 154, 156, 172, 174,
    180
Dylan, Bob 101

East Lynne and *Romance* 99, 109
economics 30, 44, 54, 57, 61, 63–66, 69,
    71, 73, 78, 88, 95, 98, 105–106, 132, 159,
    162, 171; and the Production Code 37
education 1, 13–14, 56, 60, 68–69, 90–95,
    112, 125, 140
Eyles, Allen 3, 72

Feibleman, James K. 9, 130, 141, 172–73
Fields, W.C. 51, 63, 122, 180
football 56, 84, 90–93, 153, 162–63
Ford, Henry 99
fortune hunters 105, 107, **108**
42nd Street 161

gambling 14, 149–50
Garbo, Greta 1, 157
Gehring, Wes 3, 182
Go West 23–25, 101, 103, 124, 160–61, 170,
    182, 187
The Gold Rush 123, 131
Goodbye, Mr. Chips 157, 163
grand opera 14, 23, 122, 164–68, 170–71
The Groucho Club 9
Guinan, Texas 51, 192*c4n23*

handshaking 77, 81, 114, 116, **128**
Harding, Warren 37, 76–77
Hardy, Oliver 59, 122, 138
Harris, Sam 28
Hart, Moss 13
Hays, Will 37–38, 109–110, 153
high society 6, 9–14, 28, 31, 57, 59, 67, 70,
    74, 79, 98, 100, 108–10, 112–14, 116, 118,
    137, 144–45, 149–51, 166, 168, 170, 172–
    73, 178–79, 183
Hitler, Adolf 18, 83, 88
Hollywood Production Code 2, 11, 37–38
Holm, John Cecil 1, 155
Horse Feathers 1, 18, 37, 54–56, **58**, 61–62,
    72, 89, 92, 94–97, 101, 104, 115, 126, 149,
    152–53, 155, 163, 170, 180, 186
horse races 14, 155, 172
hotels 41, 127–28, 130, 132–33; evasion of
    paying bills 121, 132; personal service and
    room service 130–31; registration 129,
    134; security 133

introductions 111, 114–18, 142–43, 148

"Johnny" (Philip Morris caller) 42,
    192*c4n5*
Johnstone, Will 32–33, 35–36, 54, 92, 119,
    152, 163, 191*c3n17*
Joyce, James 7, 154

Kalmar, Bert 14, 90, 108
Kanfer, Stefan 3, 5–6
Kaufman, George S. 13–14, 18, 21, 25, 27–
    31, 33–35, 37, 39–40, 42–45, 51–53, 64,
    101, 110, 119, 128, 130–31, 139, 142, 145,
    148, 154, 163, 173, 175, 180, 183, 189*cIn5*
Keaton, Buster 14, 34, 59, 63, 75, 122, 179
kissing 98, 119; of hands 113–14

language 16, 22, 73, 97, 148–49; destruc-
    tion of 6, 31–32, 45, 56, 65, 70, 75–76,
    95, 99, 101, 108–10, 112, 162, 171–72, 175;
    Hayakawa and pre-symbolic language
    115; as intimidation 130; legal 139–41,
    144; repetition of "thank you" 114–115
Laurel, Stan 59, 122, 138
legal contracts 1, 139–41, 144
LeMaster, David James 4
letter writing 1, 138–39, 142, 144
Lindbergh, Charles 69
Lindsey, Ben 98–99
liquor 55, 110, 138, 165; and women 57
Lloyd, Harold 59, 75, 122
Louvish, Simon 3, 29
Love Happy 26, 160–61, 187
Lyons, Leonard 7

Mankiewicz, Herman 33, 180
Marceau, Marcel 16, 179
marriage and divorce 98–99, 103–106, 108–
    110, 115, 154
Marx, Arthur 20, 23, 34
M*A*S*H 8
MGM 18, 20, 21, 23, 25, 36, 38, 64, 118,
    182
mimetic form of satire 9; Harpo as mime
    15–16, 23, 75, 179
Mr. Saturday Night 131
Molière, Jean-B.P. 10
Monkey Business 8, 15, 18, 33, 35, 54, 59–
    61, 66, **67**, 70, 75, 81, 89, 98, 100, 104–

105, 116, 118–23, 136, 141, 162, 169, 176, 178, 185, 191*c3n17*

Muir, Esther 11, 38, 110, 114–15, 133, 155, *156*

Mussolini, Benito 88

My Man Godfrey 63, 68

Nacogdoches, Texas 17–18, 29, 99, 118, 145, 183

A Night at the Opera 4, 6, 8, 14, 20–24, 34, 37–39, 57, 63, 66–69, 73, 82, 106, 111, 114, 117–19, 121, 123–26, 131–32, 139, 143, 148, 153, 157–58, 164–66, 168, 174, 176, *177*, 181–82, 186; stateroom scene 121–22

A Night in Casablanca 26, 129, 158, *159*, 187

nihilism 1, 90, 173

Ocean liners 59, 119–21, 124 ; steerage passengers 124–26

O'Neill, Eugene 1, 154–55, 163, 174

Paramount 18, 19, 22–23, 33, 36–37, 40–41, 52–54, 62, 152, 168, 174, 180, 182–183

passports 70, 122–23

Perelman, S.J. 13, 31–33, 35–36, 39, 54, 56, 64, 89, 92–93, 96, 101, 105, 119, 152–53, 163, 175, 191*c3n17*

Philip Morris 42, 192*c4n5*

Pirosh, Robert 21–22

politics and political practices 9, 10, 12, 14, 29, 30–31, 33, 39, 53, 54, 57, 64, 72, 75, 76–81, 83, 87, 109, 112, 145, 168, 171, 175–76, 182, 183

popular culture 1, 41–42, 74, 88, 162–63, 169, 172, 178, 180

Porter, Cole 8

Prohibition 14, 37, 54–57, *58*, 59–61, 76

promoters 44, 46, 48–49, 52

pronunciation 22, 80, 127, 172

radio 1, 22, 25, 32–34, 43, 50, 68–70, 82, 87, 91, 100, 142, 143–44, 162–64, 166, 192*c4n5*

Radio City Rockettes 43

real estate 14, 41, 44–45, 47–53, 130; Florida land boom-and-bust 1, 29, 41, 44, 46; land speculation 40, 47

Rhinelander, Kip 13, 157, 190*cln38*

RKO 23

romance 28, 100–101, 103, 105, 109–10, 161; dislike of sentimentality 27–28, 44, 99, 102, 110, 112

romantic love 99–106, 110

romantic myth 99–100, 105, 108

romantic poetry 102–103

Room Service 9, 18, 23, 25, 35, 69, 131–32, 138, 161, 186, 189*cln20*

Roosevelt, Franklin D. 1, 18, 30, 61, 68–69, 88, 109, 168, 176

Roth, Philip 8

Roventini, Johnny 42, 192*c4n5*

Ruby, Harry 14, 90, 108

Ryskind, Morris (Morrie) 14, 18, 21, 28–31, 33–35, 39–40, 42–43, 45, 51–53, 63–64, 68, 119, 128, 130, 142, 154, 163, 175, 180, 189*cln20*

salesmen 1, 44–45, 48–51, 60, 70, 121, 136; Groucho 121; snake oil 49–50, 89

Santley, Joseph 41

Saroyan, William 8

Sarris, Andrew 181

Saturday afternoons at the movies 11–12, 15

Seaton, George 21–22

sex 10–11, 28, 38–39, 64, 97–99, 101, 105–106, 109–10, 114, 118, 133, 142, 153, 156, 158, 175

Shean, Al 16–17

Sheekman, Arthur 24–25, 35–36, 159, 181

social anarchy 43, 168

social outsiders 59, 173, 178–79

Socialism 42, 44

Sons of the Desert 138

speakeasies 55–59, 61, 92, 115, 149; passwords 56–57, *58*, 59, 154, 180

speechmaking 1, 68–69, 89–90, 103, 142–44

stock market 66–67, 143

stowaways 32, 60, 66, *67*, 70, 100, 121–22, 124–25, 132, 144, 157

Strange Interlude 1, 103, 143, 154–55, 157, 163, 174

Sturges, Preston 70

Sullivan's Travels 70–71

Surrealism 7–8, 35–36, 85–86, 138, 169

Swain's Rat and Cat Act 26

swashbucklers 161

Teichmann, Howard 27

Thalberg, Irving 4, 18, 20–23, 34, 36–39, 73, 126, 168, 176, 181

Theatre traditions 49, 178–79

Three Men on a Horse 1, 155, 157

tipping 123–24

To Have and Have Not 158

Tolstoy, Leo 30

Il Trovatore 164–65

Truffaut, François 8

United Artists 26

Volpe, Robert 8

Vorkapich, Slavko 32, 40

war 1, 14, 28, 35–36, 53, 60, 62, 72, 74,
   77–78, 81, 83–88, 111, 148, 180, 182, 183
Warner Brothers 158–59
WASP 14, 47, 178
West, Mae 22, 63–64, 101, 175, 180
Western movies 1, 14, 84, 160–61
Wigell, Christine 4
Wilder, Thornton 7

wisecracks 27, 38, 42, 73, 126, 175, 180,
   183; Wisecrack Brothers 18, 22
Wood, Sam 22

Yann, Michael 4
You Bet Your Life 142, 155

Zolotow, Sam 26